"I couldn't put this book down. My readers often ask me, 'What will happen to suburbia once we've all right-sized our homes and communities?' Leigh Gallagher provides the data that I've been looking for, and makes the powerful assertion that our suburbs are permanently changing, not because of the Great Recession, but because of new attitudes about where and how we want to live—which is great news, both for the near term and for generations to come."

—Sarah Susanka, author of
The Not So Big House series and *The Not So Big Life*

"Through compelling expert interviews, data, and trends analysis, Leigh affirms the notion that we've hit 'peak burb.' This book presents a strong case for America's increasing preference for higher density lifestyles and the resulting trend to manage our lives via the information highway, not the paved kind!"   —Scott W. Griffith, chairman and CEO of Zipcar

"This book is a steel fist in a velvet glove. Beneath Leigh Gallagher's smooth, elegant prose there is a methodical smashing of the suburban paradigm. When all is done, a few shards remain—but only because she is scrupulously fair. This story of rise and ruin avoids the usual storm of statistics, nor is it a tale told with apocalyptic glee—which is most amusing to me but too depressing for most people. *The End of the Suburbs* is the most convincing book yet on the lifestyle changes coming to our *immediate* future."

—Andres Duany, founding partner of
Duany Plater-Zyberk & Company and coauthor of *Suburban Nation*

"The book is loaded with fascinating detail wrapped in a vivid story Gallagher creates from behind the scenes of America's greatest promotion: the suburbs."

—Meredith Whitney, author of
Fate of the States and founder of Meredith Whitney Advisory Group

"Leigh Gallagher asks all the right questions and comes up with surprising conclusions in this sweeping discussion of the future of the suburb. Spoiler alert—it's a bleak future for the burbs, but don't panic: Gallagher foretells a new world order where the conveniences of the urban lifestyle rewire our understanding of the American Dream. You'll never look at a cul-de-sac the same way again after you enjoy this book, which is simultaneously entertaining and informative, breezy and analytical."

—Spencer Rascoff, CEO of Zillow

"*The End of the Suburbs* is a compelling, insightful must read on what author Leigh Gallagher calls the 'slow-burning revolution' re-mapping the shape of America and its future. Her masterfully argued case springs to life with both impressive research and empathetic portraits of those seduced and often betrayed by suburbia's promise of a more livable life. Now, where's my moving truck? Oh, right. Stuck in commuter traffic."

—Linda Keenan, author and resident of *Suburgatory*

"No one knows how American residential preferences will change in the twenty-first century. But Leigh Gallagher's well-researched and provocative *The End of the Suburbs* makes a persuasive argument that is difficult to refute. Required reading for anyone interested in the future of the United States."

—Kenneth T. Jackson, professor of history,
Columbia University, and author of *Crabgrass Frontier*

"Have you ever wondered whether the Great Recession will halt the process of gentrification in major American cities? Or what will happen to the empty suburban sprawl that is the result of the housing boom and bust? Or how most of us will live in a world where oil is expensive? Leigh Gallagher's crisp, entertaining, and fact-filled new book answers these questions and many more."

—Bethany McLean, coauthor of
The Smartest Guys in the Room and *All the Devils Are Here*

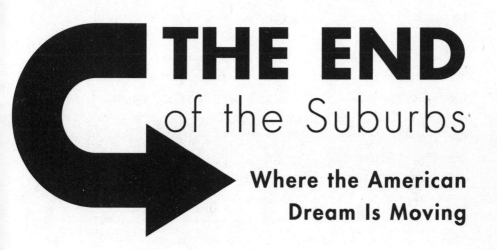

THE END
of the Suburbs

**Where the American
Dream Is Moving**

LEIGH GALLAGHER

PORTFOLIO / PENGUIN

PORTFOLIO / PENGUIN
Published by the Penguin Group
Penguin Group (USA) Inc., 375 Hudson Street,
New York, New York 10014, USA

USA | Canada | UK | Ireland | Australia | New Zealand | India | South Africa | China

Penguin Books Ltd, Registered Offices: 80 Strand, London WC2R 0RL, England
For more information about the Penguin Group visit penguin.com

Grateful acknowledgment is made for permission to reprint excerpts from the following copyrighted works:
"The Last Resort," words and music by Don Henley and Glenn Frey. © 1976 (renewed) Cass County Music and Red Cloud Music. All print rights administered by Warner-Tamerlane Publishing Corp. All rights reserved. Used by permission of Alfred Music Publishing Co., Inc.

"Mad Men," dialogue from episode no. 505. Courtesy of AMC Network Entertainment LLC.

Oh, The Places You'll Go! By Dr. Seuss, TM and copyright © Dr. Seuss Enterprises L.P. 1990. Used by permission of Random House Children's Books, a division of Random House, Inc. Any third party use of this material, outside of this publication, is prohibited. Interested parties must apply directly to Random House, Inc. for permission.

Library of Congress Cataloging-in-Publication Data

Gallagher, Leigh (Journalist)
The end of the suburbs : where the American dream is moving / Leigh Gallagher.
pages cm
Includes bibliographical references and index.
ISBN 978-1-59184-525-6
1. Suburbs—United States—History. 2. Suburban life—United States—History. I. Title.
HT352.U6G35 2013
307.740973—dc23
2013017233

Printed in the United States of America
1   3   5   7   9   10   8   6   4   2

Book design by Alissa Amell
Set in Janson MT Std

For Mom, Dad, and Drew

CONTENTS

THE END
of the Suburbs

INTRODUCTION

We shape our buildings, and afterwards our buildings shape us.

—WINSTON CHURCHILL

Aron Ralston looks out at the twenty-five hundred people gathered in the Valencia Ballroom at the Orange County Convention Center in Orlando. You know Ralston; he's the guy who got trapped by a boulder for five days while hiking in southeastern Utah in 2003 and cut his arm off with a dull knife to escape. The ordeal made him a celebrity, and a sought-after motivational speaker. On this February day in 2012, Ralston is here to kick off the opening ceremonies at the International Builders' Show, the annual gathering of the American home-building industry put on by the National Association of Home Builders (NAHB). The theme: overcoming adversity.

"I'm looking at several thousand survivors right now," Ralston says somberly. He acknowledges that the executives and industry members in the room have just come through the Great Recession, which inflicted epic unprecedented levels of pain on their business.

He is here, he tells his audience, to help them see their struggle as a gift; to help them find what he calls the "blessings in your boulders."

For the next half hour, Ralston tells the story of his own ordeal: how a sunny hike in a remote, undeveloped section of Canyonlands National Park—an area he quips could be "a ripe market for builders"—turned into a life-changing event when an eight-hundred-pound boulder dislodged and landed on top of him, crushing his right forearm and pinning him inside a canyon. He chronicles the events of the following five days—how, after futile attempts to free himself, he sipped his remaining water, drank his own urine, videotaped good-byes to his parents, and carved his presumed date of death into the sandstone. But then he recounts the stroke of joy, the "eureka moment" he felt when he suddenly realized he could break his own bones, sever his arm, and have a chance at surviving. He describes the process in wrenching detail—hitting the nerve was like "liquid metal," he says—but he emphasizes that the actual act of cutting was a beautiful thing. "I stepped out of my grave," he says. When he passed out after he was rescued, it wasn't from pain, he tells the audience; it was from joy.

At this point, a low murmur starts to roll through the crowd. Someone in the back row has himself passed out and needs attention. Soon there is a rustle closer to the stage; another person has fallen faint. Ralston stops his speech for several minutes while emergency crews enter. A third call for help comes from the left section of the audience. Then a fourth. Someone next to me leans over and whispers in concern: Could it be food poisoning? It wasn't. Ralston's speeches have incited physical reactions before, but this is the first time he's ever had to stop his act and the first time more than one person has succumbed. ("It was like a chain reaction," he said later. "They basically ran out of paramedics.")

After the ill are revived and wheeled out, Ralston steps forward on the stage and resumes, tactfully acknowledging the intensity of his story. Then he brings the message home: "It might be a challenge to look at this as the greatest thing that's ever happened to you," he tells the crowd. But he encourages them to see it that way. "You all have that same strength," he says, "to make your boulders your blessings."

The home-building industry circa February 2012 could use some blessings. In the five years since the mortgage bubble burst, setting off the Great Recession and leaving many home owners underwater, the industry has been gutted. Hundreds of companies have gone bankrupt. Attendance at the show this week is around 50,000, half the 100,000 or more at its height in 2006. Three years after the recession officially ended, things are still grim. By the time of this writing the situation would come to improve markedly, but as the attendees sit here listening to Ralston, they are sitting in their own ravine, the bottom of the wrenching housing bust. A fresh set of numbers has just confirmed it: single-family housing starts—the number of privately owned housing units on which construction has begun—and new home sales each hit new lows in 2011. More than eleven million home owners are still underwater. And despite rock-bottom interest rates and prices that dropped 34 percent nationwide and much more in some areas, here in February 2012 people still aren't buying. The Standard & Poor's index of home-building stocks lost 71 percent of its value between 2006 and 2012, nearly

twice as much as other troubled industries like publishing and airlines.

It is these statistics that have brought me to Orlando. Although the
entire housing market, and indeed, the entire country, has felt the pain
of the recession, I'm here to explore the effect it has had on one specific
area: our suburbs, that broad, catchall descriptor for the vast landscape
of leafy, low-density, residential enclaves that house the majority of our
312 million people. Because more Americans live in the suburbs than
anywhere else, it is where the builders in the room do the overwhelming majority of their business. The housing crisis, in which the binging
on residential mortgages led to the overbuilding of millions of homes,
hit the suburbs especially hard: builders erected more single-family
houses than at almost any time in history and covered record amounts
of farmland with new subdivisions. Many of those houses now sit empty.

Anyone who has read a newspaper over the past couple of years
might reasonably deduce that the suburbs have been in some trouble lately: statistics and articles about the pain being inflicted on
our bedroom communities have been appearing almost since the
financial crisis began, citing not just the number of foreclosures
among American home owners but related issues like the rise in
crime and poverty in suburban communities. ("The Death of the
Fringe Suburb," read one recent headline; "Struggling in the Suburbs," said another; a third declared, "The Housing Crisis Could
End Suburbia as We Know It.") Meanwhile, a cache of articles, papers, and popular books has heralded the resurgence of cities.

But what the headlines miss is that while much of the hurt can
be blamed on the recent recession and its immediate effects, there
are larger trends at work. Many of the suburbs affected by the hous-

ing crisis are not experiencing a temporary setback but a permanent one, the result of a powerful tectonic shift whose forces have been grinding away for quite some time.

When I set out to write a book in the spring of 2011, I originally planned to explore the future of our economy and how the aftereffects of the financial crisis would bring permanent changes to various aspects of our lives. But the more I researched, the more I discovered that the most dramatic shift involved where and how we choose to live—and it wasn't a result of the Great Recession at all. Rather, the housing crisis only concealed something deeper and more profound happening to what we have come to know as American suburbia. Simply speaking, more and more Americans don't want to live there anymore.

The reasons are varied, but several disparate factors all point to a decrease in demand for traditional suburban living: many Americans are tiring of the physical aspect of the suburbs, the design of which has changed dramatically over the years to gradually spread people farther and farther apart from one another and the things they like to do, making them increasingly reliant on their cars and, increasingly, on *Thelma and Louise*–length commutes. Big demographic shifts are seeing our population grow older, younger, and more diverse seemingly all at once, while powerful social trends are shrinking and transforming the American nuclear family, long the dominant driver of suburbia. An epic financial crisis coupled with the rising cost of energy has made punishing commutes also unaffordable, while a new-found hyperawareness of environmental issues has shaken up and reordered our priorities in ways that stand in direct conflict to the suburban way of life.

This has all been happening for years, but it's now being backed up by data. The rate of suburban population growth has outpaced that of urban centers in every decade since the invention of the automobile, but in 2011, for the first time in a hundred years, that trend reversed. Construction permit data shows that in several cities, building activity that was once concentrated in the suburban fringe has now shifted primarily to cities, or what planners call the "urban core." At the same time, demand for the large, single-family homes that characterize the suburbs is dwindling, and big suburban home builders like Toll Brothers are saying their best markets are now cities.

Many of the builders present at the NAHB show in Orlando know this and have started changing the way they do business. Like Ralston, they've started breaking their own bones by tearing up old floor plans, adjusting land acquisition strategies, and shifting their focus to include smaller houses and more urban developments. "Gone are the master bathrooms you can land planes in," said Boyce Thompson, the editorial director of the *Builder* group of magazines at the housing research and publishing firm Hanley Wood, during a presentation on market trends. Many of the attendees took part in educational sessions on "multifamily" housing units, design strategies for a shifting market, and the changing preferences of the new home buyer. During one such session, the audience watched an ad for builder Shea Homes' new "Spaces" line in which pleasant-looking suburbanites talked about what they wanted in their new homes. "A typical home in the suburbs for *me*?" one housewife asks. "It's just not the way things are done anymore." The 2012 annual *Builder* magazine "concept home," at the show, always an important barometer of where housing trends are headed, was instead a series of three different homes targeted to three different generations, all featuring smaller—or "right-sized," since "small" is still a word that goes unsaid by this group—floor plans and more efficient use of space. "Change is the only path to tomorrow," Larry Swank, chairman of the NAHB's conventions and meetings committee and a leading builder in Indiana, advised an audience in a breakout session.

Not every home builder is hurting. Floating around at the NAHB show were people like John McLinden, a longtime builder in Chicago who had spent the past few years developing a kind of replacement for the conventional subdivision: a neighborhood of compact, upscale bungalows steps from the train station in the middle of Libertyville, Illinois. His sales were going gangbusters. "Nothing exists like this—certainly not in the suburbs," he told me eagerly. "And we did it in the midst of a housing crisis." Indeed, one of the biggest trends in home building right now is remaking our suburbs to look more, well, urban. Like McLinden, developers in suburbs from Morristown, New Jersey, to Leesburg, Virginia, to Lakewood, Colorado, are rebuilding their downtowns as urbanized centers with streets that combine stores, restaurants, and apartments, while nearly every home builder now has a town house or condo division. Even Toll Brothers, the Horsham, Pennsylvania–based home builder that rose to fame on the wings of the suburban mega-home, says what it calls its "suburban move-up" houses are now roughly 50 percent of what it builds and sells, down from 70 to 80 percent just a few years ago.

This brings me to an important point: when I talk about the "end of the suburbs," I do not mean to suggest that all suburban communities are going to vaporize. Plenty of older suburbs are going strong for reasons we'll explore later, and many newer suburbs are reinventing themselves to adapt to the times. But when the people who have delivered the same kind of one-size-fits-all suburban subdivisions over the past few decades are tearing up their blueprints, venturing gingerly into urban markets, and actually fainting at the thought of what the future holds, something big is afoot. The reliable expansion of our suburbs, the steady growth of the housing industry, and the seemingly unending supply of new single-family homes—and home owners—that we became used to over the past several decades may well be a thing of the past. Robert Shiller, a Yale University economist, founder of the Case-Shiller Home Price Indices, and the forecaster who predicted both the dot-com and housing bubbles, has said we may be in for a new normal. According to Shiller, U.S. suburban development since the 1950s was "unusual" in its reliance on the automobile and the highway system; the bursting of the bubble may result in a bigger, more structural change. "The heyday of exurbs may well be behind us," he has said. "Suburban prices may not recover in our lifetime."

The suburbs have been the dominant pattern of residential growth in America for the last century. There are roughly 132 million homes across the country, the largest percent of them—almost half—in the suburbs, somewhat obtusely defined by the U.S. Census Bureau as the parts of our metropolitan statistical areas that lie outside central cities. Looking at the broadly defined "metropolitan" regions of our country, which is where more than 80 percent of Americans live, the percentage of us living in the suburbs is higher: 61 percent. To get a sense of their scale, consider that there are an estimated 64 million houses in suburbia. Over the past half century, the portion of people living in the suburbs has steadily grown, from 31 percent in 1960 to 51 percent in 2010, which amounts to about 158 million Americans. In terms of sheer size, not for a long time have the suburbs been "sub."

Of course, it's hard to paint the suburbs with one brush. Even the term "suburb" refers to many things. Broadly speaking, it refers to residential neighborhoods on the outskirts of big cities. But the American suburbs are a variegated terrain, a massive amalgam of thousands of different types and vintages. There are older, stately ones in the Northeast with centuries-old stone houses and newer ones all over the country in subdivisions lined with tracts of mass-produced homes. There are wealthy enclaves like the Main Line of Philadelphia or the North Shore of Chicago or Shaker Heights, Ohio, or Atherton, California, and blue-collar mainstays like Yonkers, New York, or Cicero, Illinois. There are big ones and small ones, boroughs and hamlets, inner-ring ones and ex-urban ones, hilly ones and flat ones. There are large swaths of suburbia, like the San Fernando Valley in Los Angeles or New York's Long Island, that are the size of small countries. Suburbs look different depending where you are: in Las Vegas front yards are filled with pebbles and cacti, in California Mediterranean red-tiled roofs rule the day, and in wealthy suburbs throughout the Northeast regal old homes line leafy streets.

Despite their differences, the American suburbs share one thing in common—they evoke a certain way of life, one of tranquil, curving streets and cul-de-sacs; marching bands and soccer leagues; bake sales and PTA meetings and center hall colonials. The phrase "the American Dream" immediately brings to mind images of the single-family home with a white picket fence; the suburbs have also provided the setting for so many of our iconic cinematic moments. They are where Macaulay Culkin got left home alone; where Ferris Bueller took the day off; where Jake kissed Samantha in *Sixteen Candles*; and where Joel Goodsen, thereafter remembered only as Tom Cruise, first strutted his stuff in *Risky Business*.

The suburbs are innately connected to America because they are a uniquely American phenomenon. No other country has such an enormous percentage of its middle class living at such low densities across such massive amounts of land. As Kenneth T. Jackson put it in his masterful book *Crabgrass Frontier: The Suburbanization of the United States*, widely considered the definitive history of the American suburbs, "affluent and middle-class Americans live in suburban areas that are far from their work places, in homes that they own, and in the center of yards that by urban standards elsewhere are enormous."

This might be a good time to mention that even though I'm writing a book about the decline of the suburbs, I don't have anything against them personally. I currently live in Manhattan's West Village (the former stomping ground of the legendary urbanist Jane Jacobs), but I had a pretty idyllic childhood growing up in Media, Pennsylvania, a suburb twelve miles southwest of Philadelphia. I lived in an old stone house in a leafy neighborhood called Bowling Green, which had a lot to offer a family like mine: a house with a lawn, a neighborhood full of kids, and the great Wallingford-Swarthmore public school district, of which our slice of Media was a part.

I have gauzy, sepia-toned, *Wonder Years*–style memories of my childhood in Media. Most of the houses in Bowling Green dated back to the 1920s—ours was a 1923 stone colonial—and the streets were lined with majestic oaks that dated back who knows how long. The epicenter of the neighborhood was a place we called the Triangle, where Mulberry Road and Truepenny Road converged in a T intersection, forming a wider paved area that provided us kids with a place to hang out, to roller-skate, and to hold street hockey tournaments. In the summer, the Triangle also played home to the neighborhood's annual Fourth of July picnic, an all-day affair during which parents would close the streets to traffic, set up half a dozen picnic tables, and wheel their grills out from their backyards. This was the party to end all parties, as far as I was concerned: there were organized three-legged races and water balloon tosses, Mrs. Desmond's famous flag cake, and a bicycle parade for which we kids would decorate our bikes and ride them proudly once around the block; I can still remember eagerly threading the spokes of my Schwinn with red, white, and blue streamers in the hope of taking the top prize. The real highlight came at the end of the day, when the professional square dancing caller would arrive. He'd set up a sound system and an elevated stage, the music would start, and everyone would spill into the Triangle, partner up, and dance in one big hoedown. I remember whirling around to the Virginia reel and doing do-si-dos to the caller's pace until I was dizzy. Later, after the fireworks, we'd stroll home and I'd collapse in bed.

One of the best things about our neighborhood every other day of the year was that it was within walking distance of downtown Media, a unique little suburban metropolis. Media's main drag, State Street, is lined with dozens of boutiques, a lively restaurant and bar scene, and not one but two five-and-ten stores. A massive, stately courthouse—Media is the county seat of Delaware County—spans at least four square blocks, anchoring the downtown and bringing a swell of lawyers and workers to the town each day. There's a 1927 vaudeville theater that's been restored, a local newspaper—the *Town Talk*—and even a working trolley. (You can distinguish the locals by how deftly they swerve their cars to avoid it when it glides down State Street.) There are annual events like the Media 5 Mile Race, a tradition since 1979, and Super Sunday, the town's annual flea market, from which I once procured a T-shirt sporting Media's slogan, "Everybody's Hometown." I went to an excellent public school that was academically rigorous and had a diverse student body. My teenage memories are those of marching band, football games, and sneaking out to drink Keystone Light in the woods behind our house. More than twenty years later, my high school English teacher still sends me her recommended reading list every summer.

Although I am a city girl now, my parents still live in Media, and I visit them often. It's rare that I bring a visitor home who doesn't remark on how central casting it all seems. (In the mid-1990s it actually *was* central casting: television producers used exterior shots of our house for the opening credits of a short-lived NBC sitcom called *Minor Adjustments*.) Once, after I invited a former boss over for dinner while he was visiting the area, he chided me about an upbringing that was almost comically idyllic. "How's everything in Grover's Corners?" he'd ask from then on whenever I returned to the New York office from a visit home.

But things have changed. Bowling Green's Fourth of July picnic has been moved to a block party in September, because people started wanting to go to their beach houses for the holiday instead. The square dance caller has been replaced with an iPod playlist, and food-safety concerns have led to new rules requiring all the dishes be kept on ice. Parents now accompany their kids to the bus stop every morning; I used to walk alone. In the late 1990s, despite a protracted and emotional fight from the residents, a developer turned a big estate that abutted one edge of the neighborhood into a subdivision of forty-three luxury homes. A Starbucks now sits just outside the neighborhood.

Our country's suburbs have changed during that time, too. Most of today's suburbs do not look like Media, and it's not just because they don't have a courthouse or a trolley. While people who live in the Northeast are more accustomed to older neighborhoods like Bowling Green, most Americans live in communities built in the last fifty years, and for reasons we'll explore in detail later, these more prevalent suburbs look a lot different. They are bigger, newer—the average age of all housing stock in this country is just thirty-nine years—and feature a more homogenous style of housing. They're also more spread out. As development has pushed farther outward from urban areas, we have had to travel ever greater distances to get to all the places we need to go. From 1969 to 2009, overall miles traveled per household annually jumped 60 percent, and today, many suburbs are located so far from their "urbs" that they're not really a "sub" of anything. Think of developments in the horse country of Chester County, Pennsylvania, or Loudoun County, Virginia, or the subdivision hamlets surrounded by cornfields in Illinois or hanging off freeways all throughout the West. Or consider Ridgecrest, California, the only incorporated town along U.S. 395 in Kern County located halfway between Bakersfield and Death Valley. Ridgecrest is located 112 miles from Bakersfield, the metropolitan area of which it is officially considered a part, giving it the dubious distinction of being the suburb furthest from its "urb."

Plenty of books have been written about the negative ramifications of this development and why the suburbs are bad for us. But this book isn't about why the suburbs *ought* to end. Rather, it's about how the suburbs—at least as we know them—*are* ending. When I started looking into this subject, I knew of some key data points that supported the main thrust of my argument. The more I looked, the more the data from all corners confirmed it. Consider the following:

⮑ Census data reveals a shift.

After fifty years of outward migration, we're starting to move in the other direction. According to census data, population growth in outer suburbs, which had been the engine of residential growth for much of the 2000s, ground to a near halt from 2010 to 2011, increasing by just 0.4 percent. Cities and high-density inner suburbs, meanwhile, grew twice as fast, marking the first time in twenty years that city growth surpassed that of the exurbs. Our largest cities, meanwhile, grew at a faster rate than any of their suburbs for the first time in one hundred years. To some degree this is a reaction to our recent housing crisis, which saw so much overexpansion especially in the exurbs. But it's also the first time since the invention of the automobile that our outward migration pattern has reversed.

An emerging body of research is starting to bolster the census data. One such study comes from a professor at Tufts University who used data from the U.S. Postal Service to track the number of occupied housing units in the suburbs (as it turns out, whether a house receives mail is one of the only reliable ways to tell whether it's truly occupied). The data showed occupancy declining in the suburbs and gaining in the cities. We'll explore these and other results in detail later, but to many policy experts these kinds of changes represent a tipping point.

↳ Home valuations have inverted.

In the wake of the Great Recession, housing values have held up far better in cities than in suburbs, a reversal from the way things normally work. During almost every recession in our history, urban home prices have suffered the most. This time, the pain has been concentrated in the suburbs. Kevin Gillen, a housing economist at the University of Pennsylvania's Fels Institute of Government, has studied this phenomenon closely in the Philadelphia area. During and after the downturn of the early '90s, home prices in downtown Philadelphia fell 34 percent while prices in the suburbs fell 14 percent. This time around, the opposite happened: prices in the most distant suburbs have fallen 33 percent, while homes downtown fell 20 percent. "The pattern is completely reversed," says Gillen, using a phrase I would hear repeatedly over the course of my reporting.

This new pattern is playing out nationwide. Studying more than ninety thousand home sales in fifteen markets across the country, Joe Cortright, president of Impresa, a Portland-based economic consulting firm specializing in regional economic analysis, found that home prices in the urban centers of Chicago, Los Angeles, Pittsburgh, Portland, and Tampa have held up much better than prices in those cities' suburbs. Other research has shown a distinction in valuation even among different kinds of suburbs: valuations in towns that are considered more walkable and contain more urban elements—things like Main Streets and downtown commercial districts—are holding up better and appreciating faster than those that are in so-called drivable suburban developments.

↳ Building activity has reversed.

Since 2000, building activity has picked up in cities and slowed down in suburbs. In New York City in the early 1990s, 7 percent of all residential building permits were in the city limits, while more than 70 percent were in the suburban fringe. By 2008, that had flipped: 9 percent were in the fringe and more than 70 percent were in the city. The city of Portland, Oregon, issued 38 percent of the region's building permits that same year, compared with 9 percent in the early 1990s. Denver proper accounted for 32 percent of its region's building activity, up from 5 percent in the early 1990s. The housing crash may have accelerated things, but the shift has been under way for some time. "It's a complete reversal," Jonathan Rose, a leading developer of sustainable, mixed-use communities, told me. And while the housing market has started to recover, with home construction and pricing data showing their first signs of prolonged, sustainable momentum, a rebound may not result in a shift in these construction patterns. One of the brightest spots in the industry's comeback has been so-called multifamily construction, the building of apartments and condominiums more commonly found in cities.

↳ Poverty has invaded the burbs.

Americans started moving to the suburbs because they considered them safe, happy enclaves where they could escape the crime and poverty of cities. But this has become an increasingly false character-ization. A series of groundbreaking studies by the Brookings Institu-tion has shined a light on one of the most striking trends in our society in recent years—the sharp rise of poverty levels in the sub-urbs. As of 2010, a record 15.3 million suburban residents were living below the poverty line in the largest metropolitan areas, up 11.5 per-cent from the year prior and 53 percent from 2000. The overall pov-erty rate is still lower in the suburbs than in cities, but during the decade, the growth rate in the number of poor living in the suburbs studied was more than twice that of cities—and the suburbs are now home to the largest and fastest-growing poor population in the coun-try. Perhaps not surprisingly, crime rates are following similar pat-terns, with new data showing that homicides are falling sharply in cities and rising in suburbs.

⤷ Cities are resurgent.

As poverty has invaded the suburbs, wealth has rushed back into cities. If you've visited New York, Los Angeles, San Francisco, Seattle, or just about any other American city lately, you don't need more proof that they are booming. Real estate prices are soaring, development is cranking, and once-blighted neighborhoods are now yuppified. This is well-trod territory; in media and "thought leader" circles, cities have become the equivalent of fashion's new black, with a torrent of books lauding their resurgence. But it's a remarkable shift, especially consid-ering the growing ranks of young families—the demographic main-stay of suburbia—now electing to stay in cities. In New York, Tribeca is now called Triburbia, and in Center City Philadelphia, a former strip club has been turned into a Daddy Day Care center. In the building world, the construction of "multifamily" housing—apartment and condo buildings—is booming, while the construction of single-family homes still lags.

Retailers, experts when it comes to following moneyed consumers wherever they go, are all over this: hardly any suburban shopping malls have been built in the United States since 2006, and big-box chains are packing up, slimming down, and squeezing smaller versions of themselves into cities and denser communities. Walmart plans to open one hundred of its new small-scale Neighborhood Market stores in 2012, triple the pace of 2011. Target, which for years relied on the suburbs for its growth, is focusing its efforts on its smaller-concept urban store called City. Whole Foods, meanwhile, that emblem of yuppification, is opening a new location in Harlem. Even PetSmart has a new urban chain, called—wait for it—Unleashed.

The biggest suburban home builders are making a play for cities, too. Toll Brothers, which became one of the nation's biggest home builders by building luxury homes in suburbia, is in the midst of an aggressive expansion into New York City with dozens of new properties in neighborhoods ranging from the most exclusive blocks of Manhattan's Upper East Side to hipster enclaves like Brooklyn's DUMBO (the acronym for the industrial-chic neighborhood named Down Under the Manhattan Bridge Overpass). New York is "our hottest market by far," Toll Brothers CEO Douglas Yearley has said.

While these moves offer solid evidence that we are moving away from the burbs as we've known them, other trends indicate the likelihood that this is more than just a cyclical or reactionary fluke.

⤷ Our households are shrinking.

Today, only half of all adults in the United States are married, down from nearly three-quarters in 1960. And fewer people are having kids: families with children used to make up more than half of U.S. households, but by 2025 they'll represent just a quarter, and, strikingly, we'll have as many single-person households as families. The suburbs are built for life with kids, and we're not having nearly as many of them. There are a variety of reasons for this that we'll explore later, but the implication is the same: "The whole Ozzie and Harriet day has passed," says Peter Calthorpe, the San Francisco–based architect and urban planner who pioneered the notion of transit-oriented development and who, as a cofounder of the New Urbanism movement, is one of the leading thinkers on alternative growth models to conventional suburban development.

⤷ Millennials hate the burbs . . .

America's eighty million so-called millennials, defined for the purposes of this book as those born between 1977 and 1995, are an enormous group—bigger than the baby boomers. As such, they're more poked, prodded, and studied than any generation. As of this writing, record numbers of the older segment of them—those that are in their early twenties and older—are still living with their parents, which presents its own problem for the economy since it creates a big logjam in the normal housing cycle. But here's the bigger problem: studies show that when millennials do leave their parents' homes, they don't want anything to do with the kinds of suburbs they grew up in. Seventy-seven percent of them prefer to live in an urban area, and whether that means an inner city or an urbanized small town or suburb, one thing it doesn't mean is the kinds of homes that will be left for them in conventional suburbia. Arthur C. Nelson, director of the Metropolitan Research Center at the University of Utah, has forecast that based on these changing demographic forces and a shift in consumer demand, there will be a surplus of as many as forty million large-lot homes—those on a sixth of an acre or more—in the United States by 2020.

↰ . . . And they hate cars even more.

Millennials may also be the first generation of young people since the automobile was invented to be indifferent about cars and driving. In 1980, 66 percent of all seventeen-year-olds had their driver's license. In 2010, the figure was 47 percent, a sharp and perplexing decline that has been discussed and dissected by millennial watchers and carmakers alike. The notion of a teenager opting to not get his driver's license, to those of us who grew up in a different time, may seem sacrilege. But watch them fawn over their Apple products and you will see that this generation, as Steve Jobs encouraged them to do, "thinks different." They don't want cars, and they don't want cul-de-sacs—two of the pillars on which suburban life depends.

↪ The price of oil is still rising.

As energy prices have climbed, so has the cost of the suburban commute. In 2008, the average suburban household spent double on gas what it did in 2003. Many suburban families now spend half their income on housing and transportation costs. Since houses are cheaper the farther they are from urban centers, lower-income suburban households can very easily spend more on transportation than on their mortgage or rent. Economists say the cost of distance is starting to get baked into housing prices, sending valuations down in remote housing markets. The rising cost of energy is also starting to impact our behavior: for most of the last fifty years, the number of miles driven has increased with every year. In 2007, those numbers peaked and have been declining since. Some experts have attributed this to the recession, but the decline started before the recession and before gas prices spiked, and it's happening even at higher income levels. This shift is major, and one *The Atlantic* pointed to in proclaiming "The Beginning of the End for Suburban America."

↪ We are eco-obsessed.

Thanks in part to Al Gore, everyone now knows suburban residents pump their houses full of hot and cool air, load gas into the SUV by the tankful, and pour gallons of chemicals onto the lawn. More recently, a powerful "anti-stuff" mentality has emerged, largely as a reaction to the excessive consumption patterns that sparked our financial crisis.

Home size has decreased over the past few years, while movements like the "Not So Big House," which focuses on building slightly smaller homes that offer greater function and higher quality, and "LifeEdited," which preaches the reduction of posessions, have gained traction. The rise of so-called collaborative consumption, meanwhile, has popularized the mass sharing of cars, homes, clothes, and more. All of these philosophies run counter to the acquisitive lifestyle of suburbia and signal a powerful shift in the consumer zeitgeist. Less is now more.

↪ The suburbs were poorly designed to begin with.

While older suburbs were built on a different model, the modern-day American suburbs were designed in a way that went counter to thousands of years of planning theory. They spread people far from each other and their jobs (though many jobs did migrate to the suburbs over the years) and the other places they need to go every day; and they make their residents wholly reliant on their cars. The financial viability of our modern suburbs, meanwhile, was flawed from the start: the lower-density pattern of development doesn't yield enough tax revenue to pay for the infrastructure needed to support them— one reason many municipalities are struggling or going broke.

People have predicted the demise of the suburbs before. The author and provocateur James Howard Kunstler's 1993 book, *The Geography of Nowhere: The Rise and Decline of America's Man-made Land-*

scape, called suburban development "a landscape of scary places, the geography of nowhere, that has simply ceased to be a credible human habitat." In an interview in the late 1990s, the urbanist Jane Jacobs suggested that sprawling-style suburbs were going out of fashion. A 2006 documentary, *The End of Suburbia: Oil Depletion and the Collapse of the American Dream*, explored the potentially disastrous implications of a worldwide oil shortage on the suburban development pattern. But never have so many forces been working against conventional suburban development at the same time. The facts laid out in the pages that follow represent a slow-burning revolution, a realignment of our societal priorities, and a reversal of the fundamental social equation that's come to define our nation. In the energy world, people talk about peak oil, the moment after which our supply of fossil fuels will begin to dwindle. After more than half a century of expansion and the housing equivalent of gas-guzzling, we may have hit peak suburb. When migration patterns are starting to head in a different direction, when the market has changed its mind on what's valuable, when Whole Foods opens in Harlem and Toll Brothers takes over Manhattan, it's hard to deny we're at the beginning of a serious transformation. "We've reached the limits of suburban development," Shaun Donovan, the secretary of Housing and Urban Development, has said.

But to say the suburbs are ending does not imply that everyone will up and relocate to city skyscrapers. Yes, cities are resurgent, but many people still want to live on a tree-lined street, have a front yard, and be able to drive to the grocery store to load up for their family of four. Schools, too, play a big role in making the suburbs attractive, and while this is now less of an issue for a variety of reasons, schools are still a major factor drawing young families to the suburbs.

Besides, some people just like their half, quarter, or whatever portion of an acre and a car. "There are certain segments of the population who would say, 'Over my dead body am I going to live in a dense situation,'" says Jonathan Smoke, chief economist of housing industry research and publishing firm Hanley Wood, publisher of *Builder* magazine. People tend to have strong opinions about this topic on one side or the other, but of all the people I spoke to for this book, Smoke might be the most measured. A hard-data-driven market analyst, he has a deep knowledge of the mechanics of the housing industry. But Smoke also spent more than a decade working as a consultant to several home builders and as an executive in strategic planning for one of them, Beazer Homes, so he shares the perspective of big builders and understands the realities of what the American home owner wants more than most housing economists. That experience has given him what he likes to say is a more "balanced" view. Yet Smoke, too, says we've reached a turning point. "Bottom line, there are going to be changes," he says.

In my quest to figure out what the future of America might mean for the future of the suburbs, and vice versa, I've interviewed people involved in many different aspects of the debate: I've talked to home builders, developers, planners, transportation engineers, home buyers, home sellers, residents of suburbs, residents of cities, residents who left the city for the suburbs, and residents who left the suburbs for the city. I've grilled academics, economists, architects, and psychologists; I've talked to toilet makers, air-conditioning suppliers, and deck builders. In exploring all the nuances of this shift, this book first explores the history of suburbia, because to understand where we're going, it's important to understand how we got here. It ponders the origins of the American Dream and how it came to be synonymous with a house and a yard. It seeks to explain the backlash against traditional suburban development and then in great detail lays out the many ways planners, builders, and developers are hard at work creating new kinds of neighborhoods—even within our existing suburbs—that are completely different. Finally, the book analyzes our changing priorities and the new types of homes and lifestyles Americans are looking for—because if our most popular way of life is on the wane, the next logical question is: Where will everybody go?

The night before Aron Ralston spoke at the 2012 builders' convention, I went to a swanky party put on by Hanley Wood. While guests dined on filet mignon and sushi, recession be damned, I approached the company's then CEO Frank Anton and asked whether he thought the suburbs were threatened. We chatted for a while; he pointed out that the most expensive real estate has always been in cities, lamenting how he can now say that firsthand after having recently put his twentysomething daughter up in a Manhattan apartment. Then he stopped and looked at me as he fully considered my argument. He gave me an imploring look. "Does the story have a happy ending?" He paused, considered what he asked, and rephrased himself: "Please," he said, "tell me it has a happy ending."

This story does have a happy ending. Roughly speaking, we rebuild once or twice a century in this country, and when we do, we have an opportunity to change things for the better. The new homes and communities being planned for the next phase of our development will be better suited to our needs. They will factor in the mistakes of the past to make things better for our future. They will reduce our dependency on the car. They will be developed around places where people can naturally interact with one another. They will be located closer to where we work and closer to the things we need, which will give us more time with our families and friends and more time to pursue all of the things we like to do. These changes won't happen overnight, but they will ultimately lead to more choice, more freedom, and richer lives. And that will be a happy ending for everyone.

THE GREAT URBAN EXODUS

The building of houses constitutes the major architectural
work of any civilization.

—LEWIS MUMFORD

People have always wanted to get out of the city. At least they have
since the days of ancient Egypt, which is where scholars have traced
one of the earliest known references to the suburbs. In the fourteenth
century BC, wealthy suburban villas with spacious gardens south of
the ancient Egyptian capital of Amarna housed estates of the city's
powerful nobles. Scholars cite later references by Cicero to *suburbani*,
big estates outside of Rome, as early as the first century BC. Historian
Kenneth T. Jackson cites a clay tablet dating from 539 BC on which a
resident of the then booming Mesopotamian city-state of Ur, whose
residents had started settling in the countryside, marveled to the king
of Persia about how his property was "so close to Babylon that we
enjoy all the advantages of the city, and yet when we come home we
are away from all the noise and dust." It wasn't a leafy subdivision, but
the appeal—to live outside the metropolis in quieter, more peaceful
environs—was the same.

But even though suburbs have been with us for some time, they were, for much of history, primarily the home of the poor. Throughout the Middle Ages and Renaissance, cities were the centers of culture, commerce, and the arts; merchants, politicians, and other elite members of society all lived and worked closest to the core, while the poor lived at the edges or outside the city walls (it's still that way in many countries, like France, India, and Brazil). Of course, the upper crust did not avoid the outer regions altogether, and while the immediate fringe might have been déclassé, pure air and the countryside appealed to the wealthy just as they do today. Throughout European history the privileged classes retreated to rural settings for restoration and contemplation; think of the English manor or the Italian villa, or the wealthy Florentines who fled the plague in the 1300s by retreating to the countryside in Boccaccio's *The Decameron*.

The modern-day suburban pattern—in which large swaths of the middle class work in the city but make their homes in comfortable neighborhoods outside it—didn't begin to take hold until the early 1800s, when the burgeoning merchant elite in England began building estates in the countryside outside London and Manchester. After industrialization began, allowing this new upper middle class to amass great fortunes, they began moving there permanently. As wealth started to spread and cities became increasingly polluted, the middle class followed.

While the suburbs have come to symbolize something quintessentially American, early suburban development in the United States actually drew inspiration from this English model. By the early 1800s, the majority of Americans were still living on farms, but the intellectual and cultural elite had begun to cluster in our cities. Merchants, lawyers, manufacturers, and magnates built big town houses on the main thoroughfares in New York and Boston close to where they worked, while the poor lived in back alleys or courtyards nearby or on the city's outskirts. But while they were the center of the action, cities were also crowded, noisy, and incredibly filthy. Since there was no sewage system, residents would empty chamber pots by throwing their contents out the window (think about that the next time you complain about your neighbors), leading to outbreaks of disease, not to mention stench and grime. A *New York Times* article in 1863 lamented that "the accumulation of garbage, ashes and all pollutions, the choked gutters, the reeking and deadly odors, in most of the back and side streets, is intolerable." Things got worse as the Industrial Revolution arrived in the United States, and with the increase in population and factory pollution, cities became even grimmer. By 1910, the population of Manhattan reached 2.3 million—today it's about 1.6 million—with most of those people living in tenement buildings. Some ninety thousand windowless rooms were for rent, and immigrants lived in small rooms with as many as ten people. The Lower East Side, now a trendy residential area filled with boutiques, restaurants, and bars, was one of the most crowded places in the country.

Gradually, those who could afford it started moving away from the dense and dirty downtown, and in our biggest cities pockets of nicer neighborhoods started to spring up—Greenwich Village or Fifth Avenue in Manhattan, Cambridge and Beacon Hill in Boston, Germantown in Philadelphia. In 1814 in New York, the arrival of the steam ferry soon led to the colonization of Brooklyn Heights, just across the East River, considered the first large-scale commuter suburb.

As they would over the course of suburbia's history, advances in transportation technology soon delivered us at faster speeds to farther-flung places, each innovation enabling a new phase of development. Stagecoaches and ferries gave way to horse-drawn streetcars, then horse-drawn railroads, and by the 1830s the first steam-powered railroads. Gradually, in New York, Boston, Philadelphia, Chicago, and San Francisco, the wealthy began settling in enclaves that formed around these railroad stations. By 1849 there were fifty-nine commuter trains running from Boston. The population of New York City's Westchester County doubled between 1850 and 1870, then doubled again by 1890, and again by 1910. This was, of course, thanks in large part to Grand Central Station, which opened in 1871 as Grand Central Depot and granted easy access to midtown Manhattan from its northern suburbs. Suburbs were blossoming in Chicago, too, where a local newspaper hailed the opportunity for businessmen to "avail themselves of the beautiful quiet of a country residence without shortening the number of hours usually devoted to their daily avocations."

Soon the railroad gave way to electric-powered streetcars, which were easier and cheaper to build, so they spread out wider and faster. Towns started to emerge around streetcar stations, forming now-iconic places like Medford outside Boston, Oakland outside San Francisco, Shaker Heights outside Cleveland, and thousands of other communities. Each of these early railroad and streetcar suburbs was unique, but they were similar in one important way: their design was compact. In the pre-automobile era, suburban residents had to walk once they disembarked from the railroad or streetcar, so houses needed to be located within a reasonable distance to the station. So while these early suburbanites lived in individual, single-family houses—that was, after all, the whole appeal of leaving the city—homes were built close together. Entrepreneurial shopkeepers and service providers set up their storefronts around the station, where pedestrian traffic was likely to be highest. The result was a village center with a grid-shaped street pattern that emerged organically around the day-to-day needs and walking patterns of the people who lived there. Urban planners describe these neighborhoods as having "vibrancy" or "experiential richness" because, without even trying, their design promoted activity, foot traffic, commerce, and socializing.

Even while these suburbs replicated urban villages, a separate vision was emerging that saw the suburbs as tranquil, pastoral places that more closely represented the country. Two seminal developments in the mid-1800s broke the gridded village mold in search of this new, more romanticized ideal: Llewellyn Park in West Orange, New Jersey, conceived by New York businessman Llewellyn Haskell and designed by Alexander Jackson Davis, and Riverside outside Chicago, designed by Frederick Law Olmsted, the well-known landscape architect who had just designed New York City's Central Park. Both developments were railroad-accessible suburbs meant to be bedroom communities for the ultra wealthy, but bearing the more bucolic imprint of landscape architects as opposed to the rigidity of urban planners, both rejected the right angles of conventional planning in favor of winding streets and hilly, natural terrain. Riverside's streets were specifically designed, as Olmsted put it, with "gracefully curved lines, generous spaces and the absence of sharp corners . . . the idea being to suggest and imply leisure, contemplativeness and happy tranquility."

But with these and other country-inspired enclaves, social and intellectual life was still rooted in the city. Most suburban residents not only worked in the cities but socialized, shopped, and dined there. So while a natural village life did emerge in new residential areas, the city was still the heart of the community; the suburbs were its limbs.

It wasn't until Henry Ford gave the middle class wheels that everything changed. The first Model T rolled off the line in 1908 for $850 ($22,000 in today's dollars); four years later its price dropped to less than $700. This newfound mobility was like a drug; once people tried it, they were hooked. Automobile registrations went from eight thousand in 1905 to more than seventeen million by 1925. Even during the Great Depression, many Americans were more likely to part with some other necessity than give up their car. As one farm woman famously told an inspector from the U.S. Department of Agriculture who'd inquired why she had a car but no running water in her house: "You can't get to town in a bathtub."

Motorized transport presented untold opportunity for suburban development, allowing households to spread out wider and faster, but it also posed new challenges—namely, the introduction of car traffic into residential communities. In the early 1900s, a planner named Clarence Perry came up with a solution for this, a new design for suburban neighborhoods that would limit the traffic going through them. He replaced the traditional street grid pattern with a network of separate, self-contained, almost pod-like communities, each populated with enough families to support a local elementary school. These discrete "neighborhood units" would contain only houses and schools and therefore draw only local traffic, and their streets were specifically designed to minimize and slow car speed by making use of cul-de-sacs and T intersections. All other traffic would be kept outside the unit on fast-moving arterial roads that would connect the neighborhoods and also host retail and commercial activity. Perry thought this plan would benefit everyone: it would excise fast-moving "cut-through" traffic from residential neighborhoods, while still allowing residents to access stores outside their neighborhoods on their trips to and from work. Retailers and businesses, meanwhile, would be better positioned to serve multiple communities at once from the connector roads that exposed them to higher volumes of traffic.

While Llewellyn Park and Riverside were the first suburbs developed with a deliberate country-like feel, Perry's neighborhood unit marked the first suburban layout designed specifically around the car. One of the first communities to bear Perry's imprint was Radburn, New Jersey. Developed in 1929 (by another Clarence, Clarence Stein), Radburn was, as its developers proudly proclaimed, a "town for the motor age." The purpose of the neighborhood unit and its implementation in places like Radburn was traffic safety, but it represented a radical revision of traditional town planning principles, and it would leave an indelible imprint on American suburbia.

The widespread adoption of the car by the middle class, providing individual mobility to everyone anywhere, anytime, forever transformed the arrangement of our landscape, as developers were finally untethered from the constraints of public transportation. As the influential urban historian and sociologist Lewis Mumford would later write in his 1961 book, *The City in History: Its Origins, Its Transformations, and Its Prospects*, "As long as the railroad stop and walking distances controlled suburban growth, the suburb had form." The automobile suddenly unhooked us from the need to keep communities compact, the freeways soon gave us unfettered access, and there was land as far as the eye could see.

From 1921 to 1936, the "golden age of highway building" saw the construction of more than 420,000 miles of roads in the United States, opening up fresh stretches of land for suburbanization and kick-starting what you could call our first housing boom. Between 1923 and 1927, new homes were built at a pace of almost nine hundred thousand per year; from 1920 to 1930, according to Jackson in *Crabgrass Frontier*, the suburbs of the nation's ninety-six largest cities grew twice as fast as the cities themselves. And soon, they would grow even faster.

By 1945, America had two big, related problems. The first was a housing market that had been nearly dead for fifteen years. During the Depression, development froze, and during the war, all resources went to the military effort. For twenty years, housing starts averaged fewer than 400,000 per year, down from a peak of 937,000 in 1925. The second problem was that as soon as the war ended, thanks to an onslaught of returning veterans and an ensuing surge in the birth rate, Americans needed homes again, and a lot of them.

But because construction had stagnated for so long, there was nowhere for people to go. The housing shortage was so severe that by 1947 six million families were doubling up with relatives or friends, and another half million were occupying temporary quarters like mobile homes, barns, and garages. Kenneth Jackson, the historian, remembers his family moving in with his grandparents. "That was our situation, with four kids," he says. "I remember sleeping in a dining room."

The crisis was so acute that the government intervened. In 1934, after the Great Depression caused a spike in home foreclosures, the government had created the Federal Housing Administration, a new agency whose purpose was to stimulate lending in order to jump-start the ailing housing market. It did this by insuring long-term mortgage loans made by private lenders, which had a transformative effect. Before the Depression, mortgages were short-term and so expensive, covering only a small percentage of the home purchase price, that only the wealthy could afford paying so much up front for the cost of a home. But with the new government backing, private lenders were suddenly willing to lend on much more generous terms, extending the length of the loan to twenty and then thirty years and ultimately lending more than 90 percent of the cost of the home to buyers. The modern-day long-term fixed-rate mortgage was born, making it possible for almost anyone to get a home loan. The mortgage interest tax deduction, a by-product of the 1913 law that established the federal income tax—and still one of the biggest incentives for home ownership to this day—provided a welcome assist. Then in 1944, the government passed the Servicemen's Readjustment Act, otherwise known as the GI Bill, which provided low-interest, zero-down-payment loans to millions of veterans.

Combined, these moves were effectively like throwing a match on a pile of drywall. Housing starts jumped from 142,000 in 1944 to more than a million in 1946 to almost two million in 1950, figures we wouldn't again come close to until the housing boom of the 2000s. The percentage of American families who owned their homes soared, rising from 44 percent in 1940 to 64.4 percent in 1980. By 1950 the national suburban growth rate was ten times that of central cities. The suburban surge continued for the next two decades, what would later be known as suburbia's heyday and becoming, as Kenneth Jackson called it, "a demographic phenomenon as important as the movement of eastern and southern Europeans to Ellis Island or the migration of American blacks to northern cities." By 1970, 38 percent of the metropolitan population was living in suburbs, up from 23 percent in 1950, and more Americans lived in suburban areas than anywhere else. "Everything had been on ice for twenty years, and at the same time everyone thought cities were deeply flawed for various reasons," says Jason Duckworth, president of Arcadia Land Company, a Philadelphia-area developer of walkable residential communities. "So all of a sudden, everything—twenty years of pent-up demand, the sentiment against the city, and the newfound adoration of the automobile—it all gets unleashed into the 1950s."

The economy was booming, too. From 1950 to 1970 Americans' incomes nearly doubled and the middle class ballooned, growth that translated into the purchase of more new houses—not to mention the sofas, TVs, dining-room tables, kitchen appliances, washers and dryers, lawn mowers, and everything else needed to fill them. Television helped reinforce the image of this new utopian suburbia, with shows like *The Adventures of Ozzie and Harriet, Father Knows Best*, and *Leave It to Beaver* depicting this new, happy, middle-class life in its full splendor.

The homes themselves were also very different from their predecessors in earlier suburbs. Previously, residential development typically took the form of either custom-built homes for the wealthy or lower-income rental housing. But the post–World War II era brought with it new developments in materials and mass production that lowered costs dramatically and enabled the commoditization of the home-building process.

The popularization of these techniques is credited largely to William Levitt, the enterprising young seaman from Long Island who returned after the war to Levitt & Sons, the building company started by his father, Abraham. A successful operation before the war, Levitt & Sons had mostly built custom homes for the upper middle class on Long Island, developing now well-established places like Rockville Centre and Manhasset. But young William returned from the navy armed with two things: the knowledge of new mass-production capabilities he'd learned from building military barracks, and the utter conviction there was about to be a massive surge in demand for housing. He convinced his father and brother, Alfred, to embark on a new development concept they called Levittown, the now iconic four-thousand-acre development in the center of Long Island's Nassau County composed of mass-produced "tract" houses designed for returning veterans and their families.

The genius of the Levittown houses was their simplicity and uniformity: the structures were little more than a rectangular floor plan atop a concrete slab, an unfinished attic, and few variations. But they featured practical layouts that were easily expandable and adaptable, and thanks to the Levitts' pioneering use of assembly-line and mass-production techniques, they were cheap. Originally available only to rent, by 1949 they were for sale, costing between $7,990 and $9,500, with a washing machine included. For this generation, many of whom grew up in the Depression, the opportunity to purchase a brand-new home was impossible to pass up. On a single day in March 1949, Levitt & Sons drew up fourteen hundred contracts, some for families that had been in line for four days. Levittowns in New Jersey, Pennsylvania, and even Puerto Rico would follow, but Long Island was the biggest, ultimately housing eighty-two thousand residents.

Soon builders all around the country were laying out tract after tract of simple, mass-produced houses as fast as they could to keep up with the demand. In 1950, a builder in Fullerton, California, set a record by assembling a two-bedroom house in fifty-seven hours and fifty-seven minutes. Lakewood, California, the fastest-growing community that same year, on one day sold 107 houses in an hour. Styles varied slightly by region, and the wealthy still opted for custom-built houses, but tract housing became the norm. The homes went up on cheap farmland that had no access to public transportation, but thanks to the car that didn't matter. In 1956, President Dwight Eisenhower signed the Federal-Aid Highway Act, paving the way for another forty-one thousand miles of highway and making it possible to build suburbs farther and farther away. New developments started covering our landscape at a breakneck pace. "We pushed the pendulum all the way over," says Christopher Leinberger, founder of the real estate consultancy Robert Charles Lesser & Co., who is now a professor at George Washington University, a senior fellow at the Brookings Institution, a leading land-use strategist, and the author of *The Option of Urbanism: Investing in a New American Dream.* "The market wanted it, we in real estate built it, starting out with Old Man Levitt, and we reoriented the entire society around this drivable suburban vision."

And yet as early as the 1950s, authors, critics, and other social observers found reason to ridicule the new suburban lifestyle. In 1957, first-time author John Keats wrote the book *The Crack in the Picture Window,* which excoriated suburbia for creating stultifying communities and blighting the landscape with mass-produced housing. "For literally nothing down—other than a simple two percent and promise to pay, you too can find a box of your own in one of the fresh-air slums we're building around the edges of American cities," he wrote. In 1962, the songwriter Malvina Reynolds wrote "Little Boxes," the now-famous satire of conformist middle-class America and houses made out of "ticky tacky," the slang term for the materials used in commoditized construction. (The song would much later gain a second life in the mid-2000s as the opening theme song for the Showtime series *Weeds.*)

Pop culture wasn't the only early critic of suburbia. As early as 1959, land-use experts started to raise concerns about the breakneck pace of development. That year, the Urban Land Institute and the National Association of Home Builders released a sixteen-minute film called *Community Growth, Crisis and Challenge*, which warned of the negative impacts of what had become known as sprawl. "Once, the land seemed inexhaustible," a deep-voiced narrator explained as the camera panned across wide-angle shots of lush farmland to the peaceful sounds of birds chirping. Then his tone became dark and foreboding: "Today the land surrounding our metropolitan areas is being swallowed up at the rate of one million acres a year, by factories, shopping centers, highways, housing developments, and more housing developments. How did it happen in the span of a single generation?"

What the somber-toned narrator didn't know was that we were just getting started.

Both the car and the government made possible one other critical building block of modern-day suburbia: single-use zoning. In 1926, the Supreme Court ruled in a landmark case that the town of

Euclid, Ohio, an otherwise unassuming Cleveland suburb, had the right to prohibit a local developer from developing land for industrial use. The ruling itself was well-meaning enough; it was an attempt to prevent the building of noxious waste-spewing factories next door to people's houses and to preserve the character of the neighborhood. But it also made it constitutional for the first time for municipalities to separate the use of their land into buckets, designating certain areas for residential use, others for commerce, and others for industrial purposes. Later, when the FHA required single-use zoning as a condition for granting mortgages, this separation became baked into most new developments. More than almost anything else, single-use zoning permanently altered the look, feel, and overall DNA of our modern suburbs.

Even now, single-use zoning is the easiest way to distinguish modern suburbs from their older counterparts. Instead of having a single downtown core with stores, apartments, and offices mixed together in one place, postwar suburbs typically separate everything: subdivisions are off in one area, stores in another, and office space and industrial spaces in others. Andres Duany, a renowned architect and planner, and, as a founder of the New Urbanism movement, one of the leading critics of sprawl, likens this setup to an "unmade omelet," with "eggs, cheese, vegetables, a pinch of salt, but each consumed in turn, raw." Consumed separately, these things aren't very pleasing, but when they're mixed together and cooked, the result is much more satisfying.

Some of the country's most charming places are examples of cooked omelets: if you've ever been to Nantucket, Massachusetts, or Charleston, South Carolina, or Georgetown in Washington, DC, or

Alexandria, Virginia, or Philadelphia's Chestnut Hill, or Boston's Beacon Hill, you know what this looks like. Many places like this are on the East Coast because that's where the bulk of the older suburbs are located, but they exist everywhere, in places like Lake Forest, Illinois, Palo Alto or San Mateo, California, the Country Club district of Kansas City, or Edina, Minnesota. These suburbs predate single-use zoning, so buildings of all uses are mixed together. There's usually a clearly defined town center, many residents are within walking distance of the necessities of daily life, and the streets are narrow and generally pleasant to walk on. Residents outside the walking zone might need a car, but the design and placement of the streets and their components naturally encourage walking once they get to town. Among homes, there might be big mansions next to town houses next to apartments, so people with different levels of income are mixed together, too.

Most suburbs built after the war look a lot different. While "Euclidean" zoning, as it's known, became law in 1926, it wasn't truly adopted and its impact was not truly felt until the post–World War II housing boom. From then on, residential communities were built around a different model entirely, one that abandoned the urban grid pattern in favor of a circular, asymmetrical system made of curving subdivisions, looping streets, and cul-de-sacs. Clarence Perry and the developers of the early automobile suburbs had used this template, but single-use zoning led developers to adopt it as the standard. As they did in Perry's design, the streets within the system adhere to a specific road hierarchy: cul-de-sacs and other small residential streets feed into larger residential streets, which in turn feed into larger, higher-volume "collector" roads that feed traffic from all the local residential streets and connect the various neighborhoods; those collector roads then feed into "arterial" roads, the giant, high-capacity thoroughfares that connect one town to another.

It's safe to say that almost all the common complaints about modern-day suburbia relate in some way or another to single-use zoning. Robert Putnam, a Harvard professor and author of the 2000 book *Bowling Alone: The Collapse and Revival of American Community*, has said this setup forces people to live their lives in "very large triangles," with one point being where they sleep, one where they shop, and one where they work—with a good chunk of their free time spent shuttling among these three places. This critique would grow more apt over the years, due to the creep of sprawl, commutes that grew longer, and the housing boom of the mid-2000s, which built new communities made of bigger houses farther away from one another in increasingly remote places. As a result, most suburban residents are not only dependent upon their car but spend an excessive amount of time in it, a ramification we'll explore in depth later on.

The suburbs have another kind of zoning baked into their DNA: race. During its early days, the FHA used a neighborhood rating system that was developed by the Home Owners' Loan Corporation (HOLC), a New Deal agency formed to help prevent foreclosures, to appraise default risk levels and determine who could qualify for a loan. Neighborhoods were colored green for pristine, blue for less so, yellow for declining, and red for slums. The HOLC's policies weren't explicitly racist, but they factored in the appraisers' very real biases of the times. Virtually all black neighborhoods were marked as slums, or "redlined" (some white neighborhoods were also redlined), and affluent white neighborhoods were commonly understood to be the most desirable areas. Since the FHA used HOLC maps to determine where they would direct federal mortgage loans, this made it virtually impossible for residents of black neighborhoods to get a federal loan. At the same time, until the Civil Rights Act of 1964, it was perfectly legal for suburban realtors to refuse to sell or rent to African Americans, and nearly all of them did. Levittown, for instance, contained a clause in its leases prohibiting renting to African Americans for the first few years. The result was a federal policy directing all money away from older urban neighborhoods and toward the suburbs, while at the same time effectively denying federal benefits to blacks that were flowing to whites.

While the suburbs in general are more diverse today, this racial homogeneity still pervades the U.S. housing market. The nationwide home ownership rate is 65 percent, but it's much higher among whites: 73.6 percent. Even at the peak of the recent real estate bubble, the figure for blacks and Latinos was under 50 percent; as of the end of 2012, the rate for blacks was 44.1 percent. While I was researching this book, I had coffee with a writer whose friend was in the process of relocating with her family from Berkeley, California, to Connecticut. House hunting in the wealthy upper-middle-class suburb of Darien— perhaps Berkeley's ethnocultural polar opposite—she asked her realtor about diversity. Was there any? "Oh, honey," the realtor replied reassuringly, "you don't have to worry about that here."

S o in solving one problem—the severe postwar housing shortage— we unwittingly created some other ones: isolated, single-class communities and the building blocks for sprawl. The federal housing policies put in place had several other consequences, too. For one, cities all but crumbled, seeing a net out-migration of thirteen million people throughout the '70s alone—mostly the wealthy, educated middle class. The establishments and institutions that served them, retail and restaurants and cultural institutions, followed, and poverty, blight, street gangs, and violence grew in their place. Whole urban neighborhoods got bulldozed to clear the way for the ever-expanding highway network developed to serve the suburbs, further destroying many entrenched working-class urban communities. The now well-known image of a gritty New York emerged during this time. In those days, you couldn't go to Central Park at night, and Times Square was infested with crime and prostitution.

Jobs followed the middle class out of the city, too. As far back as 1942, AT&T Bell Telephone Laboratories moved from Manhattan to a 213-acre campus in Murray Hill, New Jersey, which offered more space, quiet, and the same graceful curving roads and bucolic feel of burgeoning suburban subdivisions. But the '70s saw the beginning of an exodus of blue-chip companies from the cities that would continue for decades: IBM moved from New York City to Armonk, New York, GE to Fairfield, Connecticut, Motorola from Chicago to Schaumburg, Illinois, and on and on. These companies' workers—and more tellingly, their executives—lived in the suburbs, where taxes were lower and space was plentiful. By 1981, half of office space was located outside central cities. By the end of the 1990s, that share would grow to two-thirds.

Shopping followed as well—and soon took on a new form with the invention of the mall. The earliest indoor shopping centers appeared in the '50s, but they fully took hold in the '70s and '80s, adding cineplexes, restaurants, carousels, and more. The '80s brought the arrival of the "big box" movement that would see stores like Lowe's, Home Depot, Best Buy, and others open cavernous locations dwarfed only by the size of their parking lots.

Around this time the suburbs started to evolve into a new urban form entirely, sprawling self-sufficient zones that contained all the services one needed instead of being mere residential extensions of metropolitan areas. Whether called "technoburbs," "à la carte cities," or "boomburbs," these areas were characterized by long corridors of mid-rise office parks, strip malls, chain restaurants, and big-box stores; no center or core; and density and populations approaching those of a small city. These areas emerged along major corridors like Route 128 in Boston, in Silicon Valley outside San Francisco, in developments alongside Aurora outside Denver, and, perhaps most notoriously, in Orange County, California, which grew to two million people in twenty-six low-density mini regions. Sprawl in Orange County is so vast that when discussing the suburbs with me one day, the financial blogger Felix Salmon gleefully proclaimed Orange County "a suburb without an urb!" In 1991, the author and scholar Joel Garreau famously coined the phrase "edge city," his term for these concentrations of business, shopping, and entertainment that represented the new face of metropolitan growth.

We would soon expand so far out that edge cities would lose their edge. But back then, they represented our official entry into sprawl-dom. In places like Atlanta, less than 10 percent of the metropolitan area's residents lived in the city core. By 2000, metropolitan areas covered almost twice as much land as they did in 1970. That same year, a report written by Russ Lopez of the Boston University School of Publish Heath for Fannie Mae entitled *Thirty Years of Urban Sprawl in Metropolitan America* warned of the dangers of our settlement patterns. "Urban sprawl is emerging as a major environmental, health and social issue," Lopez wrote. California's Inland Empire, the twenty-seven-thousand-square-mile zone between Los Angeles and the Riverside/San Bernardino hubs, emerged as a poster child of urban sprawl, a massive region where two-thirds of residents lived more than ten miles from a central business district, and the packed highways and clogged arterial roads had led to almost unbearable rates of congestion and pollution. In 2002 a report by the nonprofit agency Smart Growth America rated it the nation's worst example of urban sprawl. "There is no 'there' there," said one of the authors of the report.

Experts, academics, and other influential thinkers have been expressing concern about our modern pattern of suburban development since the first Levittown. Intellectuals worried early on about the postwar suburbs' uniformity and lack of character. The historian Lewis Mumford denounced Levittown almost as soon as it went up, saying it was using "new-fashioned methods to create old-fashioned mistakes." In *The City in History*, he described the suburbs as "a collective effort to live a private life" and "a multitude of uniform, unidentifiable houses, lined up inflexibly, at uniform distances, on uniform roads, in a treeless communal waste, inhabited by people of the same class, the same income, the same age group, witnessing the same television performances, eating the same tasteless prefabricated foods, from the same freezers, conforming in every outward and inward respect to a common mold."

Then there was Jane Jacobs, the writer and urban activist who championed the preservation of small-scale, authentic city neighborhoods and who is perhaps best known for beating back Robert Moses's efforts to build an expressway through lower Manhattan in the 1960s. Her influential 1961 book, *The Death and Life of Great American Cities*, laid out her argument for the preservation of what she famously dubbed the "intricate ballet" of city sidewalks in their natural form, referring to the commerce, activity, and lively interplay among people that dense, varied neighborhood streets encouraged. (Jacobs spends several passages describing this ballet on her own stretch of Hudson Street, which is my neighborhood now, and I can vouch that her description of its various characters—children heading to the neighborhood's St. Luke's School, commuters heading to work, shopkeepers tending their stores, stopping taxis appearing to ferry downtowners to midtown, "beautiful girls" heading out for a night on the town, and drunk young men—has remain practically unchanged.)

Jacobs had plenty to say about the suburbs, too, her chief complaint being that they were a patronizing fake-ifying of nature. "It is no accident that we Americans, probably the world's champion sentimentalizers about nature, are at one and the same time probably the world's most voracious and disrespectful destroyers of wild and rural countryside," she wrote in *Death and Life*. "It is neither love for nature nor respect for nature that leads to this schizophrenic attitude. Instead, it is a sentimental desire to toy, rather patronizingly, with some insipid, standardized, suburbanized shadow of nature. . . . And so, each day, several thousand more acres of our countryside are eaten by the bulldozers, covered by pavement, dotted with suburbanites who have killed the thing they thought they came to find."

Jacobs and Mumford were not alone. Raymond Tucker, the mayor of St. Louis from 1953 to 1965, commented that there wasn't enough room to enable the new housing landscape that policy makers had in mind without causing serious damage to society. "The plain fact of the matter is that we just cannot build enough lanes of highways to move all of our people by private automobile and create enough parking space to store the cars without completely paving over our cities and removing all of the ... economic, social, and cultural establishments that the people were trying to reach in the first place," he said. Even Victor Gruen, the Austrian-born architect considered the inventor of the modern-day shopping mall, soon came to abhor the impact of his creation, describing them as early as 1978 as "land-wasting seas of parking."

Whatever the critics say, it is important to note that there is, of course, a tremendous amount of appeal in suburban life. On a funda-mental level, trees and grass and quiet calm are extremely inviting to humans, and it's understandable how someone who works hard in the city would want to commute home to a quiet, residential street and a house with no shared walls. Then there's the space, which a house in the suburbs lets you have in spades: a dining room, a TV room, a basement, a spare guest room or two—things that are impossible to claim for the same price in most cities. Plus, it's all private and, if nothing else, suburbia is, as Lewis Mumford said, a collective effort to live a private life. For a nation that prides itself on individualism, living on one's own quarter-acre lot gives every man or woman his or her own castle, his or her own island.

And of course, just because suburbanites live apart doesn't mean they're alone; many suburbs have extremely strong and tight-knit communities. And as formulaic as critics say cul-de-sacs are, they do have design virtues that make them appealing to families with young kids. Jason Duckworth of Arcadia Land Company points out that there's something "almost a little Jane Jacobs-y" about them, he says; when children are playing outside, the circular arrangement of homes with parents looking out tends to put multiple "eyes on the street," Jane Jacobs parlance for the natural surveillance that comes from the presence of people in homes or stores who can easily view street activity.

The biggest issue with the suburbs is the way we have developed them in recent years. You can almost chart the change over time by talking to people of different ages about their suburban experience. Like tree rings, each concentric circle of our suburban development denotes a different era, and a person's individual memories of suburbia depend entirely on what ring on the tree his or her experience dates from. The earlier the experience, I found, the more sentimental the memories. Talk to anyone who grew up in the suburbs in the 1950s, '60s, or early '70s, and you're likely to hear talk of neighborhoods chock-full of children, where neighbors could knock on one another's door and kids played freely in the streets. While I encountered many people who disliked the suburbs altogether over the course of my reporting, there was also a sizable segment of people who were highly nostalgic for the kinds of suburbs they grew up in.

But at the same time, I encountered plenty of people eager to unload their stories about how much they hated the suburbs. Writing part of this book in seclusion in rural northwest Connecticut, I struck up a conversation with a dairy farmer who'd been raised in nearby Brookfield and considered himself a firsthand witness to sprawl's wholesale consumption of much of Connecticut's farmland in the '70s and '80s. He hated growing up there, he said, because he felt it was isolated and limiting. "It's not the people," he was careful to clarify. "It's the construct." Then he lowered his voice, looked into my eyes dead serious, and spoke slowly so I would take in every word: "It is a vapid. Empty. Wasteland." During a meeting about something else entirely, a colleague I'd mentioned the book to launched into an impassioned tale of how she was traumatized during a family road trip through suburban Denver after driving past what seemed like the exact same strip mall every eight miles and how, largely as a result, she and her husband were doing everything within their power to stay in Boston and not leave for the suburbs. When I told a thirtysomething public relations executive about my project, he bluntly offered up his opinion of the Long Island suburb where he'd grown up. "I had no intention of ever, EVER going back there," he said. "I honestly can't even understand how someone my age could even think that's an option. It seems like the end of the world to me." Another business contact volunteered that while his suburb of Washington, DC, offered "room and some greenery and good schools," he was "not a big fan" of the lifestyle it meant subscribing to. "It's just so goddamn boring," he said.

Throughout the course of my research, the fact that I was writing a book about the future of the suburbs would often come up when I was at social events. About 70 percent of the time, the person would make some version of the same snide quip: "And what is it? Over, I hope?" or "Please tell me there isn't one!" or "Do the suburbs even *have* a future?" If I was more specific and revealed I was writing a book called *The End of the Suburbs*, I would get high fives and hurrahs, or once, from a New York investment banker, "Good for you!" What became abundantly clear is that the topic struck a chord with just about everyone. As my deadline loomed and I became increasingly strapped for time, I actually found myself sidestepping talk of my book at cocktail parties because I knew if I broached the subject, I would be stuck in conversation for another forty-five minutes.

Popular culture hasn't been too kind to suburbia, either. When it comes to dark satirical send-ups of cul-de-sac life, you can take your pick: the movies *Blue Velvet*, *Revolutionary Road*, and *American Beauty*, and the TV shows *Desperate Housewives*, *Weeds*, and *Suburgatory*, to name just a few. In 2011, the indie rock band Arcade Fire took home the Grammy for best album for *The Suburbs*, an entire album dedicated to teen angst and isolation inspired by band members' Win and William Butler's upbringing in Houston's master-planned community The Woodlands. The social network Twitter, perhaps not surprisingly since it acts as a proxy for general sentiment, is overflowing with gripes about the suburbs. Kate Taylor, a stay-at-home mom who lives in a suburb of Charlotte and tweets as @culdesacked, is one of the more amusing: "If the only invites I get from you are at-home direct sales 'parties,' please lose my number, then choke yourself. #suburbs." At one point I searched for the hashtag #ilovethesuburbs and found, on all of Twitter's billions of tweets, a single tweet, from Joy Kirr in Elk Grove Village, Illinois: "Ooh! It IS a good night for that! I love being able to have the windows open again! #ILoveTheSuburbs." To be sure, Twitter tends to reflect the exceptionally opinionated one way or the other. But even when you look at the more neutral patterns of Internet search requests, the result is not that different. Google the phrase "Suburbia is..." and the next word the auto-fill feature suggests is "hell."

By the early 1980s, a small group of urban planners and architects, alarmed by the rate of sprawl, started meeting to come up with solutions to it, looking to traditional European city planning as their inspiration. In 1993 they organized under the name the "Congress for the New Urbanism," with the goal of promoting the design and building of traditional neighborhoods that were small and walkable, mixed stores and housing together, and emphasized community. Their early leaders included the San Francisco urbanist and architect Peter Calthorpe and the Miami-based husband-and-wife architect team of Andres Duany and Elizabeth Plater-Zyberk. Over the years their leagues expanded to include hundreds, among them the author James Howard Kunstler, whose *The Geography of Nowhere* spoke of the "immersive ugliness of our everyday environment" and the "despair" that environment was generating among the young, and who has called suburbia "the greatest misallocation of resources in the history of the world." Kunstler likes to provoke—the article that became his first best-selling book was originally titled "Why Is America So Fucking Ugly," until his publisher, Simon & Schuster, changed it. His points resonated anyway.

But noble as the New Urbanists' intentions were, traditional builders and developers dismissed them as nostalgic idealists who paid little attention to the way the market was heading and how people actually wanted to live. Suburbia, they said, was still what America wanted. And it seemed suburbia was what it would continue to get.

THE MASTER-PLANNED
AMERICAN DREAM

Some rich men came and raped the land, nobody caught 'em
Put up a bunch of ugly boxes, and Jesus, people bought 'em
—DON HENLEY AND GLENN FREY, "THE LAST RESORT," *HOTEL CALIFORNIA*

If you looked up "Minnesota nice" in the dictionary you might see a picture of Charles Marohn. Affable and mild-mannered, Marohn, who goes by Chuck, grew up the eldest of three sons of two elementary school teachers on a small farm near Brainerd, the central Minnesota city best known as the backdrop for the movie *Fargo*. Marohn (pronounced "mer-OWN") graduated from Brainerd High School, entered the National Guard on his seventeenth birthday, and went on to study civil engineering at the University of Minnesota. He now lives with his wife, two daughters, and two Samoyeds in East Gull Lake, a small city north of Brainerd. Marohn, forty, likes the Minnesota Twins, reads voraciously, and is a proud Republican. He's the friendliest guy you're likely to meet. He's also a revolutionary who's trying to upend the suburbs as we know them.

After graduating from college, Marohn went to work as a municipal engineer in his hometown and spent several years working with the small towns around the greater Brainerd area, putting projects together that would build roads, pipes, storm drains, and all kinds of infrastructure. It was the mid-1990s, the area was booming, and Marohn was laying down the systems that helped the area grow. "I built sprawl," he now says.

Often his work required him to knock on the doors of residents, many of whom he knew from growing up, and tell them about changes that might impact their property. In order to make the town's roads safer, he would explain, engineers were going to have to widen the road in front of their house or cut down a tree in their yard. When his neighbors would get upset and ask why or try to protest—the roads were hardly trafficked at all, and sparse enough to almost be rural, they would point out—he'd explain that the town was required to make these changes in order to comply with the book of engineering standards to which it had to adhere. The code, put in place by the town but derived from state and national standards, dictated that roads must have an ample "recovery zone," or a wide berth to accommodate cars that veer off the road, and that drivers have improved "sight distance," the distance a driver needs to be able to see in order to have enough room to be able to react before colliding with something in the roadway. When residents pointed out that the recovery zone was also their yard, and that their kids played kick ball and hopscotch there, Marohn recommended they put up a fence, so long as it was outside the right-of-way. He was sorry, he told them, but the standards required it. The trees were removed, the roads widened, the asphalt paved and repaved. "I never stepped back from my own assumptions to consider that I wasn't making anything safer," Marohn says. "In reality, I was making their street more dangerous, and in the process, I was not only taking out their trees, I was pretending I knew more than them."

In 2000, Marohn found himself assigned to fix a leaky pipe in Remer, a small town north of Brainerd. It was a routine project, but it would ultimately lead him to an epiphany. A sewer pipe that sat under a highway had a leak that was allowing clean groundwater to flow in. That meant that the clean water was getting pumped out to sewage treatment ponds, which were exceeding their capacity and would soon overflow. It was easily fixable, but it would cost $300,000, a hefty sum considering the town's total budget for such projects was $120,000 a year; sure enough, the town said no. But the pipe was going to cause the sewage ponds to overflow, undermine the dike, knock down its wall, and pour into the neighboring river "in like a catastrophic way," Marohn says. So he decided to find a federal grant to pay for it.

He discovered that the project was too small; grant agencies didn't seem to be interested in a $300,000 renovation, he found, presumably because it wasn't worth the time in administration costs. So he expanded the project, proposing the government pay not just to fix the pipe but also to extend the sewers, expand the size of the pumps, and more, at a cost of $2.6 million. The grant agency gave the green light; the state and federal government put up all the money except for $130,000, which the U.S. Department of Agriculture financed at below-market rates over a forty-year time period. Marohn was hailed a hero. "Everybody was super thrilled with me because I got this project approved out of nowhere," he says. And since the project would connect more homes, it would allow the town to promote the fact that it was creating capacity for the city to grow.

But over the next several years, as Marohn went back to Remer to do additional work—he had by then gotten a degree in urban planning—and saw that the town was in the process of doing a similar project with their water system, he realized he had created an unsustainable financial situation. Thanks to the leaky pipe he fixed, the town now had to bear the maintenance costs of a system that was double the size of the one it had before. "I bought them time," he says, "but I gave them a giant unfunded liability."

Marohn started questioning the rationale of this kind of system. The government paid the up-front costs of the massive project, but there was no accounting for the significant cost to maintain the system. The town's property taxes wouldn't come close to covering those costs, which meant the city would ultimately need to take on more debt. And the system was likely to need replacing well before forty years were up—the duration of the financing he'd procured—which would require an investment of equal or larger size. Marohn began to wonder whether all the work he'd been doing to supposedly help the city grow was really necessary or whether it was going to end up hurting it and, on top of that, whether the roads he was helping to "improve" were designed to accommodate the way people lived or were that way simply because the planning books said that was the way they had to be built.

He connected with a few friends in the local planning community who shared his concerns. In November 2009 they started a Web site called Strong Towns to start raising questions about America's approach to land use and the financial impracticalities suburban sprawl encourages. Rich in case studies and educational materials, Strong Towns lobbies for communities that are financially productive and grow responsibly. But it's also a screed against what Marohn sees as development patterns that go against the logic of design, finance, and the best interests of residential communities and everyday Americans.

One night soon after he started the Web site, Marohn wasn't sure what to write about, so he composed a blog post on his experience tearing down trees in his neighbors' yards, an idea that had been bouncing around in his head for a while. Declaring his work "professional malpractice," he described how the wider, faster streets he was sent to build weren't only financially wasteful but unsafe. "In retrospect, I understand that it was utter insanity," he wrote in the essay, which he called "Confessions of a Recovering Engineer." "Wider, faster, treeless roads not only ruin our public places, they kill people," he wrote, referring to statistics of traffic deaths each year that, in his view, were a direct result of poor design. He penned the piece in less than an hour and went to bed. When he got up, his in-box was full of comments from people in the planning community with whom his words had resonated.

The Web site soon became a nonprofit, which became a series of podcasts, videos, and live neighborhood events around the country called the "Curbside Chat." A local nonprofit threw in three years' worth of funding, and in mid-2012 Marohn quit his job to focus on Strong Towns, which is now a robust site packed with in-depth articles, podcasts, a Curbside Chat companion booklet for public officials, and a "Strong Towns University" section with instructional videos featuring Marohn and his partners discussing things like the ins and outs of wastewater management. Marohn's work has brought him attention within the planning community; he now travels all over the country speaking at conferences, hosting Curbside Chats, and spreading his message. But all, he says, for the greater good. "We're not bomb throwers," he says. "We like to think of ourselves as intellectual disruptors."

Marohn primarily takes issue with the financial structure of the suburbs. The amount of tax revenue their low-density setup generates, he says, doesn't come close to paying for the cost of maintaining the vast and costly infrastructure systems, so the only way to keep the machine going is to keep adding and growing. "The public yield from the suburban development pattern is ridiculously low," he says. One of the most popular articles on the Strong Towns Web site is a five-part series Marohn wrote likening American suburban development to a giant Ponzi scheme.

Here's what he means. The way suburban development usually works is that a town lays the pipes, plumbing, and infrastructure for housing development—often getting big loans from the government to do so—and soon after a developer appears and offers to build homes on it. Developers usually fund most of the cost of the infrastructure because they make their money back from the sale of the homes. The short-term cost to the city or town, therefore, is very low: it gets a cash infusion from whichever entity fronted the costs, and the city gets to keep all the revenue from property taxes. The thinking is that either taxes will cover the maintenance costs, or the city will keep growing and generate enough future cash flow to cover the obligations. But the tax revenue at low suburban densities isn't nearly enough to pay the bills; in Marohn's estimation, property taxes at suburban densities bring in anywhere from 4 cents to 65 cents for every dollar of liability. Most suburban municipalities, he says, are therefore unable to pay the maintenance costs of their infrastructure, let alone replace things when they inevitably wear out after twenty to twenty-five years. The only way to survive is to keep growing or take on more debt, or both. "It is a ridiculously unproductive system," he says.

Marohn points out that while this has been an issue as long as there have been suburbs, the problem has become more acute with each additional "life cycle" of suburban infrastructure (the point at which the systems need to be replaced—funded by debt, more growth, or both). Most U.S. suburbs are now on their third life cycle, and infrastructure systems have only become more bloated, inefficient, and costly. "When people say we're living beyond our means, they're usually talking about a forty-inch TV instead of a twenty-inch TV," he says. "This is like pennies compared to the dollars we've spent on the way we've arranged ourselves across the landscape."

Marohn and his friends are not the only ones warning about the fix we've put ourselves in. In 2010 the financial analyst Meredith Whitney wrote a now-famous report called *The Tragedy of the Commons*, whose title was taken from the economic principle that individuals will act on their own self-interest and deplete a shared resource for their own benefit, even if that goes against the long-term common good. In her report, Whitney said states and municipalities were on the verge of collapse thanks in part to irresponsible spending on growth. Likening the municipalities' finances and spending patterns to those of the banks leading up to the financial crisis of 2008, Whitney explained how spending has far outpaced revenues—some states had spent two or three times their tax receipts on everything from infrastructure to teacher salaries to libraries—all financed by borrowing from future dollars.

Marohn, too, claims we've tilled our land in inefficient ways we can't afford (Whitney is one of Marohn's personal heroes). The "suburban experiment," as he calls it, has been a fiscal failure. On top of the issues of low-density tax collection, sprawling development is more expensive to build. Roads are wider and require more paving. Water and sewage service costs are higher. It costs more to maintain emergency services since more fire stations and police stations are needed per capita to keep response times down. Children need to be bused farther distances to school. One study by the Denver Regional Council of Governments found that conventional suburban development would cost local governments $4.3 billion more in infrastructure costs than compact, "smart" growth through 2020, only counting capital construction costs for sewer, water, and road infrastructure. A 2008 report by the University of Utah's Arthur C. Nelson estimated that municipal service costs in low-density, sprawling locations can be as much as 2.5 times those in compact, higher-density locations.

Marohn thinks this is all just too gluttonous. "The fact that I can drive to work on paved roads where I can drive fifty-five miles an hour the minute I leave my driveway despite the fact that I won't see another car for five miles," he says, "is living beyond our means on a grand, grand scale."

Marohn is one of a growing number of sprawl refugees I encountered during my reporting—people who at one point helped enable the building of modern-day suburbia but now spend their days lobbying against it with the zeal of religious converts. Some, like Marohn, focus on the unsustainability of the financial structure. Others focus on the actual physical design of the suburbs and point to all the ways it's flawed. Most of them argue for the development of more walkable communities closer to public transportation. But their unifying criticism is that our spread-out development pattern was manufactured, packaged, and sold to Americans as part of an American Dream that fails to deliver on its promises. "We've actually embedded this experiment of suburbanization into our psyche as the American Dream," says Marohn, calling it "a nonnegotiable way of life that must be maintained at all costs."

For all the ideals of freedom our country was built on, our modern residential pattern of suburban development—and the notion that it provided a better way to live—was decidedly master-planned. It started with the federal policies that laid the groundwork for suburbia, the post-Depression inventions explored in the previous chapter that suddenly made home ownership affordable for the middle class. The mortgage interest tax deduction, which wasn't even intended for mortgages but was an indirect product of the 1913 act that established the federal income tax, today provides nearly $400 billion in subsidies to home owners each year, propping up the market for single-family homes to the detriment of renters, who get no such help. The FHA put in place incentives that made it more lucrative for builders to invest in new construction than to improve existing houses—loans for repairs were smaller and shorter term than loans for new houses—as well as rules that eased the way for the construction of subdivisions. By stipulating, for example, that homes had to be built far from "adverse influences" and in areas of economic stability, FHA loans overwhelmingly favored single-family detached houses in the suburbs. The agency's rules also established minimum requirements for lot size, the distance the home had to be built from the street, and width of the house itself, all but pushing lending activity toward suburban-style homes.

In 1956, the Federal-Aid Highway Act granted funding to the construction of high-speed roads so Americans could easily access new and more distant communities. This system still exists, and while developers usually pay to build the roads in their subdivisions, and sometimes for the feeder roads that connect them, they're not required to pay for the state or federal highway construction needed to enable that growth. This subsidy amounts to nearly $200 billion a year and is enjoyed not only by millions of suburban commuters, but by the trucking industry, which, with the exception of a small percentage of toll roads, rides free to haul goods long distances. The freight rail transport system, meanwhile, is funded by private companies. "When we move goods by freight, the private sector pays for everything," says Arcadia Land's Jason Duckworth. "When we move them by truck, the truck rides on a free highway subsidized by the federal government."

Conservatives often decry any efforts to scale back suburban development as Big Government intervention. When California recently proposed new planning laws that would require new housing to be built at higher density levels or that would limit the percentage of housing permitted on or beyond the "urban fringe," for example, it sparked outrage among conservatives, who cried that the state had declared war on the single-family home. But this argument disregards the fact that suburban development itself—everything from the federal highway system to the single-family home to the low price of gasoline in the United States compared to other countries—was built thanks to, and still depends on, generous governmental subsidies.

"The suburbs are a big government handout if there ever was one," the author William Upski Wimsatt wrote in the *Washington Post* in a 2011 article debunking five myths about the suburbs. Myth number three: the suburbs are a product of the free market.

Even the way our suburbs look is guided by a thicket of government regulations. Beyond just adhering to single-use zoning, for example, conventional suburban developers must follow other zoning laws, building codes, street design regulations, and minimum parking requirements. Just like the book of standards Chuck Marohn had to follow, the codes are highly specific about these rules, which drill down into detailed requirements for things like street width, building setbacks, and the percentage of space given over to off-street parking. Some of these rules border on the ridiculous. The city of Long Beach, California, for instance, at one point required twenty parking spaces for every thousand square feet of gross floor area in "taverns," where the primary activity was drinking alcohol. "The code and standards are everything," says Marohn. As he wrote in his "Confessions of a Recovering Engineer" essay, "A book of standards to an engineer is better than a bible to a priest." Of course, these rules often defeat their own purpose. In the delightfully entertaining 2000 book *Suburban Nation*, Andres Duany and his coauthors coined the term "Pensacola Parking Syndrome" to refer to the phenomenon in which a city or municipality tears down so many buildings to create parking spaces that people stop going there because it's no longer an appealing place to visit—so named, the book's authors explain, "in honor of one of its victims."

You could argue that the initial wave of government support for modern suburban development was a reasonable, if not well-thought-out, response to our postwar housing shortage that simply didn't factor in the unintended consequences. But this doesn't fully explain the ethos surrounding suburban living, which has only become more deeply entrenched in our society in the decades since. A shortage of housing is no longer a problem, of course, and hasn't been for quite some time. So why have Americans continued to be so obsessed with owning a house in the suburbs?

This wasn't exactly an accident, either. Almost as soon as we started building the modern suburbs, we began viewing them as an ideal, almost magical way of life. At the 1939 World's Fair in New York, General Motors presented a now-famous exhibit, "The Futurama," that showed what the American landscape might look like twenty years into the future. The model featured a vast network of suburbs overlaid with an intricate web of high-speed "magic motorways." It was a car-centric vision of the future, it was awe-inspiring, and it actually seemed within reach. More than nine million people stood in hour-long lines to view it. After the Futurama exhibit, there was a palpable hope—even a dream—among the American people that this would be the way we would build our country. "It was a brilliant marketing move," says George Washington University's Christopher Leinberger. "We fell for it hook, line and sinker as a people."

But marketing works best when it taps into something deep within our psyche, and even Leinberger, who today maintains an extensive collection of Futurama paraphernalia, points out that GM would not have been able to sell us this vision if deep down we hadn't already wanted it. "You have to move people in their guts to make them really embrace something, and people fell in love with it," he says. The vision of this novel way of life did exactly that. Along with the car, the private home had long been a symbol of prosperity. The Futurama exhibit crystallized for the American people how the car, the house, and the suburban way of life could come together to symbolize something bigger: the American Dream.

Technically speaking, the original notion of the American Dream wasn't tied to having a house at all; in 1931, the author James Truslow Adams simply wrote of "that dream of a land in which life should be better and richer and fuller for every man, with opportunity for each according to his ability or achievement," regardless of "circumstances of birth or position." But when government policies made home ownership possible for the masses, owning a house suddenly presented a logical proxy for this prosperity. The difference between life before the Great Depression, when only the extremely wealthy could afford homes, and after, when almost anyone could, was night and day. Very quickly, people embraced the notion that anyone who was smart and morally and financially responsible would make it a goal to buy a plot of land and live in a house with a yard. It was as true in rural Minnesota in the 1970s as it was in Levittown in the 1950s. "I grew up believing that prosperity was suburbia," Chuck Marohn says.

Owning a home represented more than just prosperity; over the years, it came to represent patriotism, good citizenship, and the mark of a productive member of society. During the Cold War, home ownership was credited with upholding American free-market ideals. "No man who owns his own house and lot can be a Communist," William Levitt said. In 1995, Bill Clinton launched National Homeownership Day to celebrate the role home owners played in building a productive society. "Strengthening families, establishing communities, and fostering prosperity, homeownership is the cornerstone of our economy and a common thread in our national life," Clinton wrote in the proclamation. A few days later he established a new National Home-ownership Strategy, a joint initiative with the U.S. Department of Housing and Urban Development designed to boost the home owner-ship rate. In his remarks announcing the strategy, Clinton recounted a charming story about how, when he was trying to "coax" Hillary into marrying him, he finally succeeded by surprising her and buying a house the future secretary of state had admired while she was away on a trip. A decade later, in the midst of what was becoming a massive real estate bubble in 2004, George W. Bush fanned the home ownership flames by touting that we were creating an "ownership society in this country, where more Americans than ever will be able to open up their door where they live and say, 'welcome to my piece of property.'"

And then, of course, when mortgages became incredibly, artifi-cially cheap during the recent housing boom, the home-owner-as-hero ethos only became even more evident, as those who had previously only dreamed of owning a home bought up property like the good, proud Americans they had always hoped to be.

While the housing bubble of the 2000s is by now well-trod territory, it is worth mention here since it accelerated, and then accentuated, the decline of the suburbs. In 2001, the United States was struggling to emerge from the ashes of the dot-com stock crash of the late '90s that weakened our economy and the 9/11 attacks that nearly decimated it. In search of a fix, the Federal Reserve turned to home ownership, slashing interest rates to jump-start home sales and demand for new construction. What better way to juice the econ-omy, the government reasoned—just as it had in the wake of the

Great Depression—than to promote home ownership, that reliable engine of growth?

Only this time, it wasn't just the government encouraging us to live in big homes on plots of land. A giant assist came from another player: banks, which, in search of better returns, engineered a new asset class around housing. What if investors, who had tired of stocks, could buy packages of home loans instead? The American Dream had suddenly met the Wall Street Machine, two powerful engines that came together with the force of a neutron bomb. The creation of the mortgage-backed security, as we now know, was an instant success, and the cultural obsession with home ownership would play right into the banks' hands as they happily fed the voracious demand for new home loans. The whole experiment would leverage the hope and hype of the American Dream and award it to millions of new home owners.

As has by now been well documented, our housing industry ballooned. Prices rose nearly 200 percent from 1995 to 2005. Houses that sold for $300,000 were worth $600,000 two years later, then $700,000, then more. It wasn't just Wall Street making a profit: everyone wanted in on the new gold rush. Everyone became an investor; the cocktail party chatter wasn't just about the home you bought to live in, it was the home you bought to flip. A *Fortune* article in May 2005 chronicling this euphoria opened with the tale of a twenty-two-year-old in Phoenix who owned so many homes that he got lost going from one to the next.

The home-building industry exploded, too, going from constructing 1.3 million new single-family houses in 2000 to 1.7 million in 2006, an all-time high. Farmers made millions as real estate speculators and developers bought up citrus groves and cotton fields by the thousands and converted them into subdivisions. From 2000 to 2007 the United States developed close to four million acres of farmland, spending billions tilling it and filling it with fast, cheap tract houses for first-time buyers. Code inspectors couldn't keep up with the pace; years later, consumer watch groups would urge home owners who bought homes built between 1999 and 2007 to have them reinspected because so many contractors had cut corners.

At some indiscernible point, a mania started to take hold. Everyone wanted bigger, better, more. And if you couldn't afford it near where you wanted to live, you could find one in your price range if you just kept going. Builders and developers plowed farther and farther out along the periphery, where land was cheapest. Soon there were places like the plot of land earmarked by luxury home builder Toll Brothers an hour and a half drive from DC toward the Shenandoah Mountains. A *New York Times Magazine* profile described the meeting where the president of the company had presented this parcel to cofounder and then CEO Bob Toll, who marveled at the high prices other builders had been able to command nearby: "Look at these prices," Toll said. "At the end of the world, these prices." The Poconos soon became bedroom communities of Philadelphia and New York, and Poughkeepsie became a suburb of Manhattan; similar development spread out into Loudoun County outside of Washington, DC, and Gwinnett County outside Atlanta. The traditional American Dream said nothing about ninety-minute one-way commutes, but that's what people were willing to do to get the biggest, best home they could buy. By 2009, three million Americans were making "extreme commutes" of three hours or more round-trip every weekday. Sometime during this era, Bob Toll, who kept an apartment on New York City's Upper East Side, learned that one of his doormen had moved his family from Queens to the Poconos. He asked him why he did it, when it meant he had to drive an hour and a half—on a good day—to work. "I wanted my family to have their own home and their own land," the doorman said. "And I was willing to drive an hour and a half a day to be your doorman to do it."

This approach put millions more people into millions of homes. In the span of eleven years, the rate of home ownership in the United States went from 64.4 percent, where it had hovered for more than three decades, to 69.4 percent. Rising prices, meanwhile, allowed existing home owners to refinance their mortgages at higher and higher valuations, pocketing the extra cash. This further increased home owners' sense of wealth and spurred purchases of everything from SUVs to second homes to Saks Fifth Avenue shopping sprees. In addition to representing a place to live, the home had suddenly become a wealth creation machine. It was the American Dream, squared.

The homes themselves grew bigger and more ornate—Arcadia Land's Jason Duckworth refers to this as housing's "baroque" period—and soon we were identifying them with a new label, the McMansion. Though almost every builder started making them during the housing boom, the invention of the modern-day McMansion dates decades earlier; the first use of the term dates to around 1990 and was soon thereafter defined by the *Oxford English Dictionay* as "a large modern house that is considered ostentatious and lacking in architectural integrity." But identifying the demand for a new category of housing in between high-end custom-built homes and tract housing can be credited to Toll Brothers, which came to mass produce the most expensive homes of any builder in the country. In the mid-'80s Toll was a regional builder operating in Pennsylvania and New Jersey when Bob Toll identified the demand among a new upper-middle-class buyer for flourishes that suggested prestige, like large floor plans, brass fixtures, columns on the front facade, marble countertops, and the like. Toll masterminded the art of delivering these visual embellishments on houses that were high-end but mass-produced, so they could be built at a much lower cost than custom homes. Toll's houses were still twice as expensive as its rivals, but it popularized a new category in housing: a halfway point between suburban tract homes and multimillion-dollar upscale abodes. "They were brilliant about it," says Duckworth (Duckworth says this as a Philadelphia-area real estate developer himself and one with particular insight on Toll: his father was a top executive at the company for years). Toll, the younger Duckworth points out, understood that buying a house was as much about fantasy as utility. "They knew how to push people's psychological buttons," he says. "They could see the buyer saying, 'This is how I'm going to impress my brother-in-law.' You can get by with a cheap subfloor, but you had to have the Jacuzzi for two."

Toll might have popularized the notion of the McMansion, but by the early 2000s nearly every builder was making their own versions of them; soon their two-story foyers, butterfly staircases, and separate media rooms were de rigueur. The houses grew bigger—three to five thousand square feet or larger. They often matched their region— sprawling redbrick colonials outside Washington, DC, adobe castles in Phoenix, French-style chateaux in the suburbs of St. Louis—even if the bricks and adobe were coming off the same assembly line in New Jersey. Builders of these homes saved on costs wherever they could—using synthetic stucco or plywood in place of the real thing, for example, or framing corners with three studs instead of five—and sometimes they didn't get it quite right: a Palladian window might be under a French gable roof. But most buyers didn't really care—their purpose was to deliver the signals of wealth if not the actual trappings of it. Provenance and accuracy weren't as important—it was size and scale and how much it glittered that mattered.

By 2005, there were nearly four million homes with 4,000 square feet of space or more, up 17 percent from 2001. By 2006, the average home was 2,500 square feet, more than double what it was fifty years prior. The National Association of Home Builders' concept home that year was more than 10,000 square feet. As big as McMansions had become, every effort was made to make them look even bigger, with builders employing visual tricks like adding fewer trees and less vegetation, and perching the houses on a man-made hill to make them seem more imposing. The American Dream had morphed from owning a home to owning a palace.

To keep the endless supply of loans coming after the regular mortgage market got tapped out, lenders turned to people who'd never had a mortgage before. These first-timers kept the party going and fueled suburban expansion even more. Thus began what became known as the "drive till you qualify" mania, which meant going as far as you needed in order to afford your dream home. "Drive 10 miles and save $10,000," was one developer's pitch in Wright County, Minnesota, some fifty miles northwest of Minneapolis.

All told, between 1996 and 2006, more than eighteen million new houses were built, with nearly no increase in average incomes. It was almost like the housing boom of 1947 all over again, but there was one key difference: there was no increase in natural demand. This time around there was no population boom, no millions of returning soldiers needing jobs and homes. The demand was manufactured by Wall Street, and it played to our deepest desires as a country. The national narrative had become even more fixated on home ownership than it already was.

O f course, as we now know, it would all soon fall apart. By the end of 2009, home prices had fallen 29 percent from their peak; that year, the foreclosure process was begun on 2.1 million homes. Each time housing prices hit a new low, experts called it the bottom, only to have prices fall through the floor again. All told, housing prices fell 34 percent from peak to trough, compared with roughly 26 percent during the Great Depression. In some places, like Phoenix and Las Vegas, the number was closer to 60 percent. In all, more than 4.5 million homes were lost to foreclosure. "We ended up with far too many [housing] units," wrote Warren Buffett, who through his company, Berkshire Hathaway, owns modular home manufacturer Clayton Homes, in his 2011 letter to shareholders. "And the bubble popped with a violence that shook the entire economy."

That violence might have busted sprawl's march for good—it remains to be seen, and we'll get to that later. For now, we're left with an endless array of images of the American Dream in tatters. There are thousands of half-built subdivisions around our country, relics of the days of free-flowing credit and a seemingly endless supply of new home buyers. These empty subdivisions dot our landscape, sometimes little more than subdivided lots marking space for homes that were never built. In many cases the infrastructure has been paid for and teed up, with empty lots ready to pipe water and electricity into homes that will now never come. In many communities, the houses were built but now sit empty, drawing squatters. In places like the Inland Empire, the situation was particularly devastating. In the hardest-hit markets, a cottage industry emerged in companies that would spray-paint brown lawns green to mask the blight. In Perris, California, owners of ranches that had foreclosed and couldn't afford to euthanize their animals left them to starve; officials found forty-one emaciated, abandoned horses wandering the area throughout 2011.

In other places the damage wasn't as visibly wrenching, but it was still there. One weekday in December 2011, I went on a driving tour of the Las Vegas housing market, one of the hardest hit in the country. Driving through the Desert Shores community in Summerlin, one of the fastest-growing communities during the housing boom, I initially didn't notice anything out of the ordinary. The sun was shining bright, the streets were tidy, and the rows of stucco ranch homes with stone pebble landscaping all seemed to fit benignly on the gently curving streets and cul-de-sacs. Things were festive, befitting the holiday week; I noticed an inflatable Santa Claus on one house, icicle lights hanging from the shutters of another, and an entire garage door wrapped in a giant red tinsel bow.

But soon I noticed that the shutters on most of the homes were closed on the inside, even though it was the middle of the day. There were no people around, anywhere. Newspapers had piled up in a few driveways. Many of the houses had Christmas wreaths on the door and pumpkins on the porch at the same time, a sort of bipolar holiday still life that hinted at the work of lazy real estate agents attempting to mask the fact that the home was empty. I soon realized that all the homes were using the same exact type of wreath and the same exact brand of inflatable Santas, also evidence of realtors at work. In several cases, the Santas had lost their loft and lay deflated on the ground, sad-looking polyester pools that seemed representative of the burst housing bubble itself.

This blight wasn't only in places that were created by the housing boom. In Berkeley, California, a city councilman wrote to the mayor asking for help for individual home owners facing foreclosure. In Atlanta, the city's outer suburban ring, which was particularly hard hit with foreclosures, was coined the "ring of death." In December 2011, one foreclosure "heat map" showed tony Westchester County, New York, as "white hot" among New York counties for the number of homes entering foreclosure, with seventeen hundred homes listed under payment default status.

The way Chuck Marohn sees it, this carnage actually has very little to do with our housing boom and everything to do with a gluttonous way of life that never made any sense to begin with. "If I could choose what to eat every day, I'd have lobster every day," he says. "But I can't afford it, so I end up eating a lot of hot dogs and hamburgers." On the other hand, he says, if someone else was subsidizing the lobster, the way the government subsidizes suburban development, "I would eat lobster every day."

As our country's fiscal issues come to a head, many policy makers are eyeing some of the governmental support for the housing market as a possible area for cutbacks. The mortgage interest deduction is seen by many as a particularly juicy target. Policy experts and economists increasingly think it should go, and there's plenty of evidence supporting their argument. Critics have long pointed out that the deduction benefits the rich disproportionately: because its cap is a high $1 million, the more expensive the house, the bigger the deduction a home owner gets to claim. The economist Edward Glaeser has said that in this way, the policy essentially "bribes" the wealthy to segregate themselves. Glaeser and others have pointed out that the deduction also artificially inflates home prices by encouraging people to buy more house than they would otherwise be able to afford. "We have a tax code that says 'hey, let's build a lot of homes for really wealthy people that cost a lot of money,'" says Bruce Katz, the founding director of the Brookings Institution's Metropolitan Policy Program. "That's really ass backwards."

A former chief of staff of the U.S. Department of Housing and Urban Development and one of the country's leading thinkers on housing policy, Katz thinks we should take that funding and plow it into innovation instead. The problem with the American Dream, he says, is that it led Americans to see home ownership not only as symbolic of good citizenship but also as a source of wealth creation itself, as millions of Americans came to expect their home to make them rich. But if we take that same funding and use it to subsidize the right kind of economic growth, he says, housing would become a byproduct of a strong economy rather than the driver of it. And it would help us play up our strengths in intellectual capital and innovation on an increasingly competitive global stage. "Will we be better off? Damn yeah," he says. "No one will be able to come close to us."

In the spring of 2011, Katz was invited to present this idea to the home-building industry. It didn't go so well. "There were about seven hundred people there," Katz says. "And about five hundred of them went berserk." He now refers to the incident as his "food fight" with the home builders, but it's an example of just how entrenched the notion of home ownership has become. The real estate industry tends to look at any suggestion of scaling it back as an attack on their livelihood, while American home owners see it as an all-out attack on the American Dream.

Therein lies the reason why the generous federal support for home ownership has lasted all these years. All the incentives and backstops provided to suburban development solved a key problem when we were coming out of the Great Depression. But you can't just yank those things away once the shortage ends; they become ingrained in citizens' expectations. And the momentum that suburban development gathered both on the ground and in our psyche made it an unstoppable force. No matter how much economic sense it makes to eliminate the mortgage interest deduction, no elected politician is likely to touch it.

Americans, too, remain fiercely protective of their dream, even after the housing bust. A recent study by the National Association of Home Builders found that 74 percent of respondents said owning a home is still worth the risk of the fluctuations in the market, and 96 percent of home owners said they are happy with their decision to own a home. Eighty-four percent of home owners who were "underwater," or owe more than their house is worth, said they felt the same way. A recent study by the real estate Web site Trulia showed that 70 percent of Americans still consider home ownership a central part of the American Dream.

For his part, Chuck Marohn is still spreading his message and is gaining cult hero status within the New Urbanism movement and the broader planning community. He's now a Delta Gold member who's logged over one hundred thousand air miles in the past twelve months as he travels the country spreading his message. Strong towns.org gets ten thousand unique visitors each month. A video of a talk he gave for a regional branch of TED, the ideas conference, has been viewed fifteen thousand times. The highlight of the talk comes when Marohn puts up a slide of a picture of his hometown of Brainerd, Minnesota, in 1894. It's a charming sepia photo of a vibrant, densely packed Main Street chockablock with pedestrians and horse-drawn carriages. "I love this street," he says. "This place totally rocks, doesn't it?" He then shows a picture of Brainerd today, a strip mall surrounded by parking lots, to show the difference. The 1894 version, he implores the audience, is what we need to go back to. "We built this before the interstate highway act, before the home mortgage interest deduction ... before zoning, before the thirty-year mortgage," he says. "We built places that rocked back when we had to build them to be financially sound."

Marohn has not been immune from the pain of the housing crisis. His house, which he and his wife had built in 1995 and refinanced a few times, has lost value; it was assessed at $272,000 a few years ago and he thinks it would sell today for $200,000. But he's more concerned for his brother, Brent, who lives forty-five minutes from Minneapolis in the exurb of Rogers, Minnesota—an area that, as Marohn puts it, "got very caught up in the entire growth Ponzi scheme"—and commutes to an inner-ring suburb. Brent's house has dropped "tremendously" in value, Marohn says. He worries about his brother's situation; the more gas prices go up, the fewer people there will be that can afford his house, forcing prices to drop further and further.

At that point, Marohn believes, one of two things will happen: either a local economy will spring up in his brother's town to provide jobs for its people so they don't have to commute, or his brother's house is going to continue to lose value until it's ultimately worth nothing and sold for salvage. As far as Marohn sees it, the government-enabled sprawl as we have known it for sixty-plus years was finally and effectively killed off by the housing bust. "The sprawl demon is dead," he says. "It's not coming back."

"MY CAR KNOWS THE WAY TO GYMNASTICS"

First they built the road, then they built the town
that's why we're still driving round and round
and all we see
are kids in buses longing to be free.
—ARCADE FIRE, "WASTED HOURS," *THE SUBURBS*

Diane Roseman and her husband, Steven Spitz, had lived all over the world by the time they decided to settle in Westborough, Massachusetts, in 2002. Roseman grew up in the suburbs of Morris County, New Jersey, but she and Spitz had had their first child while living in South Pasadena, California. They then moved to Jerusalem, where they had their second, a girl. By the ti me they came back to the United States to live in the Boston area—where Spitz, a computer engineer, had been transferred to an office in nearby Marlborough—Roseman had three children under five years old and coveted the space and ease of life the suburbs would provide. "I wanted the minivan and the big house," she says. "I wanted to try the whole American Dream."

They looked at Newton, a wealthy, older suburb, but prices were high, so they started looking farther out. "You get into this mind-set that if I'm spending five hundred thousand dollars, I should get a big house, it shouldn't be a little house," she says. In Westborough, a suburb thirty miles west of Boston, they found a three-thousand-square-foot center hall colonial built in 1985 in a subdivision that was brimming with other young families. The schools were excellent. It was all going to be great. Their fourth child, a girl named Ella, was born three weeks after they moved in.

It didn't take Roseman long to realize the life she'd signed up for was not the one she wanted. "If you want to live in a suburb, it's a fine suburb," she says. "But I slowly realized it was not the kind of life I wanted to lead." She missed being surrounded by people of a wide range of ages and life stages; most people in her immediate neighborhood were couples in their thirties to fifties raising children. She didn't realize how much work would go into keeping up the house; her husband spent almost every weekend shoveling snow or taking care of the lawn. But her biggest issue was the one that surprised her most: she had no idea how much time she would be spending in her car.

Of course, Roseman was well aware that she and her husband had opted for a bedroom community, and she had long ago embraced the role of stay-at-home mom. (On her LinkedIn profile, Roseman calls herself "CEO, CFO, Engineer at Roseman/Spitz Household" and cheekily describes her job as "required to plan the schedules of 5 individuals, provide clean and well-designed surroundings, prepare 3 meals/day, and be available in the evenings and night when some hugs, kisses and ego-soothing are necessary.") She was extremely grateful that they could afford both a big house and for her to stay home full-time to take care of their children. But she was surprised to discover that she would have to do more driving than her husband just to get herself and her children around each day. Contrary to what she expected, kids didn't really run around outside and play in the subdivision. Instead, everything was coordinated by scheduled activity and playdate, so every day she would spend the hours from 3:00 p.m. to 6:00 p.m. shuttling her children to and from all the places they needed to be: swimming, chess, ballet, Hebrew school, jazz, soccer, music lessons, and more—what Roseman describes as "all the ridiculous things you sign them up for because they can't just go outside and do something with their friends for three hours." She estimates she was putting forty to fifty miles on her car each weekday. "I'm in my car from morning till night," she says. "My car knows the way to gymnastics."

Of all the many complaints about the modern, postwar American suburbs, most of them can be traced in some way to the suburbs' relationship with the car. There would be no suburbs without the car; and conversely, Americans would not be so completely dependent on the car were we not so uniquely suburban. The history of the suburbs has been entirely dependent on the automobile—not just because people need cars to commute between cities and suburbs (or between suburbs) but because the very design of the suburbs, in which millions of houses are spread out at low densities across the country, doesn't lend itself to any other type of transportation. "The suburbs as we knew them were a petroleum-derived derivative," says Victor Dover, a leading New Urbanism architect and planner. George Washington University's Christopher Leinberger puts it another way: "We social engineered the system to where you only have one choice to get around. It's your car. You can have any color you want, as long as it's black," he says, suggesting an alternate meaning to Henry Ford's famous quote about the Model T.

Americans are, of course, a car-loving country. Transportation planners like to talk about "mode split," the breakdown of the type of transportation people use in a society. In the United States, 83 percent of our trips are taken by car, more than in any other country (in Europe, by contrast, transportation by automobile represents only around half of trips taken). We have the highest per capita gasoline consumption rates in the world. As sprawl has grown over the years and as we've grown farther and farther apart, our reliance on the automobile has intensified. That in turn has led to a number of complicated, unintended consequences: it's impacted our health, our relationships, our finances, and the way our children grow up. Nowhere is this truer than in the suburbs. And like Roseman, a growing number of suburban residents are starting to initiate changes in their lives to make themselves less auto-dependent. They are finding other options, shifting their behavior, or, increasingly, seeking out less car-dependent ways of living. As they do, the most car-dependent suburbs will become less and less desirable.

There are many downsides to the car-oriented design of the modern suburbs. One of the biggest is that they often make walking more dangerous. The "hierarchical" street design model we explored in chapter 1—that system of curving, looping streets, cul-de-sacs, and connector and arterial roads—was designed so that cars could move smoothly and easily around and between them. But that often means it's hard for people to do the same.

This kind of design makes it easier to navigate a car, but it also sends subtle signals to the driver that make his or her driving more reckless. Streets tend to be wider in more modern suburbs, for instance, and a wider street typically encourages drivers to go faster. One study found a nearly 500 percent increase in accident rates between traditional twenty-four-foot-wide streets and newer thirty-six-foot-wide streets. Curving roads, too, encourage drivers to take curves at higher speeds than right-angle turns; think of the difference when you drive down a street that curves gently—you can take the turns with just one finger on the wheel—while corners that form right angles, like those in cities and many prewar suburbs, require a driver to slow almost to a full stop. "Curvature causes people to accelerate," says Eric Dumbaugh, PhD, associate professor and director of the School of Urban and Regional Planning at Florida Atlantic University and a leading expert on street design.

The amount of open space on either side of the street matters, too. When the buildings or houses that line the street are set far back and spaced wide apart, it creates an atmosphere of more open road—less "lateral friction," in transportation engineerspeak—which encourages speed; when buildings or homes are built closer to the road and closer to one another, it creates a sense of "spatial enclosure" and encourages drivers to go slower. "The wider the street and the less lateral friction a motorist has, the faster a motorist is going to go," says Dumbaugh. Jeff Speck, a renowned city planner and author of *Walkable City: How Downtown Can Save America, One Step at a Time*, puts it another way: "Most motorists drive the speed at which they feel comfortable, which is the speed to which the road has been engineered."

Some of the most dangerous roads in all of suburbia are the arterial roads, the faster-moving commercial thoroughfares that connect suburbs to one another. Because these roads combine fast-moving through traffic—the cars whizzing from town to town at forty miles an hour or more—with slow-moving "access traffic"—the cars that slow down and put on their blinker to turn left or right into the Best Buy or Home Depot—they can easily cause pileup accidents. Introduce pedestrians who cross at crosswalks, or, worse, dart out in the absence of one, and these roads are "one of the more dangerous elements of modern-day suburbia," says Dumbaugh, whose research shows that rates of fatal crashes are higher on these roads than other kinds of roads. Specifically, Dumbaugh found that every additional mile of arterial roadway increases a community's fatal crashes by 20 percent.

Many other studies have demonstrated the danger of modern suburban road design. A recent report authored by experts at the Centers for Disease Control and Prevention (CDC) found that while we make less than 6 percent of our trips on foot, pedestrian injuries account for 13 percent of traffic fatalities, with the most dangerous areas for walkers being "newer, sprawling, southern and western communities where transportation systems are more focused on the automobile." Another study found that 60 percent of pedestrian deaths during the time surveyed happened where no crosswalk was available, and concluded that the most dangerous cities for walkers were newer communities where transportation systems are "focused on the automobile above all else."

Our modern suburbs feature all of these car-friendly design elements. Suburban subdivisions themselves are often safe cocoons, but only until they empty into a faster connecting road. Because Diane Roseman's neighborhood was a self-contained subdivision on a closed-off loop, for instance, the loop itself was safe, but since it terminated in a fast-moving connector road, neither she nor her children could leave the subdivision on foot or on bike. Once their street fed into the larger road, the cars went too fast. "[My kids] couldn't ride their bikes to the library or anything," she says.

One informal, if unlikely, metric for how car-dependent a suburb is might be how much its residents need to spend on candy on Halloween. Where Annette Lee lives with her husband and five children in Worcester Township, Pennsylvania, lot sizes are so large that she and her husband buy one bag of candy each year and feel lucky if they get a single trick-or-treater. "Nobody wants to walk, and there are no sidewalks," says Lee, a reproductive endocrinologist, "so the only trick-or-treaters you get are the ones who get driven by their parents who wait in the driveway." Many kids in the area have taken to decamping for the denser nearby neighborhood of Sunnybrook for more efficient collecting of Halloween loot. There, Lee says, home owners awaiting trick-or-treaters "have to buy $100 in Halloween candy."

Lee and her family used to live in Boonton Township, New Jersey; there were no sidewalks on their street there, either, and lot sizes were even larger. But there, the township came up with a different solution to the trick-or-treat dilemma: everyone drove to the parking lot of the K-8 school on Halloween night, parked their cars next to one another in tailgate formation, and kids trick-or-treated from car to car. Many families decorated their cars—some went all out, incorporating cobwebs, dry ice, and the like—and given the festive aspect of the event and the easier option for kids, Lee thought this jerry-rigged simulation of a dense "neighborhood" worked well. "It was good for the kids because they got to hit more places," she says, "and it was social for the adults because they got to walk around and talk to all their friends." It was nothing like the way she trick-or-treated as a child growing up in Cherry Hill, New Jersey, Lee concedes, but she tries not to get too wistful about the old days, because things were so different all around. "Back then, your parents would kick you out the door in the summer and they'd say, Okay, be back for dinner," she says. "It was a different world."

Whether it's because everything is so far apart or because it's not possible for safety reasons or because it's just not fun, suburban residents, relatively speaking, don't really walk all that much. Studies using pedometers have found the average American takes a little over 5,100 steps a day, compared with 9,700 steps for Australians, 7,200 steps for the Japanese, and 9,650 for the Swiss. That's because most Americans use their cars for just about everything. In the United States, roughly half of all trips taken by car are three miles or less. When it comes to trips under one mile, we hop in our car 62 percent of the time; in areas of sprawl, that figure jumps to 78 percent.

This has taken a huge toll on our health. You don't need to be a rocket scientist to deduce that more time in cars means we are less active. But research has been piling up that establishes a link between the spread of sprawl and the rise of obesity in our country. By now, the obesity problem in the United States is well known: more than a third of U.S. adults and 17 percent of children and teens are considered obese. But research by the CDC and others has found that some of the biggest reasons cited for not exercising are lack of structures or facilities—like sidewalks or parks—and fears about safety. Researchers have also found that people get less exercise as the distances among where we live, work, shop, and socialize increase. As far back as 2001, a report from the CDC asserted a link between the design of our "built environment" and our increasing rates of chronic diseases like heart disease, diabetes, obesity, asthma, and depression. "There is a connection . . . between the fact that the urban sprawl we live with daily makes no room for sidewalks or bike paths and the fact that we are an overweight, heart disease-ridden society," wrote the report's author, Richard Jackson, MD, a pediatrician, chair of Environmental and Health Sciences at UCLA, and former director of the CDC's National Center for Environmental Health. Jackson has been tracking the impact of environment on health for his entire career, in recent years focusing specifically on the influence of urban planning, including sprawl, on our overall well-being. Jackson has become a fierce advocate for the design of what he calls "healthier" communities—those that have safer places to walk, designated bike lanes, green spaces, better air quality, and the like—elements that draw people out into the environment and get them walking and exercising naturally. "We have built America," he says, "in a way that is fundamentally unhealthy."

In places where people walk more, obesity rates are much lower. New Yorkers, perhaps the ultimate walkers, weigh six or seven pounds less on average than suburban Americans, Jackson says. It's not just the greater prevalence of type A perfectionists addicted to their spinning classes. Anyone who's ever set foot in Manhattan (or New Yorkers who have hosted visitors from car-dependent areas who naively pack the same high-heeled shoes they wear at home) quickly realizes that walking a single New York City block is more than most people from almost any other place in the country walk in an entire day. I learned this the hard way when I moved for a few months to a small community on Long Island while working on this book; despite eating healthier and exercising more, my pattern of walking about three-quarters of a mile a day to transport myself suddenly ceased—and I gained six pounds in two months. My colleague Pattie Sellers is perhaps on the extreme side, even for New Yorkers: she lives on Manhattan's Upper West Side, walks to work in midtown and as much as possible when going about the course of her daily life, and usually exceeds ten thousand steps a day (which she tracks using a nifty UP electronic wristband). It's not at all uncommon for her to clock eight miles or more in a single day.

The obesity rates are especially alarming for our younger generation. The prevalence of overweight children has doubled since 1980; for teens it's tripled. Rates of type 2 diabetes have doubled in the past fifteen years, and a growing number of children are now being diagnosed with heart disease and liver disease—conditions once only seen in adults. These numbers parallel a drop in physical activity. In 1969, roughly half of all children walked or biked to school, but today that figure is less than 15 percent. You can almost pinpoint when things started to change: children are four times as likely to walk to schools that were built before 1983, when most students arrived by foot, than after, when schools started to be built farther away from town and were designed to meet the needs of students arriving by car. The number of trips the average child makes each day on foot or by bicycle has plummeted over the years, dropping nearly 40 percent from 1977 to 1995. Jackson says this is directly related to our pace of suburban sprawl. Unless changes are made in the way our neighborhoods are constructed, he says, today's young people—those born since 1980—may be the first in our country to live shorter lives than their parents. "This is so unbelievably serious," he says.

Bolstering Jackson's argument that our environment is to blame for our weight issues, a telling study came out of the University of Utah in 2008 that found a correlation between the age of residential neighborhoods and obesity levels of their residents. Researchers found that on average, people who lived in walkable neighborhoods—those that were more densely populated and more pedestrian friendly, and tended to be built in earlier times—weighed, on average, six to ten pounds less than those living in less walkable neighborhoods. And they found that adding ten years to the age of the neighborhood decreased obesity rates by 8 percent for women and 13 percent for men, implying that the newer the neighborhood, the less conducive it was to exercise.

In newer suburbs, people often decline to walk even when they can. One of the tipping points in Diane Roseman's experience in Westborough came when she suggested that the parents in the neighborhood start walking the children to school, which was about a third of a mile from the neighborhood and accessible through a little-used wooded path that happened to connect to their subdivision. The route entailed an extended walk through an isolated area, so it wasn't ideal, but Roseman suggested that perhaps the parents could take turns accompanying the kids each morning. She had no takers. "Nobody would do it," she says. "I was the rabble-rouser for trying to get the kids to walk to school."

Because of the lack of serendipitous interaction this kind of residential design fosters, children in many suburbs today tend to play according to a rigorous schedule of coordinated playdates and activities—hence Roseman's forty- or fifty-mile-per-day after-school shuttle. She says she "had this dream of kids walking up and down the street and knocking on doors" but found that, instead, everything was arranged ahead of time. "Everyone has a play set, but you don't have access to that play set unless you arrange a playdate," she says. Of course, some of this is due to a shift in parenting style over the years and to our playdate-centric culture, which is thriving in cities as well. It may have more to do with parents' busier schedules these days than with the inability of children to roam free. But many people interviewed for this book lamented the lack of free play or serendipitous interaction—whether between adults or children—in today's suburbs, especially compared with older suburbs many of these parents themselves grew up in.

The wholesale reliance on the car in today's suburbs is especially hard on adolescents, who under this setup need to rely on their parents as chauffeurs until they're sixteen or seventeen. This makes them unnaturally dependent at precisely the moment developmental experts say it's most important for them to become independent. "When there is nearly nothing within walking distance to interest a young person and it is near-lethal to bicycle," says Richard Jackson, "he or she must relinquish autonomy—a capacity every creature must develop just as much as strength and endurance." In this way, even teenagers remain what the urbanist Andres Duany characterizes as "frozen in a form of infancy." To get a glimpse of the angst brought on by the limitations of suburbia for teenagers, witness any John Hughes movie from the 1980s or what may still be the best example to date, the music video of the 1982 Rush classic "Subdivisions."

The car-centric arrangement can be just as isolating for well-adjusted adults. A 2010 study by researchers at the University of California, Davis, found that neighborhood satisfaction was higher among residents of older, more traditional neighborhoods than conventional suburban neighborhoods, even after controlling for sociodemographics and other characteristics, largely because of a perception of "liveliness." The lack of interaction grew more exaggerated over the years, due to the creep of sprawl, commutes that grew longer and resulted in less time spent at home, and the housing boom, which built new communities farther away from one another in increasingly remote places. "I live within 500 meters of ten neighbors," one suburban resident posted on Amazon.com in a review of Kenneth T. Jackson's *Crabgrass Frontier*, "and I know more about the last guy I sat next to on a plane than the neighbors I have resided by for over five years."

When she and her husband left New York City for Westchester County in 2004 and then settled in the Boston suburb of Wellesley in 2007, Linda Erin Keenan found herself unprepared for the isolation she felt. She ended up writing a series of humorous blog posts about her experience, which became a book proposal, which then became the ABC sitcom *Suburgatory* (and then a book of laugh-out-loud humor essays, *Suburgatory: Twisted Tales from Darkest Suburbia*). Keenan, a former producer for CNN, says she knew she was truly lonely when she found herself missing even the overly inquisitive doorman in New York she used to go out of her way to avoid. "I started missing not just my urban friends and job," she writes, "but especially Rob, my go-to conversation machine, and all the other random faces I would bump into, sometimes literally, going about my city life." To combat the "crushing loneliness," Keenan soon started talking to anyone who would listen. "I began talking to everyone, anywhere, anytime, all the time," she writes. "Were people's facial cues telling me to back the fuck off, you crazy mommy? I didn't care." She immersed herself in Facebook, she says, both to have some kind of communication and to connect with people on current events. Roseman, too, found her life in suburbia to be surprisingly solitary. After dropping her children off at school, she would be alone in her house for much of the day. "I would have six hours in an empty house," she says, which she says was "fine, but a little weird."

This isn't to say modern suburbanites are inherently antisocial—on the contrary, many suburbs have exceptionally close-knit communities, and even residents on individual cul-de-sacs can form their own kind of tight neighborly unit. But with people spending so much time in their cars and in their houses, and with many communities lacking a walkable town center or pleasantly walkable residential streets, the spontaneous interaction that comes from, for example, walking down a Main Street or a central square or even down the block is harder to come by. And that spontaneous interaction is important, as a growing body of research has shown. Researchers have found that when people bump into each other, good things happen. Both the Harvard economist and urban scholar Edward Glaeser and the urban theorist Richard Florida have linked higher-density or pedestrian-friendly places to higher levels of innovation. Tony Hsieh, the CEO of Zappos.com, is moving his company from suburban Henderson, Nevada, to downtown Las Vegas precisely because he believes the "serendipitous collisions" that happen when people are freer to walk between the office and local cafés, restaurants, and other public places will make his employees happier, help them forge closer relationships with one another, and lead to the faster cultivation of new ideas.

Perhaps it's no surprise, then, that walking has become en vogue with the biggest tech minds in Silicon Valley. The late Apple CEO Steve Jobs loved to go for walks with friends and business colleagues to discuss ideas, and getting asked to go on a walk in the woods of Palo Alto with Facebook CEO Mark Zuckerberg was at one point a rite of passage among Valley stars and potential employees. Twitter cofounder and Square founder Jack Dorsey is also an outspoken believer in the benefits of going for walks. "The best thinking time is just walking," he has said.

He's not wrong. Studies have shown that the act of walking itself delivers physiological benefits of a higher order, or at least a different kind, than other kinds of physical activity. Jeffrey Tumlin, a transportation planner and author of the book *Sustainable Transportation Planning: Tools for Creating Vibrant, Healthy, and Resilient Communities*, has spent the past few years studying the social and evolutionary importance of walking and its effect on our bodies and brains. "We're bipedal social primates," he says; every aspect of our body systems needs not just the exercise, but the pattern and physical motion of walking itself in order to work well. The rhythmic aspect of walking helps our lymphatics function, which impacts our immune system; as the most common weight-bearing activity, walking helps bone strength. There is a socially and psychologically therapeutic dimension to walking as well; it's "the reset button for our psychology," Tumlin says, noting there's a chemical basis for people who say, "I'm going for a walk" after a tense situation. Being able to walk to a Main Street or other locus of activity, meanwhile, gives people a jolt simply by creating the anticipation of a social interaction. "There's possibility—of life, or a work connection, or a little flirtation," he says.

If the centerpiece of the suburbs is the car, the central daily activity is the commute. The average suburban resident now drives fifteen to eighteen thousand miles per year; in the exurbs, it's closer to twenty-five thousand miles or more. Most of that time is spent commuting to and from work, which has been a part of daily life in the suburbs since people started moving there.

It's actually hard to know just how long the average commute is. The Census Bureau says the average worker spends fifty-one minutes commuting each day, but it's a tough figure to accurately gauge because people tend to underreport the amount of time it takes them to get to work. (When we talk about commuting in the United States, we are talking almost exclusively about commuting by car; close to 90 percent of U.S. commuters drive themselves to work, while less than 5 percent take public transit.) And the average doesn't tell the real story. Some 3.5 million Americans now make grueling "extreme commutes," defined as daily round-trip travel of three hours or more. A few years ago local television news stations started moving their first morning news broadcast from 5:00 a.m. to 4:30 a.m. or even 4:00 a.m. in some markets to capture the growing percentage of viewers who were leaving for work earlier in the day. "Commutes have increasingly cut into what we usually describe as sleep time," one television executive quipped to the *New York Times*.

As our obsession with housing led us to push out farther along the residential frontier, commutes got longer. Like Diane Roseman, millions of Americans felt that if they were going to spend $200,000, $300,000, or $400,000 on their house, they wanted it to be the best house money could buy, which usually meant the one farthest from the urban job center and out of the range of a public transit system. One of the country's biggest drive-'til-you-qualify zones is California's Inland Empire, where over the past decade hundreds of thousands have moved to the far reaches of Riverside and San Bernardino counties for more affordable housing. Towns here are seventy miles or more from Los Angeles or Orange County, to which many residents commute—more than 40 percent of Riverside and San Bernardino county residents commute outside the already remote region. The sheer travel distance is made exponentially worse by traffic: it is one of the most polluted, traffic-clogged corridors of the country.

One of the worst tales from the commuting trenches I heard while reporting for this book came from this pocket of the country. Maribeth Reinbold is a fifth-grade teacher who lives in Temecula, California, a small city forty miles south of Riverside that saw explosive growth in the 1990s and 2000s. In 2001, Reinbold and her husband, then a university police officer, decided to move from Orange County, where they were paying pricey rent for a one-bedroom apartment in Fullerton, to Temecula, drawn by its quaint "old town" center and the three-bedroom stucco house they were able to buy for $489,000, for which the mortgage payment was less each month than the rent on their Orange County apartment. They bought the home with the intent of finding jobs near Temecula, too, but the economy had taken a turn and local work was hard to come by. So they committed to another school year in Orange County and decided to make the seventy-five-mile daily commute each way until they could find jobs near their new home.

The distance was punishing, but it was the traffic that was the killer. The trip took an hour and ten minutes with no congestion, but on the clogged freeways during rush hour it took up to three hours each way. To avoid the traffic, Reinbold and her husband—they carpooled since they worked minutes from each other—would set their alarm for 3:50 a.m., leave by 4:00, and arrive at 5:15. With nowhere to go at that hour—it was still pitch black—they would park in the McDonald's parking lot, recline their seats, and sleep, setting the alarms on their cell phones for 6:00 a.m. when the drive-through window opened. Reinbold's husband would then drop her off at school, where she'd do her hair and makeup in her classroom and get dressed in the restroom. On the days Reinbold had to drive in without her husband, she felt unsafe sleeping in the McDonald's parking lot alone, so she would go straight to her classroom and sleep under her desk instead. "I was like George Costanza," she says, referring to the *Seinfeld* episode where George gets caught by his boss, Yankees owner George Steinbrenner, taking a nap under his desk. As bad as the mornings were, Reinbold's commute home was worse: three hours of stop-and-go traffic after which she would walk into her house, go straight to her bedroom, and plop on her bed with her arms and legs stretched out while her body decramped. After a year, she still hadn't found a teaching job near her new home, but rather than face the prospect of signing up for another year of her commute, she gave up. She quit her job, trading the tenured, well-paying position for which she'd earned a master's degree for a local substitute teaching gig, which she supplemented with a job at a tutoring center in Temecula for $8 an hour. "I just could not live that lifestyle anymore," she says of the soul-sucking back-and-forth. "It killed my spirit." Shortly after that, she was hired as a full-time teacher in Menifee, a twenty-minute drive from Temecula.

Reinbold and her husband are unique in that they never intended to make that commute a permanent part of their lives. But many of their friends, and millions of Americans, do; it's the only way they can afford the houses they live in and the lifestyle they signed up for. None of them needs to be told how miserable commuting can be, but a body of research has emerged in recent years that helps to quantify its toll on our bodies and our psyches. A 2006 study on happiness by Princeton cognitive psychologist and Nobel laureate Daniel Kahneman and economist Alan Krueger (now chairman of the White House Council of Economic Advisers) found that commuting was consistently rated the worst part of people's day (sex was the best). In 2004, a pair of Swiss economists found that people with long commutes consistently and systematically report lower overall well-being and calculated that a worker needed to make a 40 percent higher salary to be compensated for a one-hour commute in order to maintain the same level of happiness. Other studies have linked long commutes to higher levels of stress, anxiety, annoyance, social isolation, and exhaustion, not to mention a litany of serious physical ailments: higher cholesterol and blood pressure, weight gain, back and neck pain, and adverse effects on cognitive performance.

Since the time spent commuting typically replaces time spent at home, it also has an impact on relationships with friends and family. Robert Putnam, the Harvard political scientist and author of *Bowling*

Alone, found that every ten minutes of commuting results in 10 percent fewer social connections. Experts have suggested a link between sprawl and the rise of teenage hooliganism in some places because parents commuting longer distances to work are spending less time at home. More recently, a study from researchers in Sweden found that couples in which one partner commutes for more than forty-five minutes are more likely to separate. Another study of commuting couples in Canada found that manifestations of long commutes frequently included guilt caused by being away from children in their growing years, poor spousal communication, and an "irregular" sex life.

Yet even though we hate commuting, we have continued to seek out housing solutions that require it. Researchers have coined this the "commuting paradox"—people consistently underestimate the wear and tear of a commute and overestimate the benefits of its rewards. It's become conventional wisdom for people to insist that they're prioritizing family life and lifestyle when they buy a bigger, nicer home with a bigger yard. Yet if that location requires a long commute, they're unwittingly doing the opposite, putting their lifestyle—and the time they get to spend with their family—at the bottom of the priority list. One explanation for this irrational behavior is that while a big house is easy to see, the commute's greatest sacrifice—free time and lost moments with family and friends—is invisible. Another, more practical reason why so many people continue to commute by car is that they don't have much choice. While big cities like New York, Boston, and Chicago are the exceptions, most U.S. suburbs don't offer robust public transit. Nationwide, roughly 40 percent of workers now commute between suburbs, for which there is often no other option than the car.

As sprawl has gotten worse, of course, so has road congestion nationwide, the amount of time we spend stuck in traffic has more than doubled in the past thirty years. In badly clogged areas, like Washington, DC, and Los Angeles, commuters spend more than sixty hours a year stuck in traffic. That in turn has led to health problems like increased rates of pollution and asthma, not to mention some $120 billion a year in lost productivity and wasted fuel. It's also led to a spike in reported incidents of "auto-induced maladaptive behavior," otherwise known as road rage. Officially given its own medical diagnosis in 2006, incidents of road rage have climbed steadily over the years. A study by the American Automobile Association concluded that the episodes were rarely the result of a single incident but of the "accumulation of stress in the motorist's life."

All this driving doesn't just make us overweight, sick, angry, and stressed out. It also makes us poor. The building of the suburbs took place when oil was cheap and relied on the assumption that it would remain so. But oil didn't keep its end of the bargain. In 2003, the average suburban household spent $1,422 on gasoline, according to the U.S. Bureau of Labor Statistics. By 2008, that had risen to nearly $3,000. That's expensive for any household, but for a middle-to-lower-income family, it can be the difference between making ends meet and not. A major flaw with "drive till you qualify" is the cost of all the driving. That shiny new four-bedroom in the hinterlands is cheap. Getting there and back is not.

Scott Bernstein, who heads the Center for Neighborhood Technology (CNT), a Chicago research outfit that studies ways to make neighborhoods more sustainable, has spent the past several years trying to convince people just how quickly the gallons of gas can add up at suburban and exurban distances. A transportation engineer with a quick wit and a modesty that belies a lustrous résumé, Bernstein is an expert on the role transportation costs play in household budgets, and his opinions have been widely sought in the wake of the financial crisis. In 2008 he testified in front of the House Committee on Financial Services, and he was later one of five experts to present papers to a White House panel to discuss ways to recover from the housing-led financial crisis.

Early in the 2000s, Bernstein began examining the true role transportation plays in housing costs on a neighborhood-by-neighborhood level. Studying the average cost of transportation in hundreds of metropolitan areas, and using a formula that takes into account gas prices as well as the cost of the car, insurance, maintenance, and repairs, Bernstein and his team found that the average family spends 48 percent of its income on the combined costs of housing and transportation. For working families with incomes of $20,000 to $50,000, the figure was almost 60 percent. This lower end of income earners, he found, was spending slightly *more* of their income (29 percent) on transportation than on housing itself (28 percent).

This counters the generally accepted rule of thumb that housing costs alone should represent 30 percent of household income. It also counters the notion that housing is cheaper if you travel farther distances. Most people think about their housing costs without factoring in transportation, but the two are inextricably linked. Plus, it's the people who can least afford it who buy at the costliest distances. For example, in Kankakee County, sixty miles south of Chicago, Bernstein's index calculated that housing costs amount to 22.5 percent of the typical household's income, but transportation costs come to nearly 30 percent. In Peachtree City, Georgia, a master-planned community thirty miles south of Atlanta, 32 percent of the average household's income goes to housing costs alone, but almost 60 percent goes to housing and transportation combined.

Bernstein and his team indexed housing and transportation costs for more than nine hundred metropolitan areas and plotted it onto a color-coded map, which they named the H+T Affordability Index. They coded the map in two colors: yellow for areas where housing and transportation together consume less than 45 percent of household income, and blue for neighborhoods where housing and transportation made up more than 45 percent. Using the conventional definition of housing affordability, where housing comprises 30 percent or less of total income, 76 percent of communities would have been considered affordable. But using the new definition—in other words, factoring transportation costs into the total housing outlay—only 28 percent of communities were considered affordable.

A few years ago, Bernstein led an effort to create a new kind of mortgage that would factor transportation costs into the overall cost of owning a home. A more "efficient" location—one that had better access to public transit and life's daily conveniences—would mean the buyer could qualify for a bigger mortgage and get a nicer house, or put less money down, or borrow at a lower interest rate. Conversely, a borrower buying the same house located far away from his or her place of work and daily needs would need a proportionally higher income to qualify for a loan for that house or would have to accept a more challenging set of terms for the loan. Location, in other words, would be factored in as a measure of risk, just like income and credit score.

The mortgages were a novel idea, and they were favorably received by the housing finance industry. Soon after Bernstein introduced the concept, Fannie Mae agreed to participate in an experimental plan to test them, and bought and underwrote some two thousand of the new "location efficient" mortgages. They performed well: of a random sample CNT studied of three hundred of the mortgages nationally, there was one default, and it never turned into a foreclosure; the home owner was ultimately able to make good.

Similar studies have shown similar patterns, even when incomes vary wildly. "Nobody's disputed this," Bernstein says. "Mortgages in location-efficient places perform better." At the time, the idea for the mortgages was a tough sell to banks because, still recovering from the housing bust, they weren't financing anything. And in the time since, they've been reluctant to lend to anyone, so the idea has languished.

Bernstein has one influential follower, though: Shaun Donovan, the secretary of Housing and Urban Development. Donovan is a long-time proponent of smart growth and a big believer in the benefits of transit-oriented, pedestrian-friendly urban communities (he has said he's trying to put the "UD" back in "HUD"), and he has long talked of a sort of fuel economy or Energy Star–style rating for homes, a required disclosure of the estimated cost of transportation to would-be buyers. "We don't have a good system today of understanding, when you buy a house, 'what is this *really* going to cost me?'" Donovan has said. Bernstein and his team are working with HUD to come up with such a system, an official locational affordability index for homes, by the end of 2013.

But even if all mortgages switch to the location-efficient kind, and even if a new mandatory fuel economy rating gets slapped on every house, it won't be enough. The suburbs have a bigger problem. They are arranged in a way that makes gasoline as vital to our daily lives as oxygen, and the price of gas is going up.

The American suburbs are dependent on cars, and, at least for now, cars are dependent on oil. From their beginning, the suburbs were based on the availability of not just energy but inexpensive energy. And for years, oil was cheap, not just back in the 1950s but for most of postwar history. But starting in 2003 it began a steady climb. From 2000 to 2008, oil prices increased almost 80 percent. In 2004, the average price per gallon topped $2 for the first time. In 2007, it crossed $3. In the summer of 2008, oil spiked to $147 a barrel, sending gas prices over $4 per gallon nationwide.

For people who live in the suburbs, especially remote ones, the cost became untenable. That year, one hundred schools in sixteen states moved to a four-day week to save on transportation, heating, and cooling costs. Ellen Dunham-Jones, architecture professor at the Georgia Institute of Technology, remembers two junior staff members coming into her office and pleading with her to let them shift their schedules; living at the outer reaches of suburban Atlanta (also known as "Sprawlanta"), they could no longer afford to drive in five days a week. "They said, 'Please, I will work four ten-hour days. I'll even work four twelve-hour days,'" she says. They went to four ten-hour days, and shortly thereafter, one left for a job closer to her home.

In truth, our gas prices are a lot cheaper than they should be. In

Europe, gas prices are closer to $7 and $8 per gallon, or $10 in Norway. Europeans pay more because they pay higher gas taxes to cover things like road pavement, pollution control, accidents, and more—things we in the United States provide drivers and car owners nearly for free. "The most socialistic thing [2012 presidential candidates Rick] Santorum or [Mitt] Romney ever saw is the American transportation system and the private car," suburban historian Kenneth Jackson told me in a phone conversation that took place during the 2012 election season. The real cost of gas if it were priced to account for things like the building and paving of our roads and oil and gas industry subsidies, he says, would be $20 per gallon; others peg it anywhere from $5 to $15.

It's no coincidence that where gas costs more—in Europe, for example—there is less sprawl. In the United States, we were so happy to spread out and make ourselves comfortable mainly because everyone could afford to. "Exurb homeowners accepted long drives and commutes as an avenue to getting the huge house and lot they wanted," writes Christopher Steiner, the author of *$20 Per Gallon: How the Inevitable Rise in the Price of Gasoline Will Change Our Lives for the Better.* "That was when cheap gas seemed a certainty rather than a fleeting perk."

But even at our subsidized prices, our consumption is so high and the price of oil has risen so much that it's a strain for many people. And while price spikes have come and gone over the years, most experts agree we're now at the start of something bigger—a combination of dwindling resources and a looming explosion in global energy demand that will continue to drive gas prices higher. Yes, recently we've been heralding lots of good news when it comes to our domestic energy supply: the discovery and extraction of shale gas in recent years has been a boon; our dependence on foreign energy imports is at its lowest point in recent memory. But most cars don't run on natural gas. And most experts, including the lauded oil economist Daniel Yergin, predict fossil fuels will remain our primary energy source for the foreseeable future.

Indeed, while the development of alternative fuel sources and electric cars show promise, the solutions so far aren't going to be enough to make a significant difference in our patterns of energy consumption in the near-term. "The various tech industries are full of MIT-certified, high-achiever status quo techno-triumphalists who are convinced that electric cars or diesel-flavored algae excreta will save suburbia," says the author and sprawl critic James Howard Kunstler. That may be giving MIT scientists, as well as the array of hybrid vehicles on the market, promising developments in alternative fuel, and advancements in electric cars, short shrift. But the main problem is that to date, none of these developments has reached significant scale. To hit the mark the way cheap oil did, whatever we come up with has to be cheap and accessible enough for the 158 million Americans who need to drive or be driven to, from, and around the suburbs and exurbs each day. If it doesn't, the ever-rising cost of energy will increasingly impact where people choose to live.

Those on the extreme side of this argument—people like Kunstler, and Steiner, and Jeff Rubin, the former chief economist of investment bank CIBC World Markets who became so convinced of the coming oil shortage that he left to write a book about it, *Why Your World Is About to Get a Whole Lot Smaller: Oil and the End of Globalization*—say that dramatic changes are on the way. Kunstler paints a picture where oil soon hits $6, $8, then $12 per gallon; when it does, airlines shut down, parts of the world become inaccessible, and public transit gets mobbed. He foresees our pattern of development reverting to dense villages and cities where food, goods, and services will need to be produced and consumed hyper-locally; the outer suburbs will be reconverted to farmland, where the land will have more value. "Places that can't grow food locally are not likely to make it," he says. (Kunstler has long derided what he calls the "3,000-mile Caesar salad" and the complex, energy-consumptive supply chains we have come to take for granted to get food from the ground to our suburban tables.) As the transport of goods by water becomes increasingly important, he predicts the decline of any community that's not near a waterway. "You can forget about Phoenix and Las Vegas," he told me when we sat down for a chat in West Palm Beach—incidentally, the kind of in-person interview that under Kunstler's logic will probably go by the wayside, too.

To hear Steiner tell it, meanwhile, cars will mostly be playthings for the rich, and gasoline prices will be so high that for the rest of us, as he writes, "driving to the supermarket becomes an exercise of coasting through stop signs in neutral" to preserve every last drop of fuel. For his part, Rubin envisions a world in which neighbors will reconnect with one another; will relearn domestic crafts like sewing, gardening, and farming; and will stay close to home or close to our villages. He predicts that sky-high oil prices will ultimately bring manufacturing back to the United States; even though our labor rates are higher, that increase will be dwarfed by the increase of transportation costs to import goods from overseas.

Some of these views may be extreme. Transportation engineer Eric Dumbaugh sees it somewhat more simply. Gas prices are inconvenient, he says, but they won't be the thing that forces us out of our cars. Real behavioral change, he says, will come from somewhere else. "I think we're going to get out of the car because it doesn't make any social sense," he says. "There's a cultural shift going on right now—and I think that right there is going to be the game changer." The cultural shift he's referring to is that for the first time since the invention of the automobile, our driving behavior is beginning to veer in a different direction.

In one of the more striking societal behavioral shifts of the past few years, after all these years of car dependency and after millions and millions of miles clocked, it seems that Americans are slowly but surely driving less. The total number of miles driven peaked in 2007 for the first time since World War II and has been declining since, according to the Federal Highway Administration. The total number of registered automobiles has fallen, too: nationwide, the figure fell 4.5 percent from 2008 to 2010; in California, it's fallen nearly 10 percent. In April 2012, a U.S. Public Interest Research Group (PIRG) report showed that by 2011, the average American was driving 6 percent fewer miles per year than in 2004. This is partly due, of course, to the financial crisis and the persistent near recession we've been in in the past few years, which has forced Americans to pare back on everything. But the changes are significantly more perplexing than that because they started happening before the financial crisis set in. When measured per capita, vehicle miles traveled started to decline in 2004. And in addition to miles driven and automobiles registered, the share of trips Americans make by car has been on a downward trend as well—one that started in 2001. "America's transportation preferences appear to be changing," says Phineas Baxandall, coauthor of the PIRG report. Some in transportation circles are calling these collective changes signs that we've reached or are about to reach "peak car."

One reason for the change in behavior may be an ever-increasing awareness about the need to be more responsible with energy use. Consider the success of the Prius and other hybrids, or the rise of Zipcar, the car-sharing service that saw membership grow to close to eight hundred thousand before rental car giant Avis bought it in early 2013. The company specifically markets its service as a way to reduce the number of cars on the road. "Less cars on the road mean less congestion, less pollution, less dependence on oil, and cleaner, fresher air to breathe," its Web site says. Originally born as a service for city residents, it's seeing more demand come from suburban markets: in early 2012, Zipcar invested in Wheelz, a peer-to-peer car-sharing service, in order to test the concept at lower densities, and it's been expanding regular Zipcar service to suburban areas like White Plains, New York, and Montgomery County, Maryland. Meanwhile, established car rental businesses like Hertz and Enterprise, and even carmakers like Ford, GM, and BMW, are getting into the car-sharing game.

More and more suburban residents are experimenting with reducing their car dependency. In suburban Dallas, Rachel Meeks and her husband gave up one of their two cars a year ago and blogged about the effort. "We've been living in the suburbs with just one car for over a year, and I must say that it's been 10% inconvenient and 90% awesome," Meeks writes. "With two cars, there was always something we had to do: Oil changes, inspections, more gas and new tires.... One car is so much easier to take care of, and we drive less in general." The post got 110 comments. In the summer of 2012, a few transportation agencies in North Texas got together to organize a "Dump the Pump" campaign, part of a nationwide effort to encourage residents to commute by means other than their cars. Commuters could bring a gas receipt to designated destinations in exchange for unlimited bus and rail rides.

An easy gauge of the heightened interest in car-optional living is the sharp growth of Walk Score, a buzzed-about Seattle-based start-up that quantifies the walkability of almost any neighborhood (its slogan: "Drive less. Live more"). Plug in any address on Walkscore.com and the site, using a blend of proprietary algorithms and publicly available data, calculates how far it is from a school, a restaurant, a store, a coffee shop, and about a dozen or so common destinations and ascribes it a "score" of 1 to 100, with 90 to 100 being the best (a "walker's paradise") and 0 to 24 being the worst ("car-dependent"). The site is part utilitarian, part social mission: its founders believe that walkable neighborhoods are one of the simplest and best solutions to the problems facing our environment, our health, and our economy. Messages reminding users of that ethos appear all over the site. ("Save money, get fit and make room for the rest of your life," reads one.) Walk Score now shows more than nine million scores a day—and it's also introduced Transit Score and Bike Score ratings—but more telling is the way it has been embraced by the real estate community. Fifteen thousand realtors now build the Walk Score search mechanism into their Web sites sharing housing listings, largely because their house-hunting clients are asking for it.

There's another earthquake happening when it comes to our driving habits as well: teens and twentysomethings seem to be expressing a surprising indifference toward cars and driving. Getting a driver's license used to be a rite of passage for any self-respecting postwar American teenager: it was a ticket to freedom, autonomy, and unchaperoned life with one's friends. It's not as significant to today's youth. According to FHA data, in 1980, 66 percent of all seventeen-year-olds had their driver's license; by 2010, that had dropped to 47 percent, despite the huge swell in the population of millennials. The PIRG study that tracked overall miles driven, meanwhile, found the decline to be especially pronounced among younger drivers: the average American aged sixteen to thirty-four drove 23 percent fewer miles in 2009 than the average young person in 2001.

The indifference isn't just toward cars, it's toward driving, and it's sizable. In a study done by MTV Scratch, the network's in-house millennial research and consulting arm, not a single car brand was mentioned in the top 10 brands preferred by members of this group. This is starting to show up in car purchase figures: while people between twenty-one and thirty-four purchased 38 percent of new cars in 1985, they accounted for just 27 percent of new cars in 2010. "Gen Y Eschewing V-8 for 4G," read the headline on Bloomberg News when the data came out. "That is inconceivable to me," the historian Kenneth Jackson said to me in a conversation about the decline in driver's licenses. "You [used to count] the hours until you got your driver's license."

Of course, many teens still do count the hours. But ask around among the teenagers and twentysomethings you know today and you will likely find a decidedly different attitude when it comes to cars and driving. "Young people aren't enamored with their cars anymore," says Arcadia Land's Jason Duckworth. "A small apartment with interesting friends and a good Wi-Fi connection are today's '57 Chevy." I recently chatted with a former colleague of mine whose oldest daughter had turned sixteen several months prior. He said when he asked her if she wanted to get her driver's license, he was bowled over by her response: "Maybe next year," she shrugged. "Maybe *next year*?" he repeated to me as he recounted the story. "I couldn't believe it."

The housing market has started to reflect a change in driving priorities. Far-flung suburban communities are losing their appeal—and their valuations. An analysis of real estate data by Fiserv Lending Solutions shows that home prices have fallen more in towns and neighborhoods far from urban centers than those closer to cities. Homes located in or near walkable neighborhoods held up better in the recession, and, as we'll explore in the next chapter, new research keeps coming out showing an increase in demand for and higher valuations ascribed to foot-traffic-friendly, less car-dependent communities. "I think cities without adequate public transportation are going to be the ones that are really screwed over in the future," says Diana Lind, executive director and editor in chief of the urban affairs magazine *Next City*.

In the end, after six years in Westborough, Massachusetts, Diane Roseman and her husband decided they couldn't do it any longer; while they recognized why many people would choose it, the car-dependent, subdivision lifestyle just wasn't for them. They sold their house and moved their family to an attached row house in Cambridge and they haven't looked back. It wasn't easy: they got a deal on a fixer-upper in Cambridge, but they still had to spend more than what they were able to sell their Westborough house for. When they explained their plans to their suburban neighbors, they blamed her husband's commute for the move. "People really dropped us," Roseman says. "They took it a little personally."

Now in Cambridge, everyone in her household is happy. Her children walk to school, or even to the museum or to cafés. "My kids have so much more freedom than they ever had in the suburbs," she says. Last year her daughter attended a summer camp at Boston's Museum of Fine Arts and for a week took a bus to the museum on her own. "There's no way anything like that could ever happen in the suburbs," Roseman says. "It can't happen because of the infrastructure." Her husband works for Google and can choose between a ten-minute walk or a three-minute bike ride to work. "He's so happy," she says. Virtually everything the family needs is accessible by walking, biking, or taking the T. They live a mile from the public school. Whole Foods is around the corner. They have a "postage stamp" backyard, Roseman says, but they love it because her husband is free from spending weekends maintaining a big lawn—and if her kids want to play outside, they walk across the street to the park.

When I first connected with Roseman, she happened to answer the phone while she was in her car, driving her kids to a museum. She apologized profusely for even being in it and swore to me it was a rarity—they had only decided to drive because one of her children insisted. She was actually embarrassed. "It's a rare day that I take the car," she insisted. And yet despite the headache of buying, then selling their suburban home and relocating four children to new schools, Roseman isn't regretful of her experience in Westborough; in fact, she thinks it made her more appreciative of her situation now. "In some ways I wish we never had that suburban interlude," she says. "But I think I always would have wondered."

THE URBAN BURBS

I can't even enjoy a blade of grass unless I know there's a
subway handy, or a record store or some other sign that
people do not totally regret life.

—FRANK O'HARA

A few months after the National Association of Home Builders' convention in early May 2012, I am sitting in meeting room 1E of the
Palm Beach County Convention Center in West Palm Beach, Florida.
I'm here for the Congress for the New Urbanism (CNU), the annual
gathering of the nation's leading anti-sprawl movement. For twenty
years, the New Urbanists have been promoting the development of
smaller-scale, walkable neighborhoods built on traditional town planning methods, and on this warm day in May some eleven hundred
developers, architects, planners, engineers, bicycle and pedestrian
advocates, and other friends of the movement are gathering to talk
about ideas, exchange practices, network, and promote anti-sprawl
principles.

This industry gathering couldn't be a starker contrast to the home
builders' show. Outside the convention center, there are shareable

bikes available for use. A temporary bookstore has been set up selling titles like *Live-Work Planning and Design: Zero-Commute Housing, In-laws, Outlaws, and Granny Flats,* and *The Cul-de-Sac Syndrome: Turning Around the Unsustainable American Dream.* Instead of a trade show with aisles of vendors hawking products, this gathering is more of a mind meld, a kind of TED conference meets urban planning graduate program. The schedule is packed with sessions and seminars from the field's luminaries; attendees can choose from lectures like "The Secret Life of Trees," "Parking: Planning to Store the Cars Properly, Amid the Pedestrians!" and "Why Did We Stop Walking and How Can We Start Again?" At night, various local CNU chapters gather at informal salons to discuss their ideas in watering holes around West Palm Beach (the Cascadia chapter would be meeting at World of Beer; the Texas group would be holding court at O'Shea's Irish Pub; CNU Great Lakes would be at Roxy's). The New Urbanists who gather here are activists as much as they are planners, designers, and developers, and they believe in walkable neighborhoods and mixed-use development with the fervor of religious zealots. They talk about things like live/work spaces, alleys, terminating vistas, and the importance of creating a "sense of place." The woman sitting next to me in meeting room 1E has an image of a mixed-use pedestrian village as her screen saver.

The Congress for the New Urbanism officially describes itself as "the leading organization promoting walkable, neighborhood-based development as an antidote to formless sprawl." Organized in the early 1990s, the movement traces its roots to a group of influential designers who had become alarmed by the growth of conventional suburban development and started meeting informally to share their ideas for solutions to it. They included Peter Calthorpe, a pioneer of transit-oriented, walkable residential development, and Andres Duany and Elizabeth Plater-Zyberk, the husband-and-wife team who had risen to fame by pioneering Miami modernist architecture in the 1980s before shifting gears to focus on more traditional neighborhood development.

These thinkers, along with several other founding members, believed there was a better way to build not just the suburbs but our entire environment, and they were looking to formalize principles they had begun to use in their residential work—mixed-use zoning, pedestrian-friendly village development, more robust public transit, and the incorporation of the kinds of urban design methods that were common before World War II. They established the Congress for the New Urbanism as their organizing body and created a charter outlining their guiding principles. "We stand for the restoration of existing urban centers and towns within coherent metropolitan regions, the reconfiguration of sprawling suburbs into communities of real neighborhoods and diverse districts, the conservation of natural environments, and the preservation of our built legacy," the CNU charter reads. Over the years, the group has grown to twenty-five hundred members, hundreds of communities, and the well-attended, ambitiously titled congress each year.

The movement's unofficial leader is Duany, the charismatic Princeton- and Yale-educated architect and urban planner who became one of the leading modernist architects in the 1980s. Born in New York and raised in Cuba and Barcelona, Duany moved to Coral Gables, Florida, with Plater-Zyberk in the mid-'70s and became influential in the contemporary architecture movement. The Miami-based firm they helped found, Arquitectonica, quickly rose to international fame for its flashy, in-vogue high-rises; one of its most iconic condominium buildings was featured in the opening credits of *Miami Vice*. But after seeing a lecture by architectural theorist Léon Krier in which Krier talked about the importance of traditional urbanism and the power of physical design to change the social life of a community, Duany—after recovering from the all-out attack Krier had made on everything he stood for— had an epiphany. Duany and Plater-Zyberk soon left to found their own firm, Duany Plater-Zyberk & Company, to start designing communities in the way Krier had described.

One of DPZ's first major projects was the development of Seaside, an eighty-acre parcel of land on the Florida Panhandle that Duany, Plater-Zyberk, and the developer Robert Davis planned in the style of a classic American beach town. With its narrow streets, front porches, and residences of varying sizes designed specifically to bring people into the community to engage with one another, Seaside was both a commercial success and a revolutionary idea; the social element of the neighborhood was as important in its design as the physical look and character of the houses and structures. Seaside brought DPZ worldwide renown—it made the cover of *The Atlantic*; *Time* magazine selected it as one of the ten "Best of the Decade" achievements in design—and established Duany and Plater-Zyberk as leaders of the burgeoning New Urbanism movement. Even now, from its headquarters in Miami, DPZ is like the Apple or Harvard or Goldman Sachs of New Urbanism; it is the sterling name, the firm that draws the best and the brightest.

If DPZ is akin to Apple, Duany is the movement's Steve Jobs—a big-picture visionary whose bold ideas upended the status quo and whose conviction, not to mention oratory skills, have given him guru-like status within the architecture and New Urbanist worlds. Outspoken, passionate, and highly opinionated, Duany is prone to bold statements and ideas that hit him at any moment on matters both large and small. (Arcadia Land's Jason Duckworth recalls Duany at a dinner party some years ago making an "incredibly refined argument" about how to load a dishwasher.) Duany has, over the years, moved from architect to New Urbanist to more general futurist and prognosticator. "The present is not my job," he likes to say. "The present is a distortion field."

The architecture and New Urbanist worlds are filled with people who have been "Duanied," meaning they saw or heard Duany speak only to have it lead to an epiphany and a reversal of course on their own work. Sam Sherman, a Pennsylvania developer who's spent the past few years revitalizing the East Passyunk neighborhood of South Philadelphia, is one. Sherman had had a successful career at some of the Philadelphia region's biggest suburban home builders in the 1980s and 1990s when he happened to hear Duany in a radio interview one afternoon in 2002 while in his car trapped in traffic on Philadelphia's Schuylkill Expressway. Duany was discussing his book, *Suburban Nation*, and talking specifically about how the design of suburban sprawl had led to painful commutes for millions of people. Sherman says in that moment, as he sat in his car, he had a revelation. "It was a soul-sucking experience," Sherman says of his home-building years. "After you build fifteen hundred of those things, it's not fun anymore—and there I was, literally, trapped in my car," he says. He went out and bought Duany's book and a few months later quit his job. "I basically walked in one day and said, 'Here's my phone, here's my pager, here are my keys,' and just walked away," he says. He has been working on urban redevelopment projects ever since; most recently, he's transformed the neglected East Passyunk area into a thriving district populated by young professionals and drawing some of the city's hottest restaurants.

It is Duany, in fact, who I am awaiting, along with my fellow congress attendees, in room 1E in West Palm Beach. He's running late, and the conference organizers are radioing one another on their headsets. "Has anyone seen Andres?" "Is he here yet?" After ten or fifteen minutes, he arrives, breezing in calm, cool, and debonair in Nantucket reds and a navy blazer. He does not disappoint. The United States has gone through "an orgy of process-based design," he proclaims to the audience, beginning a discourse against the kind of planning that, he says, has brought us sprawl. In the span of fifteen minutes he invokes Pompeii, the Mormons, the Greeks, the Beaux-Arts movement, Baron Haussmann's redesign of Paris in the late 1800s, and what he calls the "dendritic" system of suburban cul-de-sacs. After he concludes his sermon, he leaves the rest of the session to his co-panelist and *Suburban Nation* coauthor Jeff Speck, promising to return at the end to answer questions. He exits as smoothly as he arrived. (Many months later, over dinner in Washington, DC, where Duany had traveled to speak at an event but also because he felt the need to "bask in classicism," our conversation took a similar tour, traveling from the history of single-use zoning and how municipalities "downloaded the cancer" when they bought standardized development codes, to how Brigham Young was a management and town planning genius.)

Over the course of the next two days while in West Palm

Beach, I get an indoctrination into New Urbanism principles: I learn there is an inverse relationship between the length of a block and how many people will choose to walk down it, that trolleys are "pedestrian accelerators," and that the car "disaggregates the complexity of the pedestrian shed" (translation: when developers assume people will drive, things get built farther apart). Over lunch with Peter Calthorpe, the San Francisco–based architect and urbanist, I listen as he discusses the end of Communism, the evolution of the middle class, and the "flywheel" of home builders who, he says, have kept producing the same kind of product even though home owners' priorities have changed. During the conference's main stage sessions, Le Corbusier, the French pioneer of modernist architecture who envisioned a high-rise city, is invoked as many times as the movement's enemy as Jane Jacobs is as their hero.

The main principles of New Urbanism have not changed much since its founding twenty years ago. New Urbanism is not a rating or rule book like, say, LEED, the third-party green building accreditation that requires structures adhere to a set of specific standards to earn its label; rather, it's a set of basic principles and guidelines—a sort of neighborhood DNA code—for developers, planners, designers, and policy makers who wish to design neighborhoods based on traditional town planning methods. Most New Urbanism developments have certain identifying characteristics: narrower or more "modest-sized" streets, an easily identifiable town center, a Main Street lined with buildings that mix commercial and residential spaces, and a mixture of housing types throughout the rest of the neighborhood— single-family detached houses, attached town houses, and apartments—

all commingled together. New Urbanism is not architecture; New Urbanists are almost agnostic to what the houses' exteriors look like, or even to the architectural style of the neighborhood. In the same way Clarence Perry, whose neighborhood unit helped transform suburban design, had nothing to do with the design of homes in those neighborhoods, New Urbanism theories relate primarily to a community's bones, or the design and layout of the neighborhood itself. As it was with Seaside, the goal of New Urbanism is to create neighborhoods whose design serves a social as well as a physical purpose. The mix of housing stock, for instance, ensures that a wide range of economic classes lives in the same neighborhood (which also makes homes easier to sell, since the housing stock appeals to a broader range of the market), while the pleasing, diverse streetscapes are designed to be both safe for foot traffic and also appealing enough to bring people out of their homes and into the public space. Some physical attributes of the dwellings themselves have a social function, too: homes are built close to the street, and porches draw residents to the front of the house, where they might interact with their neighbors passing just a few feet away on the sidewalk. Using these principles, a better-designed community, New Urbanism thinking goes, can result in a richer life.

All told, there are an estimated five to six hundred New Urbanism villages and neighborhoods built or under construction across the United States, estimates Rob Steuteville, editor of *Better! Cities and Towns*; DPZ designed the code for many of them. The best known is Seaside, but they include places like NorthWest Crossing in Bend, Oregon; Norton Commons, twenty minutes outside of Louisville in Prospect, Kentucky; and Stapleton, a massive project designed by Peter Calthorpe's Calthorpe Associates in Colorado that is one of the largest, a 4,700-acre development on the site of the former Stapleton International Airport. Many of these communities build anti-suburban claims in their marketing materials, which can read more like manifestos. Slogans for various New Urbanism developments include "life within walking distance" and "more life per square foot"; others implore home owners to "add the charm that's missing from suburban living." I'On, a New Urbanism development just across the Charleston harbor in the South Carolina Lowcountry, makes the specific boast that its porches are eight feet deep or more, "to allow room for rocking chairs to rock; for people to put their feet up; and for dogs to be dogs." Hampstead, a community near Montgomery, Alabama, points out all the careful thought that has gone into its planning: "Residents may not know we designed a street section to be a specific width," its Web site says. "They just know it feels right when they walk to the market."

To see these principles in person, I decided to visit one of the oldest and largest New Urbanism communities, Kentlands in Gaithersburg, Maryland, a 350-acre development built on a former farm estate thirty miles northwest of Washington, DC. Conceived in 1988 by developer Joe Alfandre and designed by DPZ, Kentlands has 2,211 residences, ranging from single-family homes to condominiums and apartments, and a densely packed downtown with a million or so square feet of commercial space (Lakelands, its sister development next door, which was built a few years later, has another 2,000 residences). On a crisp November day, I drive—and drive, and drive, all the way out past conventional suburbia, off the freeway exit ramp and down a big arterial road before I make a left into a big suburban commercial retail center that includes a Giant, Kmart, Party City,

Panera Bread, and more. One criticism of New Urbanism is that the communities themselves are often built deep within suburbia on large tracts of land, and by the time I get to Kentlands I am a good forty-five miles from Baltimore and almost thirty miles from Washington, DC. But just on the other side of the shopping center's parking lot there lies a sort of parallel suburban universe: a dense, tightly woven Main Street and a walkable, sprawl-free community of narrow, tree-lined streets, stately, traditional-style townhomes, handsome single-family homes, sidewalks, and small parks. Once you enter Kentlands, it's like being in a different world; it is like Park Slope, Brooklyn, or Georgetown has been cut and pasted into the middle of suburbia.

I meet Diane Dorney, a twenty-year resident and founder of the *Town Paper*, the first New Urbanism newspaper published out of Kentlands, at the Starbucks in the Kentlands Market Square for a tour. Market Square is composed of two intersecting streets, Market and Main, and a promenade that contains a cinema, several restaurants, and commercial spaces. Heading east, Main Street turns into a narrow village street packed with small storefronts—doctor's offices, salons, restaurants, and the like. All the commercial spaces on Main Street are in so-called live/work buildings, which means that each storefront has residential units and sometimes office space on top of it. Dorney and her husband, who have three adult children, live in one of these buildings; they rent out the commercial space to a woman who runs a wellness center, and live on the two floors above it. Live/work spaces are a hallmark of New Urbanism; the stores bring the foot traffic, and the presence of residents keeps "eyes on the street," in Jane Jacobs parlance, making the area safe at night.

We start to head away from town on Hart Road, a narrow residential street lined with town houses. The densest part of New Urbanism developments is the downtown; the farther away you get, the bigger and more spread out the homes become, but that's only a matter of degree. Ninety-five percent of lots in Kentlands are eighty-eight feet wide or less. The streets are narrow, with the largest measuring thirty-six feet curb to curb—that includes room for parked cars on each side—and narrower for the many one-way streets in the neighborhood. Dwellings are built close to the curb's edge; the "setbacks," or the distance between a home's front door and the edge of the sidewalk, is as little as six feet and no more than twenty feet. That's because houses in New Urbanism communities are intended to "pull up" to the public realm, that is, the sidewalk or street. The basic rule of thumb is that the front porch, when there is one, should always be "in conversation distance to the sidewalk," says Michael Watkins, the former town architect of Kentlands—and former director of town planning for DPZ—who lives there and maintains an architecture practice in town. In addition to promoting conversation, building the houses close to the street forms a wall of sorts and creates a sense of enclosure, or "spatial containment," that helps make the streets feel intimate. The sidewalks themselves are wide and pleasant, and it takes a while before I realize we haven't walked by any garages. That's by design, too; almost all auto access has been moved to the rear of the homes, accessible by a network of alleys, another New Urbanist hallmark. By pulling car access to the rear of the house, the sidewalk maintains its "pedestrian priority"; people on foot never have to stop for a car that's backing out of its driveway. Ninety-five percent of the blocks in Kentlands have alleys, which also double as utility easements so trash collection, recycling, and all metering happens in the back.

There are eight different "neighborhoods" in Kentlands, but they all include a range of housing types and lot sizes. This variety is critical in New Urbanism, as an alternative to the formula-based identical lots of conventional subdivisions. On Selby Street, we walk by a larger colonial house that's right next to a home that's half its width and sits on a much smaller lot. A stately mansion on the corner has a "granny flat" or in-law apartment behind it, common terms for a separate living space on the same lot that is either attached or detached from a main house. The industry calls these "accessory dwelling units," and they are prohibited by most conventional suburban zoning laws. But New Urbanists love them because they add to the diversity of the housing mix; they also put more "feet on the street" by adding to the neighborhood's population density.

Instead of the closed-off loops of conventional suburban development, the streets in Kentlands form a connected network so there are a variety of routes through the neighborhood and traffic is easily dispersed. There are paved sidewalks between some of the houses. There are backyards, but they're small, which frees up much more space for public parks, of which there are several, some big, some small. Before they moved to their current live/work unit, Dorney and her husband raised their children in a single-family home here, but she says they almost never used their backyard. There are three lakes, a church, a swimming pool (the swim team has grown to 220 kids), and a few clubhouses. There's an award-winning elementary school at one end of the neighborhood; everyone walks to drop their kids off except those who come by bike, by unicycle as one family does, or in Dorney's case, by a red Radio Flyer wagon, which she uses to pick up her granddaughter every day.

Walking around on a beautiful fall day, we pass a handful of residents jogging, pushing strollers, or out for walks. I'd pictured something that looked a little more Disney-ish, but it all does seem authentic. New Urbanists talk a lot about building at the "human scale," and it strikes me as we stroll through the neighborhood that this is what they mean. It actually doesn't look too different from any older town; at a few points along our tour, I stopped in my tracks because I was struck by how much the neighborhood looked and felt like my hometown of Media, Pennsylvania. The difference is everything has been carefully designed, plotted, and placed to feel that way.

Dorney and her husband were pioneers, moving to Kentlands in 1993 as some of the original residents. Prior to that they lived in a suburb of Pittsburgh, where they lived on a cul-de-sac and where Dorney, a stay-at-home mom with a newborn, was miserable. She says she had never spent much time alone and was surprised that no one in the cul-de-sac was home during the day. "It was hell," she says. They relocated to Maryland for her husband's job, moving first to a town house community nearby until her husband saw the construction for Kentlands while he was out on a run. When they moved in, she says, "it was like heaven."

New Urbanists are not without their critics, many of whom label them as sellers of a kind of fakified nostalgia. (New Urbanists would counter that claim by saying that everything—even old historic places like Georgetown—was master-planned and brand-new at some point.) Others say they aren't solving the problems posed by the suburbs because they build on large plots often in the middle of nowhere, which has led to the nickname "New Suburbanism" (one blogger described New Urbanism as a "pretty veil over common suburbia"). New Urbanism communities can be expensive to build and their homes expensive to buy. Getting over conventional zoning codes is often problematic and requires lots of patience, and often compromise: FHA loan rules still limit the percentage of commercial real estate in vertical apartment units, making it hard for New Urbanism developers to secure financing for the mixed-use buildings they say are a critical ingredient in their neighborhoods.

Nevertheless, New Urbanism principles have been followed and copied over the years. In 1996, Disney opened Celebration, Florida, its five-thousand-acre master-planned community near Orlando, largely on New Urbanism principles, though it did not bill it a New Urbanist community. In the mid-1990s, the Department of Housing and Urban Development adopted New Urbanist design criteria in its program to build public housing projects. The Monterrey Institute of Technology and Higher Learning now offers a master's in architecture and New Urbanism. And there is some indication that when the opportunity to rebuild from scratch presents itself, the New Urbanists get called in. After Hurricane Katrina, 170 New Urbanists, led by Andres Duany, prepared redevelopment plans for eleven Mississippi Gulf Coast communities; as this book was being written, staffers from New Jersey governor Chris Christie's office had started calling DPZ for ideas about how to rebuild the Jersey Shore after Hurricane Sandy. Membership in CNU is growing, and there is a new offshoot group for the movement's younger generation.

During the housing crisis, New Urbanism communities around the country held up better than traditional suburban communities, performance that won the attention of policy makers and the conventional home-building community and led the movement to some important victories. The FHA recently loosened the restrictions on the percentage of commercial space that can be attached to residential units. Certain municipalities are starting to bake New Urbanism tenets into their planning methods—even in Texas, of all places. El Paso recently became the first city in the United States to require that architects working on city projects be accredited in New Urbanism, while the Texas Department of Transportation has adopted the rule book that guides New Urbanism street design as recommended practice. "The dynamic is changing," says Benjamin Schulman, former communications director for CNU who is now with the Chicago chapter of the American Institute of Architects. Delivering the closing night keynote speech at the CNU conference in West Palm Beach, celebrity author and urban theorist Richard Florida acknowledges these recent successes. "Isn't it interesting," he says, "that the world has come to us?"

Perhaps the biggest proof of the growing adoption of New Urbanism theories is that the large home builders, who don't tend to care much for the social aspect of the movement or the well-intended principles behind it, are starting to build New Urbanism–style communities themselves. They're not calling them that, of course, and many may not even be familiar with New Urbanism, but there are by some estimates as many as four hundred "city replicas" already built or going up in suburban America, ranging from small-scale, intimate walkable villages to giant, ambitious "lifestyle centers" that combine retail, apartments, restaurants, and sometimes high-rise apartment buildings. In one of the brightest spots in the housing market, nearly every major home builder these days is working on some effort to effectively urbanize the suburbs.

In Glenview, Illinois, a North Shore suburb of Chicago, Pulte Homes, the largest U.S. builder, is building The Glen, a master-planned community of several hundred town houses built around a town center with a movie theater, spa, comedy club, pub, and coffee shop. (You can "leave the car keys at home," the Web site says.) Not far away, it also has Arlington Crossings, a community of sixty-six stately-looking town houses from fourteen hundred to seventeen hundred square feet. In the Washington, DC, area, the company recently opened MetroWest, a transit-oriented, mixed-use community of three hundred condominiums and town houses next to the Vienna metro station. "We're seeing more of a demand for the evolution of suburbia and a desire for community centers where walking areas and retail areas are more accessible," says Deborah Meyer, senior vice president and chief marketing officer of Pulte, "where you don't have to get on a highway to get a cup of coffee."

Older suburbs are beefing up their downtowns, too. Morristown, New Jersey, a leafy railroad suburb thirty miles west of New York City, is in the middle of a $300 million redevelopment of its historic town center that has seen the construction of more than five hundred new residential units in the past few years. They include 40 Park, a seven-story luxury apartment building that went up where the old Epstein's Department Store used to be and whose loft-style apartments have Brazilian hardwood floors, open kitchens, iPod docks, and walk-in closets; the building's seventy thousand square feet of ground-floor retail space means that tenants are steps from a Starbucks and a yoga studio. The building won the "Best Mid-Rise Condominium

Community" award from the National Association of Home Builders a few years ago; last year, two of its penthouse apartments sold within days of each other for $1 million to $2 million.

Many of these developments are deliberately playing up their urban design elements. The shiny new Village at Leesburg, a massive fifty-seven-acre urban development just off Route 7 not far from the famous Leesburg outlet mall, advertises its "carefully designed streetscapes" and "traditional Main Street feel." It has shopping, apartments, and work space, the very "mixed use" style of development the New Urbanists talk so much about. On a parcel of land some thirty miles from Philadelphia in suburban Bucks County, Pennsylvania, Toll Brothers has built Newtown Station, a collection of forty-seven federalist-style town houses and condos built at higher density in a grid-style, walking neighborhood. "Echoing the style and grace of Society Hill and Boston's Back Bay," the marketing materials describe, Newtown Station was a "quiet enclave of city homes reminiscent of an earlier time." In Conyers, Georgia, outside Atlanta, Arab developers who had bought up six hundred acres in the 1980s for a shopping mall have adjusted their original plans and are building a massive New Urbanist community instead.

It's important to note that not all of these are New Urbanism developments; New Urbanists, after all, didn't invent the concept of walkable villages, and the giant urban town centers can be a lot less charming. Salon.com cities columnist Will Doig calls them a "Frankenstein of supermarkets, outdoor dining, parking lots and mock-cobblestone sidewalks." But it is all part of the same grand effort to bring an injection of urbanization to the suburbs, or to create what the *New York Times* has referred to as "hipsturbia." The mainstream home builders and developers, who tend to be hyperaware of what their buyers are looking for—or as Duany calls them, "touchingly responsive"—are simply following the market, and the market is telling them that this is what people want. When you hear the home builders starting to talk about "streetscapes," "mixed use," and "sense of place," the principles Duany and his disciples talk so much about, it's clear something is afoot. "The pendulum is swinging back toward walkable urban development," says George Washington University's Christopher Leinberger. Leinberger calls these new urban-suburban markets Walkable Urban Places, or WalkUPs, and he's intimately familiar with them. In 2012, he led an effort to define and identify forty-three such neighborhoods in and around Washington, DC, classifying them into seven different archetypes according to degree of walkability. A niche market twenty years ago, he says, this kind of pedestrian-friendly development has become "the market of the future." Says John McIlwain, senior resident fellow of the Urban Land Institute: "I don't think people have a clue that we're creating totally, radically different suburbs than what we have thought of." Out with a big group of friends one night, I was explaining this change when Neil Vogel, a New York tech entrepreneur and armchair urbanist who grew up in the Philadelphia suburbs, jumped in. "It's urban suburban," he said. "That's what everyone wants. That's the ideal."

Helping things along is an increasing amount of data that suggests that these kinds of communities are more valuable than subdivisionstyle development. Studies have shown that people are willing to pay more to live in New Urbanism communities than in conventional suburban neighborhoods. A 2001 study that analyzed more than two thousand single-family home transactions found that buyers paid a 15 percent premium for homes in Kentlands over homes of similar age in nearby subdivisions. For other New Urbanism communities the premium was 4.1 percent and 10 percent. The difference is even greater after the Great Recession, as New Urbanism communities have held up better; valuations in Kentlands were less impacted than in nearby areas. Diane Dorney and her husband bought their live/work unit for $450,000 in 2001; six years later similar units were selling for around $1 million.

Now an increasing body of research is showing that home valuations hold up better in suburban communities that have even the slightest urban-esque features. Kevin Gillen, a housing economist at the University of Pennsylvania's Fels Institute of Government, drilled down on this with a study of 340 zip codes in the Pennsylvania, Delaware, and New Jersey suburbs. Looking closely at the relationship between the physical design characteristics of a community and its home valuations, Gillen found that housing prices held their value in direct proportion to the presence of urban design elements like mixed-use spaces, access to public transit, and walkable streets. Homes in suburbs that were either in or near pedestrian-friendly town centers, for example, held up 8 percent better than average home values in the area. Homes in higher-density communities held up 20 percent better; homes in communities that had a balanced mix of houses and commerce held up 6.6 percent better; and every additional rail stop in a community, Gillen found, led to prices holding up 9 percent better.

A separate study of metropolitan Washington, DC, conducted by Leinberger and Mariela Alfonzo for the Brookings Institution, found a similar link between a neighborhood's "walkability" and its property valuations. On average, the study found that each step up a five-step scale of walkability—measured by factoring in things like density, pedestrian amenities, personal safety, and proximity of needs—added $9 per square foot to annual office rents, $7 per square foot to retail rents, more than $300 per month to apartment rents, and nearly $82 per square foot to home values. Using data from Walk Score, Joe Cortright, who heads the Portland-based economic analysis firm Impresa, studied close to one hundred thousand home sales in fifteen markets and found that on average, a one-point increase in a neighborhood's Walk Score was correlated with a $700 to $3,000 increase in home values.

Developers of all stripes are seeing this research play out in the market, and many of real estate's biggest names are coming closer to the New Urbanism way of thinking. Rick Caruso, the Southern California real estate mogul who built the Grove, a retail, dining, and entertainment complex attached to the historic farmer's market in West Los Angeles, thinks walkable suburbanism is where the future is headed. His company also operates The Americana at Brand, a massive "lifestyle center" in Glendale, California, which includes retail shops, restaurants, 100 condominiums, and 243 rental apartments. Caruso told me that during the recent real estate downturn—what he called "the worst market in the history of the world"—his company sold all the condos at The Americana at Brand except for the three he kept for himself, and of the 243 apartments, he says there's rarely a vacancy. "There's this demand to live in that environment," he says. "I think people thought that life in suburbia was the perfect life, and it's got a lot of wonderful aspects to it, but a lot of people also feel bored. People want to connect and be connected a lot more in person." He thinks another big reason for the shift is that by putting people closer to things they need, the urban-suburban lifestyle grants them the biggest gift of all: more free time. "There's almost everything in the world you can buy," says Caruso (and he is among those who would know), "but there's one thing you can't buy, and that's time. There's an overwhelming desire for people to have more free time, and part of urbanization is just that. It's so much easier to walk downstairs and walk outside and walk to a restaurant, or grab a bite."

This obsession with "walkable suburban," it should be noted, does not mean that residents never have to get in their cars again. Only in a very few places in the country is it routine for people to live car-free entirely—New York City being one of them. My neighborhood in Manhattan's West Village has a Walk Score of 100, making it a "walker's paradise," and I would say it fits that bill: in eighteen years of living in various neighborhoods in New York City, I have never owned a car. But my experience is an aberration of the highest order. All "walkable suburban" needs to mean is that a pleasant and walkable center of some kind is accessible nearby. It's great if it's within walking distance, but it's just as useful if a rich, vibrant downtown strip of stores and restaurants is within a few minutes' drive for most residents of a community. My hometown of Media, Pennsylvania, fits this description; those who live in the downtown area can walk everywhere, but almost everyone else in the zip code can get downtown with a five- or ten-minute drive. (Media's biggest problem, in fact, is parking, Mayor Bob McMahon told me.) Very rarely does "walkable suburban" mean every single person can walk everywhere for every single thing. But the difference between driving a mile to get a gallon of milk and driving fifteen miles is one that can be transformative. "Maybe it's that your kids walk to school, or you can walk to a retail area," says Marianne Cusato, designer and author of *The Just Right Home: Buying, Renting, Moving—or Just Dreaming—Find Your Perfect Match!*, a book that helps home buyers make sense of the post-housing-crisis home-buying landscape. "You don't need to have one hundred percent walk-ability to have your house be that much more valuable and usable."

Across the country, developers are increasingly playing up the social aspect of their neighborhoods in the selling and marketing of homes. In Narberth, Pennsylvania, a walkable, historic, working-class enclave surrounded by Philadelphia's wealthy Main Line suburbs, the development firm Arcadia Land Company took a large single-family home lot and subdivided it into four lots for luxury single-family homes. The houses had high-end touches on the inside, like double sinks and all the right kinds of green certification, but they were designed to invoke the Old Narberth of the early 1900s, with smaller floor plans, deep front porches, and a close-knit arrangement. The marketing materials specifically touted this social element of the houses, calling them modern and luxurious on the inside but "Narberth neighborly on the outside." Much in the way "spacious" or "palatial" might have been the marketing message not too long ago, the selling point here was the density and the "neighborly." The homes, which all went into contract within one month at prices of $900,000 or more, set a record for the highest prices ever paid in Narberth Borough.

You can even see the demand for more urbanized suburbs reflected in that age-old barometer of what's desirable and what's not: the buzzwords real estate agents use to describe things. Narberth shares a border—and a zip code—with Penn Valley, a wealthy, conventional Main Line suburb. Ten years ago, real estate agents looking to up-sell a Narberth property's appeal would label it "Penn Valley"; it was the dressier address. In the last two years, real estate agents have started cheating in the other direction, calling addresses Narberth even if they lie on the Penn Valley side of the border. "Ten years ago everything was called Penn Valley," says Jason Duckworth. "Now it's completely the opposite."

The premium that's now attached to this kind of development, say New Urbanists and conventional developers alike, is simply a result of the basic law of supply and demand. There are plenty of conventional suburban subdivisions out there; there's hardly any walkable development in the suburbs. "For the last thirty years all we've done as a country is build big, ordinary suburban houses," says Joe Duckworth, cofounder of Arcadia Land Company (and father of Jason) and a longtime home builder who spent nine years at Toll Brothers and thirteen years after that running a Toll competitor, Realen Homes, before forming Arcadia, with Christopher Leinberger and Robert Davis, the developer of Seaside in Florida. "If anybody wants one, there's a million of them out there. You want one of these things"—a walkable community—"they don't exist." Duckworth is an example of a traditional developer who came to New Urbanism ways purely for the business opportunity, not for the activism. "I'm not into the religious revivalism of New Urbanism," he says. "I think it's an underserved market niche, not a religion."

This is all part of a bigger shift in priorities that's impacting not just *where* Americans want to live but *how* we want to live. In the wake of the housing boom and bust and the Great Recession, our priorities have changed—bigger is no longer better, credit is no longer limitless, quality is beginning to trump quantity, and less is starting to become more. The housing market is starting to recognize these shifts. The average size of homes, for example, is shrinking, and it has been for a few years now. In 2007, the average square footage of U.S. homes built, which had grown from 983 square feet in 1950 to 2,521 square feet, decreased for the first time since 1995, and it's been declining since (it rose slightly in 2011, but analysts say that was due to stringent lending standards that constricted sales to wealthier buyers). A 2011 survey of builders by the NAHB found they expected home size to drop to 2,150 by 2015. The median "ideal home size" for Americans, according to a survey by Trulia, was 2,100 square feet, right around what it was in the 1990s. Demand appears to be waning for McMansions. Only 9 percent of respondents in a separate Trulia-Harris interactive survey in 2010 said they wanted homes over 3,000 square feet—which by McMansion standards isn't even that big. A majority of respondents, 64 percent, said they preferred homes ranging from 800 to 2,000 square feet. In a state-of-the-industry overview at the 2012 home builders' show, Boyce Thompson, then the editorial director of the *Builder* group of magazines for publisher Hanley Wood, told the crowd that 56 percent of builders had changed their design strategy within the past two years to build smaller homes.

The big home builders, meanwhile, are starting to incorporate the kinds of details that New Urbanists love. Porches, for example, which draw people out in front of the house, are making a comeback. Two-thirds of new homes built in 2011 had one, and the number of new homes with porches has grown from 42 percent in 1992 to 65 percent in 2011. The pace of new homes with decks and patios, meanwhile, which are typically located in the rear of the house, has plateaued. The percentage of homes built without a garage or carport is the highest since the late 1990s. And demand is growing for more responsibly designed homes that make more effective use of space, so while the home may be smaller, its inhabitants end up using more of it. The Not So Big House movement, for example, pioneered by architect Sarah Susanka, advocates an approach for designing homes that are a third or so smaller than conventional homes but in a manner such that a greater percentage of their square footage is used every single day. A home built on Susanka's plans, for instance, might have no large entry foyer and no formal living room or dining room, since her research has told her that 85 percent of people never use their formal living room and 75 percent never use their formal dining room. But it will have an oversize family room with an alcove that fits a dining table—which gets borrowed from the kitchen when it's really needed. "A lot of people have sentimental attachment to their dining room, but when you get right down to it, they don't use it," she says. Susanka's "design language" also includes specific sleight of hand touches, details designed to play visual tricks to make the space feel larger: light placed strategically at the end of a hall to give a feeling of depth, reflecting surfaces to make a room feel bigger, a variety of ceiling heights. Susanka first published *The Not So Big House: A Blueprint for the Way We Really Live* in 2001, and it has spawned a Not So Big franchise, including the Not So Big Remodeling, the Not So Big Solutions for Your Home, and the Not So Big Life. All told, her books have sold 1.5 million copies.

The big home builders are now focusing on more efficient use of space, too, designing more "right-sized" floor plans and adding flexible rooms and open floor layouts where space does double duty. "The living room and the dining room are an endangered species," says Stephen Melman, director of economic services for the National Association of Home Builders, noting that more people are willing to give up those traditional spaces in exchange for a "great room" that they can use on more of an everyday basis.

On the more extreme side, the so-called Tiny House movement has emerged in the past few years as a subculture of ascetics who take immense pride in their ability to live in spaces as small as 100 or 130 square feet. Blogs like littlediggs.com, which serves people who live in 500 square feet or less, and tinyhouseblog.com, have seen traffic skyrocket. The Small House Society, a "voice for the small house movement," now has eighteen hundred subscribers, up from three hundred in 2005. These groups are small in sheer numbers and so extreme in their ways as to represent an almost cartoonish way of living, but their vision of large homes as environmentally wasteful, excessively large "debtor's prisons" that keep us from doing other things with our lives and our time, has struck an outsize chord.

Smaller homes fit less stuff, of course, and there's a major shift in the zeitgeist taking place here, too. While the 1980s, 1990s, and 2000s saw an explosion in conspicuous consumption, the Great Recession and the housing bust and the ensuing reset that has taken place have tempered our collective materialism and ushered in a small but growing "anti-stuff" mentality. A cottage industry is emerging around Web sites and movements that promote this so-called minimalism. Take, for example, LifeEdited, a Web site and product design and real estate development firm anchored by a philosophy that advocates for reducing clutter, extra space, and extra material goods (its slogan:

"Design your life to include more money, health and happiness with less stuff, space and energy"). The company's founder, Graham Hill, previously founded Treehugger.com, one of the earliest Web sites to focus on what would become the "green" movement, and for the past few years has turned his focus on this new venture. In a TED talk introducing the LifeEdited philosophy, Hill explains our obsession with stuff (while sitting on a box of stuff) and asks the audience to "consider the benefits of an edited life." We have triple the amount of space per person we did fifty years ago, he points out, and a $22 billion, 2.2-billion-square-foot storage industry for all our stuff—and it's time to pare it back. The talk has been viewed more than 1.3 million times. The laboratory for Hill's less-space-less-stuff movement is a 420-square-foot apartment in Manhattan's Soho that he has turned into a modular exercise in sparsity: a coffee table expands into a dining table that seats twelve; a bed springs out of the wall with two fingers; a pull-out desk turns a wall into a home office. A wall can be moved to make the room bigger, or divide it when guests stay over (two more beds flip down from another wall). Hill is now developing an entire New York City apartment building based on this concept, where residents live in hyper-small spaces and, through a program he calls a "product lending library," share bikes, cars, tools, and even appliances like popcorn makers—anything they don't need every day.

Sarah Susanka, meanwhile, has expanded her Not So Big franchise to include *The Not So Big Life: Making Room for What Really Matters* to similarly advocate for a reduction in the amount of clutter. The bigger-is-better mentality that gave us McMansions, Susanka argues, also gave us McLives, her term for an over-obsession with material goods. A few years ago, she says, no one wanted to hear her message about "rightsizing" the amount of clutter in their lives and making room for more meaningful things and experiences. Now, she says, when she tours the country promoting *The Not So Big Life*, "I could sell hundreds of copies of that book when I speak."

G iven all these shifts, it shouldn't be a surprise that even the religious revivalist wing of New Urbanism is drawing some unlikely converts. Take John McLinden, a friendly, gregarious Chicago native and, like Sam Sherman in Philadelphia, a veteran conventional builder. (John Norquist, the head of the Congress for the New Urbanism, chided McLinden when he saw him walking the halls of the CNU conference last year. "He's a former sprawlmeister!" he teased.) But in 2010, in the depths of the housing crisis, McLinden came across an opportunity in his native Libertyville, Illinois, an affluent North Shore suburb thirty-five miles from Chicago. An upscale townhome community on a desirable parcel of land steps from the town's Main Street had fallen on hard times; just five of a planned thirty-one townhomes had been built before the developer went belly-up.

McLinden had recently seen Seaside, Florida, and had connected with the "romance" of the old-fashioned town, the front porches, and the narrow streets. He thought this could be the way of the future and saw particular potential in the parcel's location steps from Libertyville's bustling Main Street. He bid on the land and won—and began turning School Street into what is essentially a model of New Urbanism: a row of twenty-six arts and crafts–style bungalows nestled right up against one another, each with its own wide front porch. He invited Sarah Susanka, whose ideas had long resonated with him, to design one of the bungalows; the first-ever Not So Big Showhouse now sits at the end of the row. He turned the eponymous historic schoolhouse on the property into fifteen open-plan, loft-style condos.

McLinden named the community School Street—and his company StreetScape Development, LLC—and started marketing the idea, talking up the accessibility of Libertyville's Main Street and the coziness of the community he envisioned, where neighbors could get to know one another, hang out on their front porches, and walk less than five hundred feet to Milwaukee Avenue for errands and entertainment. Within a few weeks, with little to show other than rough sketches, he had people lined up. "Off of squiggly drawings, I got six hard contracts with 20 percent down for something that had never been done in the suburbs," says McLinden. "And we did it in the midst of a housing crisis." The buyers ranged from young families with children to aging baby boomers empty nesters looking to downsize. One couple moved out from Chicago because the husband, a medical sales rep, spends most of the week on the road and told McLinden all he wanted to do was "ditch his car on the weekends."

Within eighteen months, McLinden had sold all the homes. The local news called it an "aberration." McLinden is now setting his sights on a much more ambitious project, a seventeen-acre development on the other side of Milwaukee Avenue that would include retail, apartment buildings, single-family homes, row homes, and a public pavilion, all built around Libertyville's train station.

He's also taking the same design principles and bringing them to a different market in Skokie, Illinois, a closer-in, older suburb of Chicago. There, McLinden is developing Floral Avenue, a pedestrian-friendly neighborhood adjacent to Skokie's downtown and public transit, that will include twenty-seven single-family homes. They'll be priced much lower than the School Street homes—around $300,000 to $500,000 compared with around $500,000 to $800,000 for School Street—but McLinden thinks his company will be able to target a much larger pool of customers in Skokie, not to mention younger millennials who prefer the smaller-scale, pedestrian-friendly layouts of inner-ring suburbs.

When I sat down with McLinden at the NAHB show (he and I might have been the only two people who attended both the home builders' show and the New Urbanism conference), his enthusiasm was contagious. "It's city living in the suburbs," he says eagerly, sitting so far on the edge of his seat, he was almost falling off it. "This is the way the world's going, even if no one knows it yet."

5

THE END OF THE NUCLEAR FAMILY

Monica: "We want a lawn and a swing set and a street where
our kids can ride their bikes—"
Chandler, interrupting: "And maybe an ice cream truck will go by!"
Ross, deadpans: "So you want to buy a house in the 1950s."

FRIENDS, SEASON 10, EPISODE 10, JANUARY 2004

No one knows when exactly Austintown, Ohio, got "old," but for the people living there, there's no denying it. Once the province of young families looking for safe streets and good schools, the population of this middle-class suburb outside Youngstown is now nearly 20 percent senior citizen. And the place is starting to show its age: the library has beefed up its large-print collection; Tuesday night concerts in Township Park feature big band, polka, and groups—Ginny and the Jettz, Sunshine Riders—named for heydays gone by; and like stray gray hairs, a Bob Evans, Perkins, and other franchise purveyors of soft foods and early bird specials have cropped up along the town's main commercial strip. "Austintown used to be a party town," says resident Jim Henshaw, age seventy. "We've all aged and matured a bit."

Henshaw would know. A retired hospital executive, he's now the executive director of Austintown's senior center, which, since its founding in October 2010, has become the new hot spot in town. "Too many people were sitting around doing nothing," says Gary Brant, an active eighty-year-old who moved with his wife, Myra, and two small children to Austintown fifty-two years ago for the schools. With their need for quality education long behind them, Brant still lives in the same house, and he has no plans to leave it. His friends are all there, his son is nearby, and besides, he's having too much fun. At the senior center, he now calls $7 bingo games three times a week. "The only way I'm moving from this house is in a box," he says.

Welcome to the retirement community of the twenty-first century: the cul-de-sac. Those now sixty-five and older were once the generation that fed the subdivision boom in the '50s, '60s, and '70s. Now, due to a combination of factors including the housing crisis, longer life spans, and the simple desire to stay in the communities they've lived in for most of their lives, they're staying put. At the same time, younger generations are having fewer children, sending ever more single-person and childless-couple households into the market.

The U.S. birth rate, which reached a high of 122.7 births per thousand people in 1957, has been dropping ever since, falling particularly sharply in the past few years. In 2011 it hit 63.2 per thousand people, a record low. Meanwhile, as the percent of children has been falling, the overall population is aging. The percent of people 65 and over hit a record 13 percent of the population in 2011. From 2000 to 2010, the ranks of Americans 45 and older grew eighteen times as fast as the population younger than 45, and the median age in the United States is currently 37.2, up from 32.6 in 1990.

The change is more pronounced in the suburbs, where for the first time, the forty-five to sixty-four age group is larger than adults ages twenty-five to forty-four, and where these days 40 percent of suburban residents are over the age of forty-five, up from 34 percent in 2000. Statistically speaking, baby boomers and seniors are now actually *more* common in the suburbs than young families. Going forward, this dynamic will only become more exaggerated: one-third of all suburbs saw an absolute decline in child populations from 2000 to 2010; by 2025, an estimated 72 percent of American homes will not contain any children, a figure that could reach 80 percent in the suburbs. "The traditional family structure is really the minority," says Deborah Meyer of home builder Pulte.

You can see this playing out. Where my father grew up in Drexel Hill, Pennsylvania, a 1920s streetcar suburb outside of Philadelphia, there were forty-one children living in the sixteen or so houses on his block alone: the Janssens (four kids), the Hayeses (three), the McNultys (four), the Lombardos (four), the McDermotts (five), the Hartmans (four), the Bancrofts (three), and, of course, the Gallaghers (seven), among many others. Today there is a fraction of that; an unofficial poll puts the number at twelve to fifteen for the whole block. This trend is happening everywhere, and has been called the "demographic winter," the "birth dearth," and the "baby bust." The decline in the number of children can be partially attributed to economic conditions: from 2007 to 2009, the height of the recession, U.S. births saw the largest drop for any two-year period since the 1970s. But there are larger forces at work as well, and they touch on bigger and deeper changes taking place in our society.

For one thing, fewer people are getting married. Married households now make up a little over 48 percent of the population, down from 83 percent in 1950. Those who do marry are doing so a lot later: in the 1950s, half of men and women who married for the first time were in their early twenties; now, the average age is twenty-eight for men and twenty-six for women. For a number of reasons, marriage no longer holds the same central role in defining people's lives as it did in the 1950s. Many people delay marriage because they're focused on building their careers, and that means delaying having children, an option newly available to women thanks to advances in fertility technology. (Between 2007 and 2009, while the birth rate in the United States fell among every other age group, it rose for women over forty.) And more women—especially older women—are opting to have children on their own. This trend, of course, is due in large part to the fact that more women are now working outside the home and can support themselves and a child financially, something that was much less common in the middle of the century. Whether married or unmarried, coupled or not, the later women have children, the fewer they have. It's also become socially acceptable—and in the case of women more economically feasible—for people to live lives outside of marriage: as an unmarried couple (whether same or opposite sex), a single parent, or alone: a record 27 percent of all households—and as many as 40 percent in some cities—now consist of just one person, the highest level in U.S. history. "The extraordinary rise of living alone is among the greatest social changes since the baby boom," writes Eric Klinenberg, professor of sociology at New York University, in his book *Going Solo: The Extraordinary Rise and Surprising Appeal of Living Alone.*

Since marriage and children have for decades been the driving engine behind suburban growth—indeed, practically the whole basis for the suburban existence—these trends suggest that what we have long thought of as the typical American household—a husband, a wife, and 2.3 children living on their own plot of suburban real estate—is receding as the dominant group in suburbia. This explains places like Austintown, where, since opening in 2010, the senior center has expanded its hours, programs, and van fleet, and membership is up by a thousand. All told, the greater Youngstown area, of which Austintown is a part, saw a 24 percent drop in population under the age of forty-five between 2000 and 2010, and it now claims the nation's highest concentration of seniors outside Florida and Tucson. Meanwhile in Hillsborough, New Jersey, a suburb in Somerset County—one of the wealthiest in the state—the Kids Playway Child Care Center has seen a 40 percent decline in enrollment in the last two years.

Then there's Durand, Michigan, a suburb twenty miles from Flint and forty miles from Lansing, where the three-story redbrick building that was once the junior high school has been turned into Sycamore House, a forty-unit senior apartment complex. These days, the worn wooden doors that once led into classrooms now open into one- and two-bedroom apartments, and the old gymnasium is now a community room where residents meet to play board games. In recent years, the gymnasium has also been the venue for the Senior Citizen Prom. Starting promptly at 6:00 p.m., attendees showed up, some men in tuxedos and many women wearing corsages, and danced the night away—or the early evening, anyway—to "Mr. Sandman" under the old class banners that still hang from the ceiling.

Much of this shift is due to the overwhelming number of today's seniors who are expected to "age in place," or live out their golden years in the same homes where they raised their families. According to an AARP survey, nearly 90 percent of seniors want to stay in the same home as long as possible; 80 percent say it's the only residence they'll ever live in. One reason for this is the recession, which wiped out many boomers' retirement savings and made it difficult for them to sell their homes and move into more traditional retirement enclaves. But there's also been a renewed desire in recent years for seniors to remain in the homes and communities in which they have friends, family, and deep roots. Instead of investing in condos in the Sun Belt, many of them are moving to retirement homes in the same communities where they lived much of their adult lives, or adapting their homes to accommodate the needs they'll have in their twilight years. And while the AARP study only surveyed current seniors, the association predicts the coming tsunami of baby boomers will express the same desire to stay put. "In some ways, current senior growth is just the lull before the storm," says William Frey, senior fellow with the Brookings Institution and one of the nation's leading demographers.

A cottage industry has emerged in Web sites and consultants offering services to help the elderly stay in their suburban homes, whether it's delivering meals, providing transportation, or installing senior-friendly tweaks like raised dishwashers and handrails in the bathroom. Many municipalities are adapting to this new reality. Fairfax County, Virginia, has created a "50-plus action plan" that has helped make pedestrian traffic signals more visible, held seminars on how to make kitchens and bathrooms more senior friendly, and set up a course on coping during retirement. The police department has established a unit to investigate financial fraud committed against the elderly. In nearby Montgomery County, officials have developed a Web site listing services for senior citizens and established a "village" system where younger residents make themselves available to drive seniors to appointments. Austintown, Ohio, is rejiggering its services to meet the needs of its aging population, adding new public transit routes and Senior Crime Watch patrols. In Westchester County, New York, dozens of aging-in-place programs have sprung up, grassroots organizations that, for fees of $50 to $400, provide transportation to shopping and appointments, referrals for in-home and medical support, and services like meal delivery and yard work. At Home in Scarsdale Village was formed in 2010; Staying Put in Rye and Environs—affectionately known as SPRYE—has 120 members after launching in October 2011. A group called Gramatan Village services Bronxville, while Staying Put in New Canaan and At Home in Greenwich serve the neighboring Connecticut communities.

If you're a parent raising young children, these changes may be hard to see because chances are you live near many other families in the same situation—and if that's the case, your community may in fact have lots of children. That's because families with children tend to cluster near one another, so the result is a patchwork of sorts, with some neighborhoods filled with children and others oddly devoid of them. But on the whole, the suburbs are graying, and that will lead to more than just demographic consequences, because young families with children do more than just bring youth and vibrant energy to a town; they bring an economic force. They buy more things, spend more money, and invest more time in building ties to the community. With fewer of them, housing needs change, the retail mix shifts, and more people are free to pick up and leave at any point—unburdened by the need to remain in one place until their children graduate.

This has a major impact on schools, which are seeing declining enrollments in many suburban communities. In Levittown, Pennsylvania, an elementary school, a middle school, and one of two high schools have closed since the late 1970s and early 1980s, and enrollment has dropped 18 percent during the past decade. The district is considering eliminating full-day kindergarten. The Austintown school district recently shuttered two of its four elementary schools, and in 2009 it opened enrollment to students outside the district and introduced online K–12 education to raise enrollment; students can use their own computers or can go to labs supplied by the district. In Munjoy Hill, a suburb of Portland, Maine, only one elementary school remains where there were once three; the others have been knocked down to build affordable housing.

The aging of the suburbs is changing the political conversation in many municipalities as well; as older voters become the most powerful base, tax revenue will increasingly get allocated away from schools and toward resources for seniors. "These older folks are going to be politically involved and will have political expenditures go where they want," says Brookings' William Frey. The more taxpayer revenue gets allocated away from schools, the more the schools will suffer; and once schools and services for young families start to suffer, those young families will choose to live elsewhere.

At the same time, more families are doing what Diane Roseman, the stay-at-home mom who briefly experimented with the Massachusetts suburb of Westborough, did (see chapter 3), and are opting to

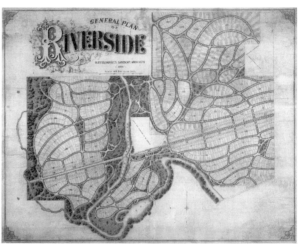

Built in the mid-1850s, the communities of Llewellyn Park, in West Orange, New Jersey (*above*), and Riverside, Illinois, designed by Frederick Law Olmsted, were the first suburbs designed specifically to mimic the bucolic feel of country life.

The history of the modern-day suburbs begins with Levittown, the massive development on Long Island built immediately after World War II.

By the mid-1950s, the suburban way was the only way.

The earliest U.S. suburbs sprouted organically around railroad stations. With their villa oriented town centers, these suburbs are better positioned for the future than their more mode subdivision-style counterparts. Here, the Village of Scarsdale, New York, in April 2013.

Tract housing developments like these in Las Vegas now blanket much of the country.

The strip mall is one of the most identifiable elements of modern-day suburbia. Instead of a centralized downtown, commercial activity takes place in a series of shopping centers like this one on Route 59 in Rockland County, New York.

The author's suburban experience: her family circa 1992 (*right*) and childhood home in Media, Pennsylvania (*below*)

The author's hometown, Media, has unique elements like a main street lined with boutiques, bars, and restaurants and a working trolley (*above*); a courthouse; and a restored 1927 theater (*left*).

Warner Bros./Courtesy Everett Collection

The rise and fall of American burbia has been mirrored in pular culture. *The Wonder ars* (*above*) depicted idyllic burban family life in the late 60s. References later turned rk in the 1999 film *American auty* (*right*). In 2005, Showtime buted *Weeds*, which portrayed e life of a pot-dealing mother the fictitious suburb of grestic, California.

Everett Collection

Michael Desmond/©Showtime/ Everett Collection

In the suburbs of Gaithersburg, Maryland, lies Kentlands, an anti-sprawl community built on principles like narrower streets, a smaller scale, and a mixture of home sizes and types.

©Leigh Gallagher

There are hundreds of New Urbanist communities across the country like Kentlands and New Town at St. Charles near St. Louis, Missouri; big commercial builders are now replicating their concepts.

©Srenco Photo 2008/Courtesy of Duany Plater-Zyberk & Company

Anti-sprawl activists point street design at the turn of t century as the ideal. Chu Marohn, founder of StrongTow .org, uses this picture of Brainer Minnesota, in 1905 in his TE talk to demonstrate a street "th rocks."

Morristown, New Jersey, has given its downtown a dose of urban chic, adding penthouse loft apartments, boutiques, restaurants, and a walkable promenade.

In Libertyville, Illinois, John McLinden developed School Street, a neighborhood of twenty-six houses in dense arrangement just off the town's Main Street. Many buyers are McMansion refugees who tired of the wasted space and relying on their car.

Developers are turning dead suburban shopping malls into residential villages. In Lakewood, Colorado, the old Villa Italia shopping mall is now Belmar, a community with one thousand housing units, as well as restaurants, boutiques, cafés, and outdoor entertainment plazas.

Toll Brothers/www.JimWilsonPhotography.com

Toll Brothers' big luxury suburban homes—like this one in Southlake, Texas—used to make up 70 to 80 percent of what the company builds and sells. Now it's more like 50 percent.

©RobFaulkner.com

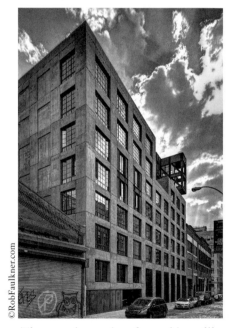

The rest is coming from things like this new forty-story glass tower in Manhattan (*left*) and a chic condo building in Brooklyn's DUMBO (*above*). New York City is "our hottest market by far," CEO Douglas Yearley has said.

Design by Atelier Christian de Portzamparc, courtesy of Toll Brothers, Inc. ©AECDP Permission to publish this image raise their children in cities instead. While this trend can be seen in almost every large city, from Boston to Dallas to San Francisco, New York City is perhaps the most telling example simply because of its extraordinarily high prices and lack of space. The average Manhattan apartment costs $1.4 million to buy, and eight hundred square feet for a one-bedroom is considered roomy. And yet the once-gritty city has become overloaded with young families. There are now twenty-six hundred more married families with children under the age of eighteen living in Manhattan than there were in 2000. Many are settling in the traditionally family-friendly Upper East Side and Upper West Side, but in recent years they have been elbowing into new neighborhoods like Tribeca, the former edgy artists' haven that now has so many strollers it's been nicknamed Triburbia, or the financial district, where fifty-seven thousand people—a quarter of them couples with children—now live south of city hall, more than double the figure before 9/11. Luxury condo buildings in lower Manhattan now include playrooms and other amenities to accommodate the number of families moving into the area long dominated by financial institutions, law firms, and the like. Ads for high-end Manhattan condos now target couples with young children: "floor plans that rival many suburban homes in space and grandeur," claims Extell Development Company in an ad for a new Upper West Side building; a Corcoran Group ad for a nine-room duplex on Central Park West implores young families to "forget the suburbs." Schools are overcrowded; strollers clog the streets; mommy groups are taking over coffee shops. As a former colleague recently posted on Facebook after getting glared at by a pedestrian while pushing her child in a stroller on the Upper West Side: "That old kid-free New York that was the exclusive domain of singles and childless-by-choicers is dead. Get over it already. And if you don't like it, YOU move to the suburbs."

If the suburbs are less of a draw for young people, you certainly don't need to tell that to the group that's next in line to change our country's makeup: the millennials. Representing roughly a quarter of the population, millennials have the power and might to throw their weight around even more than their boomer parents did (and do), and they present big issues for the future of the suburbs.

For one thing, large numbers of them have yet to fully launch into adulthood. Not since the 1940s have so many in this age group been living with their parents. In 2011, 22 percent of twenty-five- to thirty-four-year-olds were living with their parents or grandparents, according to a Pew study, up from 11 percent in 1980. Overall, 53 percent of all adults ages eighteen to twenty-four say they either live with their parents now or did temporarily in recent years. And those who haven't know someone who has.

Much of this is due to the fact that much of Gen Y came of age in the Great Recession. Many of them graduated from college in 2008 or after, as the global financial system fell apart, and it's hard for even the most qualified graduates to find work, a phenomenon that was perhaps best captured by a *New Yorker* magazine cover that showed a young, brainy graduate hanging his PhD in his teenage bedroom next to his high school trophies as his horrified parents looked on.

But the millennials' delayed adulthood has other causes that have nothing to do with the recession. One of the defining characteristics of this generation is a general reluctance to separate from their parents physically or emotionally until well into their twenties or thirties. Compared with earlier generations, millennials don't seem to feel the same kind of pressure to marry, move out, or start having children that earlier generations did. Psychologists have coined a term for this new phase—"emerging adulthood"—to refer to the elongated development process exhibited by this group, much in the way researchers first identified "adolescence" as a new phase at the beginning of the twentieth century. Experts have attributed this slowdown in maturation to a number of causes, ranging from the practical—the need for more education to compete in the job market, and thus the extended need for parental support—to the social and scientific advances of the last several decades: we live longer, can have children later, and so on, so what's the rush? These factors might also help explain the lack of stigma associated with moving back home for this group: the Pew Research Center found that 80 percent of those twenty-five- to thirty-four-year-olds who have moved back in with their parents are just fine with the arrangement—something that would have been unthinkable a generation ago.

Another oft-cited factor for the millennials' failure to launch is that so many in this group were raised by "helicopter parents," so named for their tendency to hover over their kids at all times. Helicopter parents don't want to see their children suffer the harsh realities of the real world, the thinking goes, and their children, having been raised to believe their parents will always be there to solve their problems, are reluctant to separate. Nadira Hira, author and Gen Y expert, sees it a little differently: "We've always been close to our parents because they've always been so invested in us," she says, adding that technology has only made it easier and more acceptable for millennials to consult with their parents on just about everything. "It isn't such a great leap from talking every day on the phone or via text to chatting and hanging together every night under the same roof. As strange as it might sound, we *like* each other." The result is a multi-generational commingling that has millions of twenty- and even thirtysomethings living in the suburbs in big houses—with their parents.

William May moved back into his parents' house in Hicksville, Long Island, in the fall of 2011 to finish his college degree at Hofstra University. He'd been on his own for a few years while attending school in Manhattan but decided to save money and focus on his grades. Now twenty-three, he'd like to move out soon, to be closer to the city, but in the meantime he says it's fine—he spends most of his time at school or at Starbucks studying anyway. He says his parents had no problem with him moving home—quite the opposite, in fact. "They want to keep me at home, and I want to get out." May considers it normal for kids his age to live with their parents beyond high school, though he says he has a forty-five-year-old relative who lives with his parents, which he thinks is too old. "There are limits."

Nicole Miller, also twenty-three, graduated from Denison University with a degree in religion and environmental studies in 2011. After a few stints in California and Ohio, she moved back in with her parents in Mt. Lebanon, Pennsylvania, a suburb fifteen miles outside Pittsburgh, and decided to stay there even after she got a job working for AmeriCorps. She wanted to save money, and many of her friends were also living with their parents. Her father, an architect, and her mother, a psychologist, welcomed her. Her twin brother had also lived at home after college for nine months, and her older siblings had lived rent-free in her father's fixer-uppers in Pittsburgh—in exchange for helping out with the family business—early into their adult lives. For Nicole's part, she said she craves the sense of independence she had in college, and she feels out of place in a way. "There are all these nice things," she says. "I look around, and I think, 'This is a bigger house than I'll ever live in.' It's like I'm living someone else's life." But she's enjoyed the time with her parents—they eat dinner together most nights, and they have regular television-watching rituals as well. (When reached by phone, she had to end the call when her parents summoned her—it was time to watch *Modern Family*.) She says, in a way, her relationship with her parents is better now than it was before. "Being here, I've showed them parts of my life before they didn't understand," she says. "And I've seen parts of their lives I didn't understand before my adult life. In some ways, this needed to happen."

While millennials may not see a problem with this setup, housing economists do, because their failure to set out on their own is disrupting the normal economic cycle. Typically—or at least in the post–World War II era—the housing market turns over when one generation ages out and the next moves in, either to new homes or the homes the previous generation vacated for them. It's not working that way now. From 2009 to 2011, just 9 percent of twenty-nine- to thirty-four-year-olds got a first-time mortgage compared with 17 percent a decade ago. Along with aging seniors moving in with their adult children and an increasingly ethnically diverse population with many families for whom living together is part of the culture, this is contributing to the record 30 percent of households now living in "doubled up" accommodations, defined as having at least one other adult who is not the home owner, spouse, or cohabitating partner of the home owner.

Not to miss an opportunity, and sensing a sea change that could last at least a generation or more, the home-building industry is responding with houses that can accommodate all of these people under one roof. So while most new homes are getting smaller, there is a subsection that is getting slightly larger: the new category of so-called multigenerational homes.

These houses typically have an extra self-contained suite, typically five hundred or six hundred square feet either on the first floor or over the garage, complete with its own bathroom and kitchenette and, often times, a separate entrance to preserve the illusion of living independently (for young twentysomethings, call it the "don't ask, don't tell door"). "As echo boomers move back in to live with their parents, having that flexible home design with extra bedrooms and secondary entrances to minimize disturbing the other occupants of the home is important," says Kira Sterling, chief marketing officer for Toll Brothers. These suites—also called granny flats or "Fonzie flats" in an homage to the most famous upstairs tenant in television history—can be used for twentysomethings, aging in-laws, or extended immigrant families for whom living together is a custom. In 2011, Lennar Corporation, one of the country's biggest home builders, introduced a new concept it calls its "Next Gen—The Home Within a Home," a series of houses that come with a separate private living space attached. "Your family is constantly evolving," a cheery female voice-over advises on a promotional video. "The kids move out . . . the kids move back. Maybe Grandma moves in! You need a home that will grow with you *and* your family." At the National Association of Home Builders' annual trade show in 2012, all three of the annual *Builder* magazine concept homes featured so-called multigenerational suites. Home Builders don't adjust their floor plans lightly: that new homes coming off production lines are coming baked in with these features suggests the trend is here to stay. Some builders are even experimenting with "compound" concepts, two or more separate single-family homes on a single lot with a common space in the middle—and a single mortgage for the two homes on the same parcel of land. This takes the multigenerational concept even further. "It's not just about the parents aging," says Jonathan Smoke, chief economist for Hanley Wood. "This is about people coexisting and living together for a very long period of time."

Even when millennials do set out on their own—and they certainly will eventually—by most accounts, they're not going to be the least bit interested in the conventional, car-dependent suburbs most of them grew up in. Thanks to the overwhelming amount of research that has been conducted about this group ("21 percent of millennial moms use their phone in the bathroom!" trumpets one study), we know a lot about their habits, desires, and tastes. And every time they are asked about housing preferences, their answers are the same: they want to be in urban areas and they're not that interested in owning a car.

An oft-referenced 2011 survey by real estate firm Robert Charles Lesser & Co. found that 77 percent of millennials said they plan to live in an "urban core." A National Association of Realtors study found that 62 percent of millennials surveyed say they'd rather live in a neighborhood with a mixture of houses and businesses near transportation than in a community with large lots and no sidewalks. They are already huge users of public transportation, and many are willing to pay for the ability to walk to shopping, entertainment, and the like.

Things millennials *don't* want: lawns to groom, extra or "museum" rooms that don't get used, long commutes, too much space. What they do want: lots of space for entertaining, enough room for the Wii, open kitchens to cook for themselves and their friends, outdoor fire pits, maybe a space for their dog. Oh, and they want to rent. Because of their lack of job security, interest in preserving freedom and flexibility, and the fact that many of them were spooked by the recent housing market crash, millennials don't see home ownership the way generations before them did. Some demographers have taken to calling them "Generation Rent."

"We have a different mentality than our parents, dramatically different," wrote a commenter in reference to a 2011 *Slate* article about changing housing preferences. "Our song was 'The Suburbs Are Killing Us.' Our American dream is different: a good education and high mobility." (The lyrics in question, from the 1990s indie band My Favorite, are the chorus: "The suburbs are killing us / asleep when we should be dancing.")

Skeptics of the anti-sprawl movement like to say that's all well and good, but just wait until the millennials start having children; they'll decamp for the suburbs just like their parents before them. Everyone wants to be "where the action is," they say, until practical issues like schools and space come into play. Perhaps. But the birth rate for this group is especially low; the 2011 figures showed birth rates for women ages twenty to twenty-four hit their lowest rate ever recorded, 85.3 per 1,000 people. Besides, no one is suggesting that this group is going to rush entirely to the center of big cities. The right urbanized suburbs will do the trick just fine for many in this generation. "We don't hate the suburbs, we just hated to be bored—or boring," says Gen Y expert Hira. Indeed, the economist Edward Glaeser points out that when it comes to the younger generation, there is little distinction between city and suburb if all needs and services are within walking distance. "If they can walk everywhere and there's tons of stuff that they can walk to, then it's a city." Even, he says, if it happens to be an urbanized neighborhood in a suburb. The question is whether the boom in those walkable, urban-style developments in the suburbs will be enough. If even a fraction of the 77 percent of millennials prefers urban areas, as the studies show, and they act on these preferences, it will have enormous impact on conventional subdivision-style suburbs.

There's also a rush to build what the market thinks millennials are going to want in cities: hyper-small apartments and condos, like the dozens of tiny, more affordable 275-square-foot studio apartments Mayor Michael Bloomberg is leading the charge on in New York City. (Graham Hill, the founder of the LifeEdited movement in chapter 4, helped design one of the finalists in the New York competition to win the contract.) Similar efforts are under way in San Francisco, Chicago, Seattle, and Boston.

Arthur C. Nelson, the director of the Metropolitan Research Center at the University of Utah and a leading scholar on metropolitan development patterns, has studied the existing housing inventory and the current and future demand for it. Taking into account these big demographic changes and the dramatically different housing preferences of the next generation, he predicts a surplus of as many as forty million large-lot homes—those built on a sixth of an acre or more—by 2025.

Even those with a more moderate view acknowledge that demographic shifts are setting the stage for a vast imbalance between supply and demand. Hanley Wood's Jonathan Smoke says that between baby boomers staying where they are and millennials not buying anytime soon, the market has been all but frozen. The boomers are the big question, Smoke says; whether they do choose to age in place or decamp to more urban environments or move in with their children is still largely unknown—and it will determine what happens to the market. "We really don't know what the boomers are going to do, and following them and understanding the decisions they're going to make is the million-dollar question," he says. Even if half of all baby boomers, who principally live in suburbia now and plan to stay there, do move to retirement communities or into central cities, he says, "then who on earth is going to occupy all their suburban homes?" There's an argument to be made, he says, that the level of demand for housing is not going to be anywhere near what it's been in the last decade. And even if the level of demand remains intact, it won't be for the kinds of homes that are going to be vacated. "We have an enormous housing stock that is not going to be optimal."

William Lucy, professor of urban and environmental planning at the University of Virginia and coauthor of *Tomorrow's Cities, Tomorrow's Suburbs*, has studied these numbers closely. From 2000 to 2010, the number of households age fifty-five and over grew by nine million, according to data Lucy studied issued by HUD. Over the same time period, the number of households ages thirty to forty-five and the number of households of married couples with children fell by 3.5 million. That kind of ratio of the older group to the younger group, Lucy says, "is just vastly different from the past." Even before factoring in shifting demands, he points out, the numbers don't add up—and that lopsided demographic picture "greatly diminishes" potential demand for the types of housing and locations that fueled suburban sprawl.

Sure enough, after a few months at home in Mt. Lebanon, Pennsylvania, Nicole Miller decided to try to make a go of it and find an apartment with a friend in downtown Pittsburgh. "It's not worth my youth" to stay in the suburbs, she says. As of this writing, she and a college friend were actively looking for a place.

When the modern-day suburbs were conceived, the majority of households consisted of a husband, a wife, and two or more children. The needs and preferences of those families, and the boomers that grew up out of those households, almost single-handedly drove the development of our landscape and our communities for six decades. But we're at a demographic crossroads. We are a nation of single-family homes, and yet our families are in decline. We're getting married later or not at all. We're having fewer children. Single-person households are multiplying. When 61 percent of households now have just one or two people, and when the two largest demographic bulges—aging boomers and millennials—are childless and attracted to more urban lifestyles where they don't need to drive, our traditional pattern of development isn't going to do the trick.

What will replace it is the trillion-dollar question the entire home-building and development industry is trying to figure out. But you can already see seeds of new landscape possibilities forming in pockets around the country. Our population may be splintering along different demographic lines, but the development trends at work mean there will be more choices to fit this increasingly diverse and jumbled-up society. Whatever category or slice of our population individuals or households happen to fit in, they will increasingly be able to choose their own adventure, whether that's a house in classic suburbia, an urbanized suburb like the ones the New Urbanists and a growing number of traditional developers are creating—or, as ever-increasing numbers of singles, boomers, and even young families are opting for, the urbanized lifestyle of settling down in a big city.

WHERE THE WEALTH IS MOVING

I'm going to close my eyes and when I open them
I want to see skyscrapers.
—DON DRAPER, *MAD MEN*, EPISODE 505, APRIL 15, 2012

At first glance, the sleek new condo building at 205 Water Street in the DUMBO neighborhood of Brooklyn doesn't seem out of the ordinary. It is certainly striking—nine stories high with a rust-colored Corten steel cantilevered penthouse jutting out from the top floor over Plymouth Street. But this slick-looking structure is very much in tune with the industrial chic of the neighborhood, a onetime manufacturing district where factories churned out paper boxes and Brillo pads. The lobby of 205 Water is all exposed concrete, the floors steel-plated. A reflecting garden awaits in the courtyard; there is an indigenously landscaped garden on the roof. All sixty-five apartments are lofts.

But the most striking quality about 205 Water is not obvious from looking at it. The building was conceived, built, and developed by Toll Brothers, the Pennsylvania-based production home builder and the patron saint of the luxury suburban mega-home. You wouldn't know it from looking at it; the only time the Toll Brothers name appeared on this urban dwelling was during construction when the scaffolding surrounding the site advertised the builder. Even the New York real estate press said the building blends in in an "unerringly contextual" way: the angles on the cantilever structure are inspired by the Manhattan Bridge and the walls of the lobby are made of reclaimed boardwalks from Coney Island. But the master home builder is still having a little trouble adapting to the urban landscape. When Toll's CEO, Douglas Yearley, came to see the property and saw that the concrete floors in the lobby were cracked and the graffiti had been left on the wall of an adjacent building that was viewable in the courtyard, he told his crew these kinds of things were unacceptable—"we're Toll Brothers," he insisted—until they gently informed him the floor was cracked on purpose to give it an industrial feel and the graffiti had been left by design, to create urban charm. "I'm a suburban guy." Yearley shrugs.

He won't be able to get away with that line for much longer. Toll is midway through a little-noticed but extremely ambitious push into big-city real estate. The property at 205 Water is one of sixteen in New York City open or in development as of this writing, and the company has slowly but surely been putting up luxury condo buildings at the most desirable addresses in town. Not even Carrie Bradshaw could have done a better job doing the location scouting: in the hipster enclave of Williamsburg, the company has built Northside Piers, two thirty-story all-glass modern luxury condo towers with open floor apartments, a screening room, and a pool. On the tony Upper East Side there's the Touraine, a twenty-two-unit ode to Old

World elegance with modern services including a concierge, gym, rooftop terrace, library, and wine cellar—and an average selling price of some $5 million per unit. A few blocks away, a sixteen-story building is planned for Eighty-ninth and Park, the white-glove epicenter of the *Gossip Girl* set. A few miles south in the Gramercy neighborhood sits 160 East Twenty-second, a modern, twenty-one-story, full-service doorman building aiming for LEED certification that will offer studio, one-, two-, and three-bedroom luxury condos. There's One Ten Third, a Mondrian-inspired boutique building that opened in the formerly gritty East Village in 2006, and there are three communities in neighboring Hoboken. The company will soon test its limits even more, with a hotel and condo community being developed on Brooklyn's waterfront in partnership with Starwood Capital Group and with the purchase in 2013 of two new properties on First Avenue and in Soho. And at the corner of Twenty-eighth and Park Avenue South, what is now a massive hole in the ground will soon give way to a forty-story glass skyscraper designed by the award–winning architect Christian de Portzamparc. Developed in partnership with the real estate mogul Sam Zell's Equity Residential and nicknamed by blogs the "Fortress of Glassitude," the building will house 364 units and will alter the lower Manhattan skyline.

Is it crazy for the suburban home builder to plant such stakes in one of the world's most cosmopolitan markets—let alone when the overall economy has yet to fully recover from the mortgage meltdown? Not quite. At 205 Water, where prices ranged from $400,000 to $2.5 million, the condos sold out in a year. The Touraine sold twenty-one of its twenty-two units within four months; as of this writing all that remains is the top duplex, which is on the market for

$20 million. Toll's City Living division, which it formed in 2003, has grown to become one of the biggest bright spots in the company's portfolio, making up 10 percent of the company's revenue by units delivered, a figure that could rise to 15 percent. The division recently established a new branch in Washington, DC, and is now eyeing other cities including Boston, San Francisco, Seattle, and even São Paolo. Toll Brothers City Living "is our best market in the country," Yearley told the *New York Times* in 2011.

Toll is just one of many icons of suburbia pushing into urban markets. Within a mile or two of the Touraine, there are three Whole Foods, and a stone's throw south there's the Container Store, Home Depot, Walgreens, Victoria's Secret, and the Gap. Across the nation, everything from store retail chains to sports stadiums to corporate headquarters to young families have been moving into cities and leaving the suburbs behind.

To see that cities are resurgent centers of wealth and culture, all you need to do is set foot in one. Or you can simply set foot in a bookstore. A litany of volumes have come out in the past few years praising cities and urbanism, titles like Richard Florida's popular *The Rise of the Creative Class: And How It's Transforming Work, Leisure, Community and Everyday Life* and *The Great Reset: How the Post-Crash Economy Will Change the Way We Live and Work; Aerotropolis: The Way We'll Live Next* by John Kasarda and Greg Lindsay; *The Great Inversion and the Future of the American City* by Alan Ehrenhalt; and Edward Glaeser's love letter to cities, *Triumph of the City: How Our Greatest Invention Makes Us Richer, Smarter, Greener, Healthier and Happier.* Highbrow publications like Salon.com and *The Atlantic* have launched new sections of coverage devoted entirely to cities.

Our nation's big cities have bloomed in the last decade. Reversing a ninety-year trend, in 2011 our largest cities grew more quickly than their combined suburbs. In many of the biggest cities, downtown populations grew at double-digit rates from 2000 to 2010. It's particularly pronounced in cities like New York, which saw the population within a two-mile radius of city hall grow by nearly forty thousand people from 2000 to 2010—even in the wake of the 9/11 terrorist attacks—and where new census numbers show a net population inflow for the first time in fifty years. In Philadelphia, the 2010 census revealed its population grew for the first time in sixty years, with the fastest growth occurring in the eight zip codes that make up its Greater Center City downtown area. Of all cities, Chicago showed the biggest gain to its downtown area, with forty-eight thousand people moving in. The population of the Loop area alone—Chicago's central business district—has tripled over the past decade. The influx isn't stopping: Manhattan is expected to add almost three hundred thousand people by 2030, roughly one new neighbor for every six current residents.

The transformation has been particularly remarkable in neighborhoods that were once the grittiest. In Washington, DC, Logan Circle has been transformed from a crime-ridden haven for drugs and prostitution into one of the highest-priced residential areas in the city. A few miles away, H Street NE, a onetime blighted stretch of boarded-up buildings, is now filled with restaurants and bars that draw young revelers at night. Nearby, Fourteenth and U Streets, the very corner where riots erupted in 1968 after the assassination of Martin Luther King Jr., is now one of the chicest strips in the city, with coffee shops, restaurants, independent fashion boutiques, and a thirty-three-thousand-square-foot Room and Board store. When it was mulling locations, the seller of upscale, stylish modern furniture analyzed zip codes to identify where the majority of its wealthy young professional customers were; Fourteenth and U showed up as the epicenter.

Developers have turned many of these neighborhoods into some of the most desirable new enclaves in town. In St. Louis, an old abandoned shoe-manufacturing warehouse is being turned into luxury loft apartments. In Denver, the trendy Lower Downtown, "LoDo," neighborhood has emerged amid what was once a red-light district. In Boston, a West Coast development firm is building a twenty-story residential tower in Fort Point, the former industrial district that was the setting for much of the Martin Scorsese movie *The Departed*.

This is, of course, a stark contrast to the destruction and decay that once plagued our cities, which in the '60s saw street riots, in the '70s suffered from white flight, and in the '80s and '90s experienced an influx of crime, prostitution, and a crack epidemic that ravaged urban areas across our nation. It's hard to imagine now, but in New York, it wasn't all that long ago that Times Square was dangerous, prostitutes trolled the Meatpacking District, and Central Park's Belvedere Castle was boarded up and covered with graffiti. In 1975, the *New York Daily News* ran the now-famous headline "Ford to City: Drop Dead," referring to Gerald Ford's reluctance to bail the city out from bankruptcy and encapsulating a sentiment that our cities weren't worth saving.

But over the years lower crime rates and new public works projects, not to mention major reinvestment, have transformed our urban centers. Across the country, cities that were once left to deteriorate now have so many waterfront marinas, multiplexes, loft apartment buildings, convention centers, and sidewalk cafés that they more closely resemble amusement parks than the dangerous places they used to be. In New York, Times Square is now an only slightly more urban version of Disneyland, and the Meatpacking District on weekends fills up with so many dolled-up twentysomethings, it looks like a nationwide casting call for *The Bachelorette.* The Upper West Side has enough multiplexes, gargantuan-size restaurants, and national chain stores that it seems more suburban than some suburbs. ("Put a roof over the whole thing, and you could be at a mall in Iowa," wrote the *New York Times* about the neighborhood. That was in 1999.) The grit of shows like *Taxi* and *NYPD Blue* gave way to the Jimmy Choo Manhattan of *Sex and the City* and, now its younger, Brooklyn hipsterized progeny, HBO's *Girls.* One night last summer, walking home by myself down an abandoned block in Tribeca, I felt my guard go up—a rare event—as I saw two figures walking toward me in the shadows. Then I got closer and realized it was two preteens talking about the boarding school Andover. That Toll Brothers had to pay someone to crack the concrete to make its Brooklyn building look appropriately urban perhaps says it all.

Even more striking than the reduction in crime is the fact that cities are attracting and keeping young families with children, a group that in the past almost universally decamped to the suburbs. In Philadelphia, much of the population increase over the past decade has come from young households flocking to or staying in its downtown area; the number of adults aged twenty to thirty-four grew 15 percent to nearly four hundred thousand at a time when that age group's share of the overall population was declining. Similar trends are happening in Providence, Rhode Island, Austin, Texas, Boston, and many other metropolitan areas in the country. Young families are increasingly going out of their way to stay in cities.

Bethany Daily and her husband always thought they would move from their apartment in Boston's North End to the suburbs once they had their two children, but the longer they stayed, the more friends they made—and the more they realized they didn't want to leave. So they moved from their cramped one-bedroom apartment to an only slightly less cramped two-bedroom in the financial district, dividing one of the rooms in two to fit both kids. It's a tight fit—the kids' bedrooms are seventy square feet apiece—but Daily says she and her husband will squeeze as much as they have to in order to stay in Boston. She loves the vibrancy of the city, and she thinks her children are getting exposed to things they wouldn't see in the suburbs. "They see architecture and culture and all sorts of people every day," she says. "I feel like they'll take life a little more in stride because things won't shock them."

Daily also values the extra time she's able to spend with them. To get to her job as a hospital administrator, she either walks twenty minutes or uses Boston's bike share and gets there in half the time. "I'm able to pull off my job and still see my kids and still get to work out most days and do all the things that are important for me because I don't have a commute," she says. "It's about how I want to spend my time." The day after we spoke on the phone, Daily e-mailed me to say that our conversation had got her "brain spinning about how much I love our lifestyle." She listed ten more benefits she'd forgotten to mention, including access to free events like fireworks and "cliff" diving into Boston Harbor; more time because they didn't have to take care of a big house; and easy access to museums that makes even shorter in-and-out "kid-length" visits worthwhile.

It's one thing to stay in the city, but it's another for young families to beat the traditional path to the suburbs only to pull up stakes and move back to the city again. Yet many are doing just that. Jason Duckworth, the Philadelphia developer who appears throughout these pages, and his wife, Angela, settled in Narberth, an old railroad suburb of Philadelphia, just after their second daughter was born in 2003. Duckworth had been working in venture capital in San Francisco, but both their families were in the Philadelphia area, Jason had the opportunity to run Arcadia, and Narberth seemed like the perfect place, with its walkable urban charm: it has a downtown with shops, a five-and-ten store, and a historic movie house, as well as excellent public schools, a gardening group, and even a rugby team. Downtown Philadelphia is a reasonable ten miles away.

When I first started talking with Duckworth for this book, I thought he would end up serving as an example of just how great suburban life can be. Then one day in passing, he mentioned he was moving his family into Philadelphia's Center City. When I pressed him, Duckworth shrugged. He and Angela realized they are happier in urban places, he told me, but they were really moving for their daughters, now ages nine and eleven. In the city, he thinks they'll have a more diverse group of friends and acquaintances. "I want them to have more exposure to the world," he said, "and not be so sequestered as I fear they will be." He said he got some flack from a few of his suburban neighbors, one of whom said she thought they were making the move solely for themselves and not for their children. "It's okay if that's your reason," she told him, "but just admit it."

Toll Brothers, for its part, is looking to market its new city developments to families just like the Duckworths and the Dailys, but the company is also targeting empty nesters returning to an urban environment, international buyers, wealthy Wall Streeters, retirees, and incoming millennials. "The reason New York is so hot and is our best market is because it's 'all of the above,' " says Toll's Yearley.

For the clearest picture of where American wealth is moving, it's always a safe bet to watch what retailers do. In increasing numbers, they're charging into cities, too. Walmart, the retailer known for its enormous footprint above all else, has been fine-tuning new formats designed for more urban areas: Neighborhood Markets, which are less than a quarter the size of its supercenters, and an even smaller Walmart Express format, which measures about the size of a standard-issue CVS. Walmart has said it is planning "hundreds" of these smaller stores across the country in the coming years. By 2016 Best Buy plans to double the number of its smaller-format Best Buy Mobile stores. Even Target, which more than other big-box stores tied its strategy to the growth of the suburbs, is going in the other direction, opening a new urban format store—called, simply, City—that's two-thirds the size of its typical store. The first opened in downtown Chicago, and stores are planned for Los Angeles, Seattle, and San Francisco. "You have a massive rush throughout retail to get small," Leon Nicholas of market research firm Kantar Retail told the *Wall Street Journal.* "Honestly, I am not sure what's going to happen with a lot of these giant boxes." As of this writing, JCPenney, the quintessential old-school mall anchor, had just announced plans to lease a high-profile building in Manhattan's Soho.

Company headquarters, too, are starting to relocate back to cities from their massive suburban office parks. This has been particularly true in Chicago, whose suburbs have long housed some of the bluest of blue-chip corporate campuses—McDonald's in Oak Brook, Kraft in Northfield. But in 2007, United Airlines left suburban Elk Grove for downtown Chicago. This year, Hillshire Brands (formerly known as Sara Lee Corporation) will move from its headquarters in Downers Grove to a new space in downtown Chicago. Motorola Mobility is shuttering its Libertyville campus and moving all three thousand workers to Chicago's Merchandise Mart. "The whole corporate campus seems a little dated," Joe Mansueto, CEO of Morningstar, which has always been in Chicago, told *Crain's Chicago Business* in an article about the city's many corporate campus reverse migrations ("Like the disco ball, the regional shopping mall and the McMansion, the suburban corporate headquarters campus is losing its charm," the story began). It's not just Chicago. In New York City, UBS is said to be mulling plans to return to Manhattan from Stamford, Connecticut, where it moved in the mid-1990s. In 2011, Quicken Loans relocated from suburban Livonia, Michigan, to downtown Detroit. In Philadelphia, venture capital firm First Round Capital moved from suburban Conshohocken to University City. The list goes on and on as companies competing for younger workers realize they need to move to where the talent wants to live.

Nowhere is this more obvious than in San Francisco, where some of the hottest tech start-ups are forgoing Silicon Valley for the city itself. Twitter, Zynga, Airbnb, Dropbox, Uber, Pinterest, and Yelp are among those that have opted to build new headquarters in San Franciscos proper instead of the stretch of suburbs that make up the Bay Area peninsula. Several venture capital firms, too, longtime fixtures of Menlo Park's Sand Hill Road, have recently announced plans to either relocate or open satellite offices in San Francisco. In the mornings, the traffic on the 101, the main commuting freeway out of San Francisco toward the Valley, is now heavier heading out of the city than the reverse.

One of the more interesting company relocations these days is happening in Las Vegas, where Zappos, the online shoe giant, is getting ready to move from a cookie-cutter suburban office park off a highway interchange in Henderson, Nevada, to a brand-new headquarters in Las Vegas's old city hall. The company's CEO, Tony Hsieh, is something of a guru when it comes to building workplaces, and the zany, quirky Zappos offices are legendary both for the employees' cubicles, which are decorated with streamers, foil, kitschy figurines, faux-jungle greenery, and more, and for its stated mission to "create fun and a little weirdness."

But even with all the office whimsy, Hsieh, a big believer in the benefits of the spontaneous "collisions" that occur among employees when they are encouraged to socialize and have places to do so, felt his company's culture was stifled by its suburban location. The closest place workers could "collide" after work or outside the office was at a bar a half mile away across a few parking lots. So when the opportunity arose to move to the city, Hsieh jumped, leased the building, and set about planning to move his company there in 2013.

He didn't stop there. Hsieh decided to invest in reenergizing the entire neighborhood, the neglected Fremont East area a few miles north of the Strip. He committed $350 million—the soft-spoken thirty-nine-year-old is worth hundreds of millions thanks to the sale of Zappos to Amazon.com in 2009—to develop the neighborhood surrounding the company's new headquarters and fill it with all the necessary ingredients for a thriving urban culture. That means things like loft apartments, hipster cocktail lounges, great Thai food, a thriving arts scene, yoga, doggie day care, coffee shops, and plenty of places for residents to interact with one another. In keeping with the findings of economists like Harvard's Edward Glaeser, who has found that innovation happens faster in cities because proximity to others breeds creativity, a big part of Hsieh's plan is to draw entrepreneurs from all over the country with a network of co-working spaces where dozens of start-ups can set up shop and work in close proximity to one another.

Hsieh wants as many of his employees—and those of the other start-ups—to live in the area as possible, and he knows that having good schools is critical, so his team is working on building an early-childhood school set to open later this year. He's investing in bringing displays of artwork from the Burning Man festival to the area, and his team is developing bike-sharing and car-sharing programs. "The idea went from, 'Let's build a campus' to 'Let's build a city,'" Hsieh says over shots of Fernet, the bitter digestif that has become the team's signature drink, at his new neighborhood's Cheers equivalent, the Downtown Cocktail Room.

Hsieh has a vision to create his own version of the sidewalk "ballet" Jane Jacobs described, a place where people can live, work, and play without leaving their neighborhood. (It's actually Jane Jacobs meets Ed Glaeser; the economist and author has become a hero of the

Downtown Project team.) Hsieh himself has moved, too, vacating his suburban Vegas house for one of the loft-style apartments. "I haven't been back there in months," he told me.

In addition to home builders, retailers, and corporate office parks, the urban migration can be seen in that most iconic emblem of America: our sports stadiums. For most of the 1970s, the trend in stadium construction and financing was to build "concrete doughnuts," massive, multipurpose cement structures usually placed at or close to highway interchanges accessible only by car. Built in the '60s and '70s, like everything else, they followed the move of Americans to suburbia. But starting in the mid-1990s with the opening of the Camden Yards Sports Complex, the new home for the Baltimore Orioles based right in the city's central business district and near its popular Inner Harbor, ballpark construction has been moving downtown. Coors Field in Denver, Petco Park in San Diego, and others soon followed, channeling the storied historical design of old urban ballparks like Boston's Fenway Park and Chicago's Wrigley Field. In an informal survey of twenty-three ballparks built since 1990, all but two can generally be described as "urban," with most being built in a city's downtown area.

Suburban expansion sports teams are following this path, too. Late last year, the National Hockey League's New York Islanders announced they were moving from their home in the Nassau Veterans Memorial Coliseum in Uniondale to Brooklyn, where, beginning in 2015, they will play in the shiny-new Barclays Center. It was a seminal moment in sports, one TheAtlanticCities.com called a "harbinger of suburban decline." Forty years ago, as one blogger pointed out, Nassau County was "given a gift" in the form of the first professional sports team for suburbanites. The team was a sign that the suburbs had grown large enough to compete economically with the urban center of New York. Now, the story argued, that trend is happening in reverse. "It may seem like a simple, 30-mile move from one arena to another," the Web site wrote. "But really, it's just one more reminder that the mid-century suburb has peaked."

One could argue that the resurgence of our cities does not necessarily portend the fall of the suburbs. But while many cities have been benefitting from an influx of wealth, the suburbs have been suffering a rise in poverty. From 2000 to 2010, the number of poor in the suburbs or the nation's largest metro areas grew by 53 percent to a record 15.3 million. And while poverty has increased in cities as well, the growth rate in the number of poor living in the suburbs was more than twice that in cities during the decade—and the suburbs are now home to the largest and fastest-growing poor population in the country. This isn't just the Great Recession at work; as early as 2005, the suburban poor outnumbered their city counterparts by almost a million. "We think of poverty as a really urban phenomenon or an ultra-rural phenomenon. It's increasingly a suburban issue," says Elizabeth Kneebone, Brookings fellow and coauthor of a recent Brookings book on the topic, *Confronting Suburban Poverty in America*.

The reasons for this shift are many. During the growth years of the 1990s and 2000s, low-skill construction and service jobs boomed in the suburbs. Soon immigrants began bypassing cities and immigrating directly to the suburbs and exurbs. But these low-skill jobs were the first to vaporize in the housing bust and ensuing recession. At the same time, the longer-term collapse of the manufacturing industry outside midwestern cities pushed many people into poverty. Some of this is also due to the squeeze on the middle class in general. Indeed, the rapid rise in the poor population in the suburbs in the 2000s can't be explained simply by more low-income residents moving there; a wide swath of the new suburban poor are longtime suburban residents who weren't poor in the beginning of the decade but fell below the poverty line as incomes stagnated and home prices increased.

According to one study, nearly three-quarters of suburban non-profits are seeing new visitors with no previous connection to safety net programs of any kind. In Grand Rapids, Michigan, Steve Gibson, executive director of Byron Community Ministries, says many people he sees seeking help were until very recently members of the middle class. "I hear it over and over again," he told a reporter for *Next City* magazine. " 'We used to donate to you.' " In Long Island's Suffolk County, the number of food stamp cases jumped 55 percent from 2010 to 2012, and the emergency-housing caseload hit a ten-year peak with nearly five hundred families and three hundred individuals living in shelters and motels.

Suburban poverty poses different kinds of challenges than urban poverty. There are fewer social services in the suburbs, so the safety net is "patchier and spread thinner" than in large cities, says Brookings' Kneebone. And even when services do exist, it's difficult for the poor to get to them if they lack access to a car. Suburban poverty also tends to be hidden behind closed doors as its residents fear the stigma of having their neighbors learn they're getting government assistance.

Falling below the poverty line, after all, is not exactly keeping up with the Joneses. "Soaring poverty rates threaten the very foundations of suburban identities, suburban politics and the suburb's place in the nation's self-image," wrote Lisa McGirr, professor of history at Harvard and the author of *Suburban Warriors: The Origins of the New American Right.*

Along with poverty, crime rates have gone up in suburban counties at the same time as they have declined in cities, and suburbs are increasingly seeing gang, gun, and drug activity, and worse. In 2012 federal prosecutors in northern Virginia charged alleged members of the Crips gang with luring high school girls in its wealthy suburban areas into teen prostitution rings. "Slavery in the suburbs," read the special logo on the local news the night the story broke. After a tragic gang rape in a park in a planned community in Moreno Valley, California, the accused teens were said to have ties to a local gang. There has always been crime in the suburbs, of course, but increasingly it seems to be more of the sort once reserved for cities. While overall homicides have been falling nationwide—they fell sharply from 2001 to 2010, including a 16.7 percent decline in big cities, as places like New York City saw rates hit forty-year lows—they rose 17 percent in the suburbs. "People used to leave the city because they were afraid," says the historian Kenneth Jackson. "Now, if you throw car crash danger in, you're really in more danger in the suburbs than the city most of the time."

Some experts say this shouldn't come as such a surprise. The suburbs may have started out as safe, peaceful enclaves for the middle class, but as they grew, they came to more closely mirror the country in general. There are now suburbs for every society, age, race, housing type, and income, and the suburbs now contain all the good and bad things that come with those things, too. As Brookings demographer William Frey puts it, "If it's part of America, it's part of the suburbs."

Other aspects of the suburbs have fallen into decline, too. Take the shopping mall. Once a hallmark of suburbia, it had by the mid-2000s become an anachronism. On the one hand, Internet commerce enabled shopping from the living room, and on the other, suburban shoppers now have other options in newer, open-air shopping centers that more resemble shopping on a Main Street. Only one enclosed indoor shopping mall has opened in the United States since 2006, and at existing malls, vacancy rates are soaring, hitting their highest level since the early 1990s. (A Web site, deadmalls.com, started by two retail historians, now tracks the "demise of these great giants of retail.") But because mall construction is so expensive, once the massive structures are built, they're stuck there. To stem the tide of vacancies, mall developers have been getting creative about finding new tenants, filling them with call centers, art galleries, car showrooms, even farmer's markets. Cleveland's Galleria at Erieview is now closed on weekends because there are so few visitors, and part of the mall has been converted into a vegetable garden. "I look at it as space," Vicky Poole, a Galleria executive, told the *New York Times*. "I don't look at it as retail."

Some developers have actually turned their focus on these dead or dying malls. Ellen Dunham-Jones, architecture professor at the Georgia Institute of Technology, and June Williamson, associate professor of architecture at the City College of New York, have documented this phenomenon in their book, *Retrofitting Suburbia: Urban*

Design Solutions for Redesigning Suburbs, a comprehensive look at efforts to retool, reinhabit, or return to nature abandoned suburban forms. In some cases, this means turning gargantuan forgotten malls into hip, urbanized residential villages. One such experiment is under way in Lakewood, Colorado, an affluent suburb west of Denver. The former Villa Italia shopping mall, a 1.2-million-square-foot indoor mall built in 1966 that had fallen on hard times, has been turned into Belmar, a 104-acre pedestrian-friendly community that has apartments, condos, town houses, office space, artists studios, and a shopping and entertainment promenade on twenty-two walkable, urbanized blocks. Now, instead of turning into the mall's giant parking lot, you end up cruising along a downtown main drag, Alaska Street, which is lined with old-fashioned streetlights, coffee shops, boutiques, and restaurants. There are more than a thousand housing units, which range from town houses to loft condominiums to small-lot single-family homes, as well as a row of ground-floor artist studio and business incubator spaces. A public art project called "Urban Anatomy" has installed small works of art and fragments of poetry on manhole covers, sidewalk joints, and grates throughout the development, highlighting overlooked details of the urban environment.

The whole setup is definitely still suburban—the new urbanized village includes a Zales, Yankee Candle, and Sur La Table—but these suburbanites can leave their loft apartments on foot, pick up an espresso, and go hear a poetry reading, all on a site where Foley's, Dillard's, Montgomery Ward, and JCPenney once sat. There are dozens of these projects at other malls around the country. "It's time to let the suburbs grow up," Dunham-Jones says.

Suburban chain restaurants are in the middle of a retrenchment, too.

The number of restaurants in the country grew by more than one hundred thousand from 1996 to 2008 as mid-priced mass-market restaurateurs like Friendly's, Applebee's, TGI Friday's, Olive Garden, and others chased the boom into the suburbs and the exurbs; after the recession and housing bust hit, analysts said at least twenty thousand restaurants needed to close in order to bring the industry back to equilibrium. Now, so-called zombie restaurants languish everywhere. "I don't think we're overbuilt," Paul M. Mangiamele, the CEO of Bennigan's Franchising, told the *New York Times*. "I think we're underdemolished."

The one area where we may be the most underdemolished of all, of course, is in houses. Our recent housing boom and bust was primarily a suburban crisis, and the overbuilding and resulting excess inventory still weighs on our residential landscape. When the music stopped, once-booming suburbs and exurbs quickly went bust, many emptying out almost as quickly as they'd been built. Because the boom had ended so abruptly, many subdivisions were halted in mid-development. While industry-wide housing inventory figures have improved, hundreds of these "zombie subdivisions" still dot our landscape, many with infrastructure teed up and ready to pipe water and electricity into homes that will never appear.

Residential land values plummeted so much—falling nearly 70 percent from 2006 to 2011—that developers who had bought up raw land during the boom started selling it back to the farmers they bought it from. It was a reversal from the boom years, when the amount of land used for farms fell by two to four million acres a year as developers paid huge premiums to get their hands on farmland that they could develop. Now, farmers who sold during the boom, making multiples they never dreamed of on their land, were able to profit on the other side as well, buying that very same land back for a song. In an additional dose of irony, crop prices had soared, jumping 20 percent from 2007 to 2011, at the same time that home values plummeted, so the land was now more valuable to the farmers than ever. The *Wall Street Journal*'s Robbie Whelan recounted the tale of the Englands, an Arizona cotton farming family that paid $731,000 for 430 acres of cotton fields sixty-five miles southeast of Phoenix in 2004, flipped the property to an apartment builder in 2009 for $8.6 million, then bought the farm back out of foreclosure for $1.75 million. "It was a pretty good deal," Don England Jr. told the paper.

The fact that suburban tracts intended for development were reverting back to farmland was little noticed at the time, but it was a shocking turn of events, says Frank Popper, a renowned land-use expert and professor at the Edward J. Bloustein School of Planning and Public Policy at Rutgers University. The conventional thinking in the planning world, Popper says, is that every time a farm goes into development, it's lost to agriculture forever. That reversal, he says, is "a mind-blowing thing from a planning point of view."

Popper is an expert in the planning world for his work studying the depopulation and decline of urban and rural areas, and how policy makers and land-use regulators can best manage depopulation. It's a topic few in the planning world have liked to talk about—in planning, real estate, and development worlds, "growth" is religion, and words like "shrink," "contract," "decline," or even just "small" have typically been verboten. In the late 1980s, Popper and his wife, Deborah, now a professor of geography at the City University of New

York's College of Staten Island, conducted an in-depth study of the ailing rural areas of the Great Plains. The area had lost a third of its population since 1920, and much of the land had dried out to such a degree that it was unsustainable. In a seminal article published in 1987, the Poppers argued that the land should be returned to native prairie in order to create a vast nature preserve. Returning the land to native grasses and reintroducing the buffalo, an approach they called the Buffalo Commons, would be vastly better for society than letting the local economies continue to depopulate and disintegrate into near-ghost towns.

That was what was already happening: several hundred thousand square miles of land had just six people per square mile—the definition of frontier settlement, the most rural category of settled land—and the area was seeing rising bankruptcy rates, foreclosures, and human suffering including psychological stress, family violence, suicide, and mental illness. It would be better for everyone, the Poppers argued, if much Great Plains land—they called its settlement the "largest, longest-running agricultural and environmental miscalculation in American history"—was returned to its original "pre-white" state.

They faced intense criticism for their work. The controversy around their idea inspired a novel, Richard S. Wheeler's *The Buffalo Commons*; a Pulitzer Prize finalist book, Anne Matthews's 1992 *Where the Buffalo Roam*; and several documentaries. In recent years, after the Poppers' predictions for the region's demise had started to come true, several politicians and high-profile thinkers reversed course and started endorsing their idea, with the *Kansas City Star* publishing two editorials in 2009 and 2010 supporting the creation of a million-acre Buffalo Commons National Park.

Now the Poppers also study shrinkage in large and midsize cities, former industrial centers such as Buffalo, New York; Flint, Michigan; Youngstown, Ohio; Pittsfield, Massachussetts; and Woonsocket, Rhode Island, that have seen excessive depopulation. According to the Poppers, shrinkage presents one of the century's great settlement and housing issues. It saps communities and people of income, housing, and a sense of community, But it doesn't have to, they say; they emphasize what they call "smart decline," ways to shrink that can be productive: razing structures that are no longer needed so children don't grow up amid blight, playing up a town's strengths by boosting Main Streets, retaining old buildings with history, and otherwise adjusting the urban environment to fit its population. They point to Detroit, which experienced the largest depopulation of an industrial-age American city and in response bulldozed hundreds of homes and turned over much of its land to fields and farmland that lay there before. As radical an idea as that might seem to the layperson, it was lauded in the planning world. These other industrial cities, the Poppers say, need to follow similar patterns or risk sinking into blight. Buffalo, they point out, is a "size-40 city in a size-60 suit."

Justin Hollander, an assistant professor of urban and environmental policy and planning at Tufts University and a former student of Frank Popper, took this concept to the suburbs, conducting an analysis of the depopulation brought on by the recent housing bust. Using data from the U.S. Postal Service to track the number of occupied housing units—whether a house gets mail is the best determining factor of whether it is truly vacant—Hollander found that one-quarter of all U.S. neighborhoods have fewer occupied homes now than they did in 2006. He found the depopulation in the suburbs to be far greater than cities; suburban areas registered 43 percent more declining zip codes from 2006 to 2009 than from 2000 to 2006, while for urban areas the figure was just 2 percent. In policy planning worlds, Hollander's results were significant and a major challenge to the long-held belief that cities are most prone to decline while suburban growth will continue forever. "The face of declining cities and regions in America has begun to change," Hollander wrote. "Decline is no longer limited to older manufacturing towns, urban cores and declining rural farming communities."

Hollander takes issue with the government's idea to turn our excess housing inventory into rentals; he suggests a better use would be turning abandoned suburban homes into offices, storage facilities, and artist studios—and when there's no demand for any alternate use, he says, regulators should demolish the homes and sell the land for parks or community gardens, or, much like the Poppers suggested for the frontier towns of the Great Plains, return the land to wilderness.

As our housing crisis deepened and millions of home owners forfeited their homes, this is just what some banks started to do with some of their repossessed properties. Since so many of the homes were entry level and in undesirable neighborhoods, many of them were worth so little that they actually did more damage just by existing. If they stayed on the market, they added to inventory and the banks had to pay to maintain them. If they sold, it would be for a price so low, it would pull down the average. In many cases the best answer was simply to level them. In 2011, major lenders like Bank of America, Wells Fargo, Citigroup, and JPMorgan Chase decided to bulldoze or donate the repossessed homes they owned. In California's San Bernardino County, when a local bank decided to raze sixteen new homes it couldn't sell, residents from neighboring streets came by to watch the demolition, taking video on their cell phones to capture the live-action manifestation of the mistake Wall Street had made.

Besides tearing them down, another solution to mop up the extra homes came from the government. In late 2012 the Federal Housing Finance Agency came up with a plan to sell off thousands of foreclosed properties owned by Fannie Mae and Freddie Mac to big institutional investors who, the idea went, would buy them in bulk and turn them into rental properties at considerable profit. Wall Street giants like Blackstone Group and Colony Capital, along with a gold rush of opportunistic entrepreneurs, have invested billions buying up thousands of foreclosed single-family homes, serving as landlords to what they think is likely to be a thriving rental market as the home ownership rate continues to float back down to its natural level.

Some say this is a flawed idea. For one thing, many of these homes are in the wrong place, products of a manufactured, bank-led demand that vaporized when the market tanked. These homes may be of no more interest to renters than buyers. Creating a rental market for these properties has its own set of downsides, the biggest being that renters and landlords don't usually take the same kind of care of their homes and neighborhoods as home owners do. But it is helping mop up the excess. Thanks to these efforts, the low pace of new home construction, and the strengthening of the housing market, much of the excess housing inventory has been worked off. As of this writing, we have a 4.4-month supply of existing homes, the lowest housing supply since early 2006.

But the migration of wealth from suburb to city started well before Wall Street concocted the no-income, "no-doc" loans that led to the housing crisis. Cities' renaissance started as early as the mid-1990s, urban housing prices have been rising since 1980, and crime rates have been falling for almost as long. Toll Brothers started moving into the New York City market in 2003. The trend might have been accelerated by the housing crisis, but it was happening already.

Home valuations are now reflective of the shift inward. Christopher Leinberger, analyzing data from the online real estate database Zillow, found this to be the case by comparing real estate prices in center cities and inner suburbs with their far-out suburban counterparts in the late 1990s and today. In the late 1990s, when measured per square foot, wealthy outer suburbs contained most of the expensive housing in the United States. Today, the most expensive housing is in center cities and inner suburbs. In Seattle, for example, in 1996 the price per square foot in suburban Redmond was equal to Seattle's Capitol Hill; today, valuations in Capitol Hill are almost 50 percent higher. In Columbus, Ohio, prices in 1996 were highest in Worthington, and values were 135 percent higher than Short North, a neighborhood near the city's downtown. Today, Short North prices are 30 percent higher than Worthington's, while the highest prices of all are in downtown Columbus. In Denver, home prices in Highlands Ranch, a master-planned community twenty miles south of downtown, were 21 percent higher per square foot in 1996 than Highlands, a neighborhood next to downtown Denver. Now Highlands' valuations are more than 60 percent higher than Highlands Ranch's. "Simply put, there has been a profound structural shift," Leinberger wrote in the *New York Times*, "a reversal of what took place in the 1950s, when drivable suburbs boomed and flourished as center cities emptied and withered."

A new kind of Great Migration is taking place. Rather than a cyclical phenomenon, many are suggesting these trends taken together, combined with the demographic shifts in the makeup of our population, signify a permanent shift. "The suburban project is over," says the author James Howard Kunstler. "The people who deliver suburbia—the realtors, the production builders, the mortgage originators—are kicking back waiting for, quote, 'the bottom' to kick in so they can resume doing what they were doing. It's a vain hope."

That may sound extreme, but just looking at Toll Brothers' activity alone shows that something is afoot. While we chatted on the phone, CEO Yearley—a man who has a framed proverb on his desk that reads "You can buy more land in an afternoon . . . than you can get rid of in a lifetime"—told me the company had ceased operations in some of the most remote areas it ventured into during the height of its expansion. "We have completely shut down and mothballed the Poconos and West Virginia," he says. "They're too far out right now. Maybe one day we get back there." That means Toll is completing whatever homes it sold in those markets and isn't developing new communities there right now. Toll doesn't build homes unless they're sold, so it doesn't have an inventory problem there; it's just not expanding outward.

That said, Yearley still thinks there will be a strong market for what he calls the "suburban move-up" home buyer—the upwardly mobile young family that still wants to live in a subdivision. "I think for most families, once the kids hit kindergarten, most people still want to move to the suburbs and have their own home with their own backyard with the swing set and the little league team playing down the road and with a great school district," he says. And unlike people like Kunstler or Chuck Marohn in Minnesota, Yearley thinks there will one day be a revived market in some places where the company has stopped expanding, if only because there's limited land available. "That 'next frontier' went away," he said. "It will come back." Yearley describes these changes—the company's move into cities and the cessation of expansion plans in remote markets—as a "shift, but not a monumental shift."

Even so, Toll's mix of what it sells to whom is changing. Those "suburban move-up" homes used to constitute 70 or 80 percent of the company's business, Yearley says; today they're about 50 percent, with the other half coming from a combination of city-suburban town-home developments, active adult communities, and pure urban developments like its new projects in New York City.

And the success of the company's New York properties has surpassed even Yearley's own expectations. "I would have never thought we'd be building that building at Twenty-eighth and Park Avenue South," he says. "I would have never thought we'd be building at Sixty-fifth and asking twenty million dollars for a penthouse." All told, with the new plans including the hole in the ground on Park Avenue South, Toll Brothers had close to thirty separate buildings in the New York City market when I spoke with Yearley in late 2012. Before we hung up, he told me there were plans for close to a dozen more.

7

THE FUTURE

With your head full of brains and your shoes full of feet, you're too smart to go down any not-so-good street.

—DR. SEUSS, *OH, THE PLACES YOU'LL GO!*

Even as he has led the movement against sprawl, even as he colorfully lambasts the people and policies responsible for it, Andres Duany freely admits he sees the objective benefits of suburban living. He likes to tell the story of how, when he was first setting up his planning firm in Coral Gables, he asked to commute home with his landlord, a guy in his thirties who lived in South Florida's outer suburbs, to see what it was like. The commute itself was "awful, awful, awful, awful," Duany says. They were stuck in horrendous traffic, the sun was setting in their face, and the drive seemed to take forever. But, as Duany describes it, once they pulled into the "semi-gated" community and arrived at his home, it was "complete heaven" inside. There were tall ceilings, a refrigerator full of "cool-looking things to eat," a long, welcoming L-shaped couch, a big TV, sophisticated lighting, cozy rugs, good acoustics, and more. Duany says he realized in that moment that when people say they like the suburbs, what they like is what he calls the private realm. "The private realm is objectively fantastic," he says. He understands why so many people want to live that way. "It's very appealing."

It *is* very appealing, and it's why most Americans still live in the suburbs. We are a nation that values privacy and individualism down to our very core, and the suburbs give us that. But somewhere between leafy neighborhoods built around lively railroad villages and the Inland Empire, where two-thirds of residents have to drive ten miles to reach a central business district, or shiny new subdivisions in cornfields near Iowa that bill themselves as suburbs of Chicago, we took our wish for privacy too far. The suburbs overshot their mandate.

The modern American suburbs were a product of many things: a booming middle class, the early wonder of mass production and the automobile, a heavy assist from federal housing policy, and spring-loaded, pent-up demand for housing after the war. When you're in a rush to solve a problem, you look for the most efficient solution, and in this case the easiest, most efficient solution was the suburbs.

But things have changed, and many factors—from the resurgence of cities to rising gas prices to our fast-changing household demographics—are lining up that point to the end of the suburbs as we know them. It's not overstating it to say that we are at the beginning of a transformational shift in our landscape, one as big as or bigger than the shift that took place immediately after World War II.

There is a group of authors, scholars, and demographers who say this is all a bunch of hogwash, that the suburbs are not changing or losing favor in any way. Americans love their suburbs, these critics say, pointing out that while suburban development was encouraged by the government, government leaders were simply following demand.

Joel Kotkin, executive editor of the Web site Newgeography.com and author of the 2010 book *The Next Hundred Million: America in 2050*, is one of the most prolific of these critics. Kotkin's own analyses of census data show that it's suburbs, not cities, that posted most of the household growth in the United States from 2000 to 2010. He also cites preference studies that show that everyone—even millennials— wants single-family houses in the suburbs. But those on the urban side of the debate say that Kotkin includes many urban hubs in his definition of suburbia. The census definitions he uses, they say, define places like New Jersey's Hoboken and Jersey City as suburbs—metropolises in their own right whose growth might offer more proof of the increasing popularity of cities.

The debate is complicated by the fact that it's hard to define much of the American landscape as strictly one or the other. Our cities and suburbs are such a patchwork that for every study that proves one point on this topic, there's another that proves the opposite. Add to that the fact we're still recovering from a housing crisis—which makes census data even more difficult to analyze because our migration patterns were so exaggerated during the years of both the boom and the bust—and you'll see why for every statistic-backed expert assertion there seems to be some other expert claiming fallacy.

The critics are right about one thing, though: we do love our suburbs. And many residents are fiercely protective of them. Andres Duany says he has met people who think he's crazy when he asks them if they would prefer living in a denser community. "They look at me and say, 'Why would I want to know my neighbor? Why would I not want to drive my child everywhere? That's the only time I ever get to see them.'" When he once suggested eliminating drive-through restaurants, a suburban mother stared at him point-blank and asked him: "Have you ever tried to take a baby out of a car seat?'"

So while some people might ridicule cul-de-sac life, others wouldn't have it any other way. For example, the car-to-car trick-or-treating tradition described in chapter 3 that Annette Lee and her family experienced when they lived in suburban Boonton Township, New Jersey, might not be for everyone, but Lee and most in her community who participated in it loved it. It ended up becoming a social event for the parents, who drank wine (the nondrivers anyway) and decorated their cars, and the kids collected much more loot than they would have otherwise been able to given the large size of the lots in the community. Lee now lives in a different community with similar zoning, but she still loves her setup. "We always look for the bigger the lot the better," she says, noting that her husband in particular likes the privacy a large-lot setting affords. "He wants to be able to wash his car without having all the neighbors looking at him," she says. Even though they've been in their community for five years, Lee says she and her husband don't know many of their neighbors well enough to do anything more than wave and say hello. But she points out that she knows a lot of people who live in town house developments, and they don't know their neighbors, either. And she doesn't mind one bit having to drive to go to the grocery store. Even if she could walk to one, she points out, shopping as she does for her family of seven, "what am I going to do—carry all my groceries?"

Gary Cooper has a unique perspective. A retired broadcast producer who grew up in Harlem and relocated to the suburbs of Kansas City—where, he says, what "used to be farms and cows is now all upper bracket subdivisions"—he loves suburban life. "It is like living in Nirvana," he says. "You drive up to the bank, drive up to the cleaners, drive up to the pharmacy, and everyone smiles and says hello … they have more Pilates and yoga classes than Carter has liver pills, and you can park anywhere." Since Johnson County, where he lives, is the richest in the state, its school district is one of the highest ranked. "I must admit," he says, "the quality of living is quite outstanding."

To get a sense of the vitriol thrown at those who question the viability of suburbia, just scroll through the comments on any article about the subject. A recent public radio story about the looming demographic changes that threaten suburbia's growth drew some fiery responses. "Suburbs are only 'dull and boring' if you are lazy and unimaginative," wrote one listener. "I can get to the city when I need to, and leave it when I need to … and I will never, ever have to worry about being stuck in a 'hipster enclave'—hipsters hate suburbs. If that's not a reason filled with win, I don't know what is. Viva suburbia!" Chimed in another: "What gives with the suburbs being 'soulless'? The people who live in the burbs feel the same level of connection as the people in the city. What does that statement mean for rural people? Would they be soul-less-less?"

Christopher Leinberger, the author and scholar and one of the most influential voices in the city-suburb debate, has been called an elitist and a socialist for his pro-urbanist positions. Even rabble-rouser and anti-sprawl proselytizer James Howard Kunstler acknowledges that the suburban status quo is a mighty force. "So many generations of Americans are used to it, and it has become so normal, that there's going to be a tremendous struggle to maintain it," he says.

These struggles are already playing out in many places as communities attempt to make changes. The resistance is particularly vocal in the Washington, DC, area, perhaps because the region is leading the country in efforts to urbanize its suburbs. In Maryland, a showdown is going on between not-in-my-backyard suburban residents and the local government, which has approved the construction of a $1.6 billion new light rail line that would connect Bethesda and New Carrollton. In Prince George's County, residents are fighting a new town center that would include a Whole Foods despite the fact that it would bring hundreds of jobs to the area. In Lower Merion, Pennsylvania, meanwhile, during a debate over rezoning the town's main commercial strip to accommodate apartment towers, some residents said they objected because it didn't "fit their image" of suburbia.

A more legitimate argument than any of these might be that we are a free market, and suburban living is what many people choose. Even as the government was putting in place the policy building blocks that would push the country toward a suburban settlement pattern, we devoured and demanded more of it. "This is a free country," says Leinberger. "We wanted it. This was a market-based trend." The American home-building industry is perhaps the most responsive consumer-product industry of all, with an uncanny ability to read and deliver what its customers want—and, for the most part (the Wall Street–generated demand of the housing crisis notwithstanding), it builds houses that are in direct response to what Americans are asking them for. So in many ways, like it or not, the suburbs are a reflection of us.

B esides, if the suburbs as we know them are over, then what on earth will the future look like? It's hard to tell what the country will do because we are still, as of this writing, only starting to emerge from an epic housing freeze. Household formation is picking up, but it's still much lower than it needs to be, and for all the talk about where Americans are moving, we're not moving anywhere right now. New single-family home construction is still way off from its peak. We have the lowest level of migration since the end of World War II.

Even so, after so many false starts, a housing market recovery is beginning to take real shape. Starting in late 2012 and continuing into 2013, sales of both new and existing homes showed signs of rebounding, while inventories have come down significantly and home prices seem to be on their way up from the bottom. The annual builders' show in 2013 in Las Vegas stood in marked contrast to the show in the dark days of February 2012 when Aron Ralston spooked the crowd. This year, the mood was one of hopeful optimism; the attendees arrived in Las Vegas just as positive data came out showing that single-family housing starts had climbed 18.5 percent in December and new home sales were on track for a 20 percent–plus increase over 2011's rock bottom. Vendors showed off high-tech gadgetry like hands-free faucets, touch-screen dead bolts, and elevators aimed at multigenerational households. Learning their lesson from last year, the conference organizers went in a sunnier direction, securing Michael Eisner, the former CEO of the Walt Disney Company, as the keynote speaker, and ordering up a comedic performance by the political satire troupe the Capitol Steps.

But things are still far from rosy, and where the market heads when things kick back up again is the billion-dollar question. There is almost unanimous consensus that a higher proportion of building is likely to be closer to centers of jobs, entertainment, and lifestyle needs. You can glean some indication of this by looking at the current bright spots in the housing market. One of the hottest areas is in multifamily construction—the market for apartment and condo buildings and other structures containing four or more housing units, whether in cities or in suburbs. Construction of this kind of housing has more than doubled since the housing crisis set in. Part of this growth is due to a boom in the market for rental housing. The number of renters surged by more than five million in the 2000s, the largest ten-year increase since World War II. Vacancy rates are down and rents are soaring across the country, even in markets with lots of foreclosures. The vast majority of multifamily housing starts these days are rentals, whereas in the height of the housing crisis they were predominantly condos for sale.

Meanwhile, the urbanization of the suburbs has only just begun. It's not just New Urbanists and other urban or "green" activists that are preaching this idea. Traditional planners, academics, and even home builders and real estate developers are coming to this way of thinking, too, as evidenced by the hundreds of walkable developments going up around the country—many being planned and developed by the biggest traditional home builders. Whether it's a massive town center complex like Rick Caruso's mega-centers in Los Angeles, or traditional villages based on 1800s town planning principles, or Toll Brothers' recent plans to build a seven-story luxury condo building in downtown Bethesda, Maryland, three blocks from the train station, there has been a shift in the residential development world away from distance and toward proximity. Even though almost no one walks everywhere and you will likely still have to get in the car, in places like these it becomes a matter of driving a mile or two instead of ten or twenty; or maybe it means a household can own one car instead of two. Shyam Kannan, formerly a principal at real estate consultancy Robert Charles Lesser & Co. and now managing director of planning at the Washington Metropolitan Area Transit Authority (WMATA), describes this as an entire paradigm shift in real estate. "We're moving from location, location, location in terms of the most important factor to access, access, access," he says. People in the industry insist this is more than a trend; it is a lasting transformation.

Indeed, one of the biggest challenges going forward is likely to be that there aren't enough places with these characteristics to suit the coming demand. Christopher Leinberger estimates that "drivable" suburbia still represents as much as 95 percent of the housing market. But he has found that, surprisingly, a minority of the "walkable urban" housing inventory is in central cities; the majority of it is in the suburbs already, and that, he says, is where the bulk of the change will take place.

Demand for these kinds of neighborhoods within the suburbs is indeed surging. You can see it in real estate prices, which are falling in remote, car-dependent suburbs but holding steady in those that are more compact. Studies explored in the previous pages have demonstrated a link between neighborhood walkability and stronger housing prices. Real estate agents now tend to play up these attributes, talking up Walk Scores and "community" and in many cases focusing on selling in the very neighborhoods that were passé during the heyday of the sprawling 1990s and early 2000s. "What was perceived as a niche market has become *the* market," says Leinberger.

William Lucy, the professor of urban and environmental planning at the University of Virginia who studied the housing market's demographic imbalances, has also conducted research establishing a telling connection between real estate prices and the age of a neighborhood's housing stock. Traditionally, newer housing has held up better and maintained a higher value, while the market has historically tended to assign lower values to older housing. (There are many reasons why Americans prefer new construction, but those of us who think old stone homes are the most charming are in the very small minority.) Lucy found that in the mid-1990s, during the height of suburban expansion, in half of the thirty-two metropolitan areas he studied, the oldest houses—those built before 1940—were also the least valued ones. But in 2010, that was true only in three out of thirty-five markets—and in six markets, including Washington, DC, and Seattle, the oldest houses were the *most* valuable. Along with a shift in priorities that has led more people to see the virtues in smaller homes and less stuff, Lucy's research shows a similar reversal in value between old and new; older has taken on greater worth. Lucy argues that this is driven not by these houses' charming older bones and better construction, but by their location, since older homes tend to be located in older, closer-in, village-oriented suburbs. This, Lucy argues, is what the market wants now.

The simple ability to walk to town is a big reason why Denise Gibson and her family are moving from a sixty-two-hundred-square-foot house on a one-acre lot in Long Grove, Illinois, to School Street, John McLinden's innovative new suburban village in nearby Libertyville. Gibson and her husband were "on the McMansion track," she says, living in a house with six bedrooms, a three-car garage, a circular driveway, and a two-story great room. But over time, Gibson, a retired telecommunications CEO, came to feel that everything about her living situation was a bit unnatural: the scale of the homes, the distance between them, and the fact that she had to get in her car for everything. "You drive absolutely everywhere," she says. "And your children don't play with other children unless you schedule playdates."

Gibson and her husband decided they would move to downtown Libertyville, to a home where they could walk to the town's Main Street. She'd heard about McLinden's development but thought it seemed too "radical" since the homes didn't have full yards. But when her realtor showed her the community of bungalow-style homes right next to one another, she was intrigued, and when she and her husband toured one of the houses more seriously a few days later, she was sold. One of the things that clinched the deal for Gibson was when one of the neighborhood's residents invited her into her kitchen after their tour. "In ten years I can count on one hand how many times I've stood in a neighbor's kitchen" in Long Grove, Gibson says.

A growing number of suburban Americans are craving more of those kind of moments. Stories like Gibson's and others suggest that the future of our suburbs might come down to a survival of the fittest. There are, after all, plenty of livelier suburbs out there. In 2010, *Travel and Leisure* magazine published a list of the nation's twenty-six "coolest suburbs," towns like Evanston, Illinois; Montclair, New Jersey; Lakewood, Ohio; Bellevue, Washington; Alameda, California; La Jolla, California; West Hartford, Connecticut; Birmingham, Michigan; and more. Every one of them had a thriving Main Street and all its requisite components: coffeehouses, cool bookstores, restaurants, indie movie theaters. In a recent travel section write-up, the *New York Daily News* called my hometown of Media, Pennsylvania, "as lively as a pop-up book," which is indeed an apt description and probably would apply to many of these "cool" suburbs, too—as the *New York Times* has called them, "hipsturbias."

You can also see a glimpse of the future in our "first ring" suburbs, the older suburbs that fell out of favor during the sprawl boom of the '80s, '90s, and 2000s as migration kept moving outward. These suburbs, many now populated by blue-collar workers after the wealthy headed out, are seeing a second life in many markets as millennials—those who *are* starting off on their own—flock to them. They're attracted to these neighborhoods' smaller-scale houses, more intimate feel, sidewalks, and traditional street grids (think the neighborhood Jennifer Lawrence and Bradley Cooper lived in in the movie *Silver Linings Playbook*). "Millennials want my childhood without my immigrant-accented grandparents," one boomer parent wrote in a comment to a *Wall Street Journal* article on the trend, "... art deco–inspired small homes within walking distance to the grocer, the ice cream shop, hardware store and local movie theater all owned by my neighbors. It was a special time." In Pittsburgh, the former rust belt inner-ring suburbs like Lawrenceville and Dormont are seeing a second life as enclaves for twenty- and thirtysomethings. One of Pittsburgh's first middle-class suburbs, Dormont has a housing stock of attached row houses and small single-family homes, all within walking distance to a downtown that is getting filled with eateries, cafés, and services. It's a fifteen-minute commute to downtown Pittsburgh by the T. *Pittsburgh* magazine proclaimed it as "where hipsters go to have kids." Los Angeles and Detroit's inner rings are seeing similar gentrification among this demographic.

These communities, right down to their street width, mix of hous-

ing stock, and setback distances, are precisely what the New Urbanists take great care to study and re-create. "The good news is, we have
the model," says the developer Jonathan Rose, who helped redevelop
Morristown, New Jersey, and modeled the project after the components of historic streetcar and railroad suburbs. "We don't need to
reinvent it. We know it. The model is Shaker Heights, Ohio, and Garden City, New York, and Stamford, Connecticut. The model is the
streetcar."

As the country resettles along more urbanized lines, some suggest
the future may look more like a patchwork of nodes: mini urban areas
all over the country connected to one another with a range of public
transit options. It's not unlike the dense settlement of the Northeast
already, where city-suburbs like Stamford, Greenwich, West Hartford, and others exist in relatively close proximity. "The differences
between cities and suburbs are diminishing," says Brookings' Metropolitan Policy Program director Bruce Katz, noting that cities and
suburbs are also becoming more alike racially, ethically, and socio-
economically. Katz sees the sea change hitting the suburbs as a long-
overdue correction. "The United States was so completely out of
balance," he says. "We were so pro-sprawl, pro-decentralization, and
so auto-dependent," he points out, that the development pattern was
unsustainable from an energy perspective. "What's happening now is
that we're becoming more in balance," he says, citing the increased
prevalence of the "urban form" in many suburbs.

There are twists on this idea floating out there in "thought leader"
circles, and many experts are attempting to categorize, label, and
identify the precise areas the development industry should focus on
for the future. Demetri Baches is an urban planner and former direc-

tor at Duany Plater-Zyberk & Company who now runs a planning consultancy called Metrocology out of Beaufort, South Carolina. Baches argues that 30 to 40 percent of suburban residents will stay where they are while the rest—the people who were "forced into suburbia" because they had children, couldn't afford cities, and there was nowhere else to go—will move to new kinds of markets. Baches thinks a major potential area of growth for this group is smaller cities, those with populations between ten thousand and three hundred thousand, like Augusta, Georgia, and Charleston and Greenville, South Carolina. He calls these places "Top Tier Towns" because they offer the best of both worlds: a high quality of life and an urbane and connected lifestyle, within a locally grounded place that's "easy to get one's arms around." These places "punch above their weight," he says—and they are the future.

Others are betting on a reconcentration in the opposite direction: huge cities. In their book *Megapolitan America*, Arthur C. Nelson and Robert E. Lang point out that America is not as sparse as we think; our population is concentrated in a small number of large urban regions. The authors foresee a reconcentration of the country into twenty-three massive megapolitan areas and argue that those dense areas should claim the lion's share of planners' attention and public investment. America 2050, a think tank arm of the Regional Plan Association, takes a similar approach, suggesting new population centers around eleven mega-regions in the United States and Canada, including Piedmont Atlantic, the Texas Triangle, and the Great Lakes region.

What everyone agrees on is that things are going to change. "If demographics hold the course—and nobody can see any reason why they won't—and the price of energy stays at least as high as it's been," says Scott Bernstein, the director of the Chicago-based Center for Neighborhood Technology and pioneer of the location-efficient mortgage, "then we should get serious about building a very different kind of housing stock."

That, of course, raises the question: What will happen to all those extra houses we built over the years? The answer has developers, land-use planners, housing economists, and home builders racking their brains. Some foreclosed McMansions in exurbs are finding creative new second lives as things like film collectives, rehab centers, art galleries, or, in Merced, California, dorms for college students. Coeds at the University of California, Merced, have been filling up emptied-out luxury home subdivisions in a trend the *New York Times* called "Animal House, 2011." In other pockets of California, foreclosed homes are being used as marijuana grow houses, becoming a life-imitating-art incarnation of the Showtime series *Weeds*. Some creative underwater owners of multimillion-dollar properties are renting out rooms for the night to help pay the now-inflated mortgage. In still other developments, foreclosed McMansions are being bought up by extended immigrant families in what experts say could become a viable use for many subdivisions if there's enough demand.

An increasing number of housing experts are coming to believe that the glut of extra homes in the most remote exurbs is simply too large for these clever and creative uses, and that these subdivisions will ultimately become slums. The demand for these vacated homes from traditional buyers, that argument goes, is not likely to come back. It's possible prices could fall to a point where the homes become so affordable that it would be irrational for any housing consumer *not* to consider them attractive. But if demand doesn't pick up even then, they could become the next location of affordable housing, snatched up by landlords and converted into duplexes, triplexes, and apartments. Many zoning laws prohibit the subdivision of single-family homes, but if the demand is great enough, the market may force a change. Ever since the FHA proposed turning this shadow inventory into rentals, private investors have been swooping in and buying up portfolios of hundreds of foreclosed-upon homes with the intent of renting them out. But since so many of these neighborhoods are located far away from urban centers, some say the only way the houses can become inhabitable and therefore financially viable will be if new communities spring up nearby to offer residents local employment.

Many housing watchers say the most remote exurban developments could, with enough time, fall apart. Construction on these homes was breakneck, and many were built on the cheap. It's not inconceivable that if they don't sell, without care and upkeep many will deteriorate. This could be bad: without proper policy programs to manage their depopulation, these neighborhoods risk becoming hotbeds for crime, squatters, and blight, speeding their decline. James Howard Kunstler has been saying this for years. "The suburbs have three destinies," he says. "As slums, salvage yards, and ruins. And those are not mutually exclusive."

Much of the future of U.S. residential development will be dictated by policy. If, for example, the government decides to move forward with location-efficient mortgages, that would increase demand for those kinds of places. Right now, our housing policy still encourages the purchase of single-family homes. "It's pretty damn easy to securitize the single-family product," says Brookings' Katz. "This isn't something that our policy system has responded to yet." Katz also points out that having choices is only going to become more important: unlike other mature countries—like, say, Germany or Japan—we're still experiencing massive rates of growth; the U.S. population is growing at the rate of thirty million a decade. Our racial and ethnic makeup is evolving. We have many different cohorts and a continuum of housing preferences. "People really just want more alternatives," Katz says. Now, they will undoubtedly get them.

But there's still some of what Chuck Marohn of Minnesota would call "lobster-eating" going on. Driving around the far reaches of Summerlin, Nevada, after my visit with Zappos's Tony Hsieh, I found myself at what seemed like the end of the earth. It was really just a small subdivision up a hill right off Paseo Breeze Drive, but as I drove up the half-developed street, it seemed like the final frontier, the edge of the developed United States itself. Soon the pavement turned to dirt road, and I pulled over when the road ended and got out of my rental car. There was a chain-link fence with alarming DANGER/NO TRESPASSING! signs. All I could see in front of me were vast acres of arid land and mountains in the distance.

And yet as I faced the empty desert I heard a familiar sound ring out, that of a single spare hammer hitting away, its familiar echo reverberating across the neighborhood and signaling new home construction. On one side of the street behind me a few new homes were going up, and crews were toiling away on top of the roof working in the hot sun. This was Barcelona, a sign soon told me, a new upscale community from Toll Brothers. I walked inside the completed showhouse across the street and toured the thirty-three-hundred-or-so-square-foot home, which had all the trappings of suburban Toll: a two-story foyer, a great room, gourmet kitchen with a large island, dual vanities in the master suite. The house was opulently decorated and highly staged, complete with fictitious handwritten notes on the bulletin board in the girl's bedroom ("don't forget! sleepover @ Emily's"). It was high quality: walls were thick, doors heavy, carpeting lush; all the touches seemed just right for the upscale buyer. "The ideal destination for moving up," the materials advertised. But *were* there any upscale buyers anymore, especially here in housing's post-bust wasteland? I asked the real estate agent why they were building new homes when there was still so much for sale. The foreclosure glut had actually only increased the demand for new construction, she told me. If you buy a foreclosed home, she pointed out, you don't know if the insides will still be there; your money could be held in escrow for six months, only to have an all-cash buyer come in and pull it out from under you. New homes were safer. I signed the guest book, and when I got home, I got a nice thank-you card from Toll Brothers for taking the time to view its exciting new community. Less than one year later, all seventeen Barcelona homes had sold out.

But what gets built in Vegas might very well stay in Vegas. Elsewhere in the country, the market, consumer demand, demographics, and consumer preferences are all pointing in a different direction. "The notion that we're all going to be living in cities is wrong," says Diana Lind, editor of *Next City*. "But the idea that we'll have suburbs that have a different kind of lifestyle than we have right now is just inevitable." Even Toll Brothers' CEO, Douglas Yearley, says there will be a broader mix of choices available to meet the demands of an in-

creasingly diverse population. The urbanist and architect Peter Calthorpe likens the discussion to the debate over gay marriage. "We're
not saying that the suburbs are wrong or should go away," he says.
"Just like we're not asking to stop heterosexual marriage just because
we want gay marriage. We just want to have a choice." There will still
be exurbs for people who like to live that way and can afford to do so.
But the changes afoot mean that there will be many more options.

N one of this will happen overnight. Right now it's a challenge to
build anything when the economy is stalled and incomes are
stagnant. But like most big changes, the reconstitution of our landscape will happen a little bit at a time. "It doesn't mean that all of a
sudden there will be these huge wagon trains moving in and deserts
in the cul-de-sacs," says the Urban Land Institute's John McIlwain.
It's a shift that's just beginning, he and others point out, and we won't
know until we look back, census by census, to see how it played out.

If the changes suggested in this book sound extreme, that's because
they are. But consider other transformations that have happened over
the course of our nation's history. In 1910, no one could have looked
forward and imagined cities turning into the slums they did in the
'60s, '70s, and '80s, just as in today's city-as-Disneyland era, we can't
now imagine them that way, either. Or imagine the 1950s, when most
women didn't work; now, that's hard to fathom. Or similarly, imagine
the '80s and '90s, when smoking was considered cool. That same kind
of reversal can happen again when it comes to how and where we
choose to live. The suburbs as we know them had an exceptionally
long run, remaining basically unchanged for more than half a century.

"We're turning what happened in cities fifty and sixty years ago on its head," says Sam Sherman, the urban developer in Philadelphia. "Don't ever say it can't happen. It happened before."

Besides, it's when trends are just beginning that they're the hardest to spot. "When a strong trend is in its early stage, it doesn't look strong," says the University of Virginia's William Lucy. The 1950 census, he points out, did not contain clear evidence proclaiming what would happen during the next half century. And yet a slightly visible trend soon became a wave, which became a movement, which became a contagion, which became our suburban-majority country. "In ten years," says housing economist Jonathan Smoke, "we'll know what happened."

Whatever things look like in ten years—or twenty, or fifty, or more—there's one thing everyone agrees on: there will be more options. The government in the past created one American Dream at the expense of almost all others: the dream of a house, a lawn, a picket fence, two or more children, and a car. But there is no single American Dream anymore; there are multiple American Dreams, and multiple American Dreamers. The good news is that the entrepreneurs, academics, planners, home builders, and thinkers who plan and build the places we live in are hard at work trying to find space for all of them.

ACKNOWLEDGMENTS

This book took a village, or at the very least a pedestrian-friendly suburb. The contributions of many people show up in these pages.

The End of the Suburbs would never have come into being were it not for Lew Korman, who gave me the nudge off the ledge I needed. Thanks, Lew, and to all the Kormans—Sharon, Raina, Mike, Cynthia, and Eric—for their support. I owe a debt of gratitude to Eileen Cope for her clear vision and expert guidance early on. From there I am grateful to have landed in the savvy and skillful hands of Melissa Flashman at Trident, who might have been an urban planner in another life and whose enthusiasm was more critical than she knows.

My thanks to the entire Portfolio team: to Adrian Zackheim, who saw the potential for this idea when it was little more than a few sentences and committed to it on the spot; to Will Weisser, Allison McLean, Kristen Gastler, and Tracy Brickman for their strategic guidance and tireless work; to Katie Coe for deftly managing our many moving parts; and to Julia Batavia, Bria Sandford, Dan Donohue, and Sharon Gonzalez. I'm especially grateful for the editing firepower of Brooke Carey, who is a gifted wordsmith and a master of structure, and who gingerly ushered this project from its earliest days. This book is as much Brooke's as it is mine.

I am deeply grateful to *Fortune* managing editor and my spirited boss, Andy Serwer, who was a champion of this idea from the minute he heard about it. Stephanie Mehta and Hank Gilman gave me their early and unwavering support (Hank also gets a hat tip for the Don Henley epigraph in chapter 2). I'm grateful to several other colleagues at *Fortune*: Nick Varchaver read the entire first draft—talk about sprawl—and weighed in with editorial suggestions along with encouragement that helped me soldier through the rewrite. Adam Lashinsky and Carol Loomis shared lessons they had just gleaned writing their own excellent books. Pattie Sellers not only cheered me on but lent me her apartment for a week when I was displaced during Hurricane Sandy (Pattie: I wrote my favorite chapter in your living room). Special thanks to Dan Roberts, who was an eager reader and who weighed in with sharp suggestions and copy edits; to Omar Akhtar for skillful fact checking and research; and to Erika Fry for lending her research and reporting talents. Other *Fortune* colleagues including Ryan Bradley, Brian Dumaine, Brian O'Keefe, Jennifer Reingold, Jessi Hempel, Chris Tkaczyk, Megan Barnett, Steve Koepp, Mina Kimes, Kate Flaim, Julie Schlosser, Mia Diehl, Alix Colow, Armin Harris, Kelly Champion, Carolyn Walter, Marilyn Adamo, John Needham, and Lisa Clucas all helped in specific ways; Michelle Wolfe calmly and coolly saved the day with eleventh-hour photo research.

I could not have written this book without Doris "with enough time, you can find anything" Burke, *Fortune*'s senior research editor. Doris signed on late in the process, probably against her better judgment and without a doubt not knowing what she was getting herself into. Doris is part research sleuth, part story whisperer, and part shrink; I can't imagine getting loopy on census data and giggling over bad suburbs jokes with anyone else.

I'm grateful to Ali Zelenko, Daniel Kile, Danny Leonard, and Vidhya Muregesan for their daily and invaluable guidance. My deep thanks to Terry Rooney for his support and generosity, and to David Goldin for sharing his time and counsel for this book and always.

Writing a research-intensive book on a limited schedule required some help. In chronological order, thanks to Maggie Boitano, Catherine Siskos, Amanda Erickson, Dave Plotz, Tracey Samuelson, Caroline Fairchild, and Betsy Feldman for their research. I'm also grateful to David Dobkin, who, after a a serendipitous encounter during which we bonded over Jane Jacobs, agreed to be my "eyes on the story," reading for accuracy, history, and context. Whatever the future of cities looks like, Dave will probably have a hand in it.

I am indebted to several sources who were generous with their time. Thanks to Jonathan Smoke, Chuck Marohn, Scott Bernstein, Jeff Tumlin, Andres Duany, Diane Dorney, John McLinden, Sam Sherman, Graham Hill, Tony Hsieh, Spencer Rascoff, Scott Griffith, Kenneth Jackson, and Frank and Deborah Popper. Special thanks to Jason Duckworth, who was a go-to source on all matters, and Irina Woelfle, who connected me with many of the aforementioned people and provided festive builders' show hospitality in Orlando. I'm grateful to Linda Keenan, Diane Roseman, Maribeth Reinbold, Annette Lee, and Bethany Daily for sharing their personal stories.

I leaned heavily on my author friends Kate Kelly, Bethany McLean, Joanne Gordon, and Katherine Eban. Jim Ledbetter, Erin Arvedlund,

Jon Friedman, David Kaplan, Mark Halperin, and Meredith Whitney all contributed wise counsel. Jonathan Dahl was a key reader at a critical point, John Brodie offered early support, and Dan Mandel lent his publishing savvy. Thanks to Joe Scarborough, Mika Brzezinski, Alex Korson, Jesse Rodriguez, and the entire *Morning Joe* team, and to Alex Wagner, Dana Haller, and the team at *NOW*. Deep gratitude goes to Robyn Twomey, Barbara Vesely, Ariel Lawrence, Brian Cook, Christos Karantzolas, Richard Prinzi, and the ever-helpful Samantha Baker.

My friends deserve a special mention for understanding why for almost a year I couldn't see them or talk to them much, and for staying friends with me anyway. You know who you are and I couldn't have done this without you. Special thanks to Wendi Nix, Joanna Popper, Rachel Shechtman, Peter Kafka, Lauren Winfield, Laura Brounstein, Eva Chopra, Caitlin Magner, and Jeremy Smerd, each of whom contributed material that shows up in these pages. The wise and talented Alison Brower was an early reader, a late-stage editor, and, as she is always, a source of constant counsel on matters large and small. Sylvia and Fred Fogel deserve special mention for their support that knows no bounds, for their generosity of spirit and of real estate, and for not decamping to the suburbs—yet. Deep gratitude goes to Gil Kreiter for reading every word and every note, for untold amounts of patience, and for keeping me calm, centered, and, most of all, loved.

Stephen King says a writer needs little more than a desk and something to write on to do his or her best work, but a pretty setting sure doesn't hurt. Joel Greenberg provided the picture-perfect writing cabin in Vinalhaven, Maine, and Allison Storr and Jeff and Sally Booth rented me their very special homes in Sag Harbor. In Media,

Pennsylvania, thanks to Emily and Jay Farrell, Nancy Gabel, Leonard Ellis, and the Sutton and Neuspiel families.

My family has been unbelievably supportive. Thanks to the extended Gallagher, Pelizoto, and Salamanca clans, to Anita Soar and Carl Pelizoto for their smart suggestions, and special thanks to Nana, Grandmom, and Mom-Mom. My brother, Drew, provided encouragement, sharp edits, and his trademark no-sweat attitude; Adrienne Sack showed me her unwavering support. And last but by no means least, thanks to my beloved and wonderful parents, Jack and Joan Gallagher, who are my biggest champions, my best friends, and the source of all of my strength.

NOTES

INTRODUCTION

1   **Churchill quote:** House of Commons meeting in the House of Lords, October 28, 1943. In discussing whether and how to rebuild the House of Commons after it was destroyed on May 10, 1941, Churchill spoke in favor of rebuilding it to its old form, which was too small to seat all its members. The House would be mostly empty most of the time, he argued, and during critical votes it would fill beyond capacity, which would give it a "sense of crowd and urgency." For more, see www.win stonchurchill.org.

3   **single-family housing starts . . . and new home sales each hit new lows:** U.S. Census Bureau, new residential construction and sales monthly and annual data.

3   **prices that dropped 34 percent nationwide:** S&P/Case-Shiller U.S. National Home Price Index, April 30, 2006, to January 31, 2012.

3   **here in February 2012:** CoreLogic, number of residential properties in negative equity, first quarter, 2012.

4   **312 million people:** US Census Bureau, 2011, U.S. population estimate.

4   **builders erected:** U.S. Census Bureau, new residential construction statistics.

4   **record amounts of farmland:** American Farmland Trust, www.farmland .org.

4   **statistics and articles about the pain:** Christopher Leinberger, "The Death of the Fringe Suburb," *New York Times*, November 25, 2011; "Struggling in the Suburbs," *New York Times* editorial page, July 7, 2012; Steve Yoder, "Housing Crisis Could End Suburbia as We Know It," *Fiscal Times*, July 5, 2012.

4   **Meanwhile, a cache:** Edward Glaeser, *Triumph of the City: How Our Greatest Invention Makes Us Richer, Smarter, Greener, Healthier, and Happier* (Penguin Press, 2011); Hope Yen, "Census Finds Record Low Growth in Outlying Suburbs," Associated Press, April 5, 2012; Hope Yen and Kristen Wyatt, "Big Cities Boom as Young Adults Shun Suburbs," Associated Press, June 28, 2012.

6   **in 2011, for the first time in a hundred years:** U.S. Census Bureau, "Texas Dominates List of Fastest-Growing Large Cities Since 2010 Census, Census Bureau Reports," June 28, 2012.

6   **Construction permit data shows:** *Residential Construction Trends in America's Metropolitan Regions*, 2010 ed., Development, Community and Environment Division, U.S. Environmental Protection Agency.

8   **Robert Shiller:** Yen, "Census Finds Record Low Growth in Outlying Suburbs." On March 27, 2012, in an interview with Yahoo! Finance's Aaron Task, Shiller also suggested that dispersed single-family homes are not adequately built for management as rentals, and "that's one reason why dispersed suburban housing may not do well in decades to come."

8   **There are roughly 132 million:** U.S. Census Bureau, 2011 American Housing Survey. For growth of suburbs 1910–2000: U.S. Census Bureau, *Demographic Trends in the 20th Century*, Census 2000 Special Reports, November 2002.

10   **As Kenneth T. Jackson put it in his masterful book:** Kenneth T. Jackson, *Crabgrass Frontier: The Suburbanization of the United States* (Oxford University Press, 1985), p. 6.

10   **former stomping ground:** Jane Jacobs's former residence is located at 555 Hudson Street in Manhattan's West Village. A two-story mixed-use building with an apartment above a storefront, it sold for $3.3 million in 2009. In recent years, another Jacobs has taken over the rest of the

neighborhood: there are at least six separate Marc Jacobs boutiques in the small neighborhood, prompting graphic designer Mike Joyce to start a guerrilla campaign calling for "More Jane Jacobs Less Marc Jacobs."

12 **More than twenty years later:** Thanks goes to my high school English teacher, Emily Farrell. Some of the works appearing on her 2012 reading list: *We Had It So Good* by Linda Grant, *State of Wonder* by Anne Patchett, *The Cat's Table* by Michael Ondaatje, *The Brooklyn Follies* by Paul Auster, *The Newlyweds* by Nell Freudenberger.

13 **most Americans live in communities built:** U.S. Department of Housing and Urban Development and U.S. Census Bureau, American Housing Survey, 2011. While people who live in older regions of the country, like the Northeast, may be used to seeing homes built in the 1920s and earlier, suburbs in the rest of the country look a lot different. The average age of all housing stock in the United States is 1974, and homes built before 1940 make up less than 15 percent of U.S. housing units. In places like Loudoun County, Virginia, more than 40 percent of the housing stock was built between 2000 and 2009.

13 **overall miles traveled per household:** Federal Highway Administration, 2009 National Household Travel Survey.

13 **Ridgecrest is located 112 miles:** Research conducted by Jonathan Smoke, chief economist, Hanley Wood.

14 **According to census data:** William H. Frey, "The Demographic Lull Continues, Especially in Exurbia," Brookings Institution, April 6, 2012, and William H. Frey, "Demographic Reversal: Cities Thrive, Suburbs Sputter," Brookings Institution, State of Metropolitan America series, June 29, 2012.

14 **One such study comes from:** Justin B. Hollander et al., "The New American Ghost Towns," *Land Lines*, Lincoln Institute of Land Policy, April 2011.

15 **During and after the downturn:** Kevin C. Gillen, PhD, "The Correlates of House Price Changes with Geography, Density, Design and Use: Evidence from Philadelphia," Congress for the New Urbanism, October 2012.

15 **Studying more than ninety thousand home sales:** Joe Cortright, Impresa Inc., for the organization CEOs for Cities, "Walking the Walk: How Walkability Raises Home Values in U.S. Cities," August 2009.

16   **In New York City in the early 1990s:** *Residential Construction Trends in America's Metropolitan Regions,* 2010 ed., U.S. Environmental Protection Agency.

17   **A series of groundbreaking studies by the Brookings Institution:** Emily Garr and Elizabeth Kneebone, "The Suburbanization of Poverty: Trends in Metropolitan America, 2000 to 2008," Brookings Institution, January 20, 2010; Elizabeth Kneebone, "The Great Recession and Poverty in Metropolitan America," Metropolitan Policy Program at Brookings Institution, October 2010.

17   **new data showing:** Cameron McWhirter and Gary Fields, "Crime Migrates to Suburbs," *Wall Street Journal,* December 30, 2012.

17   **a former strip club:** Lisa Thomas-Laury, "Three Fathers Solve Their Day-Care Dilemma with 'Nest,'" abclocal.go.com, January 19, 2012.

18   **Walmart plans to open:** Laura Heller, "Hundreds of Small Walmarts Are Coming Soon," *Daily Finance,* March 11, 2011, and Tom Ryan, "Walmart's View from 15,000 Square Feet," Retailwire.com, March 14, 2011; store information, corporate.walmart.com.

18   **Target . . . is focusing its efforts:** Matt Townsend, "Target's City Ambitions," *Bloomberg Businessweek,* May 31, 2012.

18   **New York is "our hottest market by far":** Oshrat Carmiel, "Toll Brothers CEO Sees NYC as Best Home Market in 2012," Bloomberg, January 11, 2012.

19   **Today, only half of all adults:** U.S. Census, Statistical Abstract of the United States, 2012, and Pew Research Center, "The Decline of Marriage and Rise of New Families," November 18, 2010.

19   **families with children:** Arthur C. Nelson, "Leadership in a New Era," *Journal of the American Planning Association,* Autumn 2006.

19   **America's eighty million so-called millennials:** Most experts put the number of millennials at seventy-eight million to eighty million. There is no standard definition for the cohort's age range; experts use beginning birth dates as the late '70s to the early '80s and ending dates as late 1990s or the early 2000s.

20   **Seventy-seven percent:** Shyam Kannan, "Suburbia, Soccer Moms, SUVs and Smart Growth," Robert Charles Lesser & Co., Public Strategies Group, February 2, 2012.

20 **Arthur C. Nelson:** Heather LaVarnway, "The Changing American Dream: Shifting Trends in Who We Are and How We Live," February 2012; coverage of Nelson's December 2011 address at Pace University Land Use Law Center's conference on sustainable development.

20 **In 1980, 66 percent:** Federal Highway Administration statistics.

21 **In 2008, the average suburban household spent double on gas:** Burerau of Labor Statistics.

21 **for most of the last fifty years . . . In 2007, those numbers peaked:** Federal Highway Administration, Highway Statistics 2010.

21 **This shift is major:** Alexis C. Madrigal, "The Beginning of the End for Suburban America," *The Atlantic*, September 14, 2011.

22 **The author and provocateur:** James Howard Kunstler, *The Geography of Nowhere: The Rise and Decline of America's Man-Made Landscape* (Simon & Schuster, 1993).

23 **In an interview in the late 1990s:** Stewart Brand, "Vital Cities: An Interview with Jane Jacobs," *Whole Earth*, Winter 1998.

23 **A 2006 documentary called *The End of Suburbia*:** *The End of Suburbia: Oil Depletion and the Collapse of the American Dream*, written and directed by Gregory Greene, 2004. A prescient and informative film; see http://www.endofsuburbia.com.

23 **"We've reached the limits":** Joel Connelly, "As Suburbs Reach Limit, People Are Moving Back to the Cities," *Seattle Post-Intelligencer*, February 4, 2010.

CHAPTER ONE: THE GREAT URBAN EXODUS

23 **Mumford quote:** *Modern Architecture: International Exhibition*, exhibit catalog, Museum of Modern Art, 1932.

23 **Historian Kenneth T. Jackson:** Kenneth T. Jackson, *Crabgrass Frontier: The Suburbanization of the United States* (Oxford University Press, 1985), p. 12. While the historical facts referenced in this chapter are the result of research from dozens of current and historical sources, books and volumes, this entire book, and this chapter in particular, owes much gratitude to Jackson, whose *Crabgrass Frontier* is still considered the definitive history of the American suburbs. (Though Jackson himself writes, "I make no

claim to comprehensiveness. Any account that covers all important suburbs is certain to be exhausting before it is exhaustive.") Jackson's observations about American suburban development and its divergence from residential patterns throughout the rest of the world, and its implications, are as true today as they were in 1985. "This book is about havens," Jackson writes in his introduction. "It suggests that the space around us— the physical organization of neighborhoods, roads, yards, houses and apartments—sets up living patterns that condition our behavior."

29 **By 1910 ... crowded places in the country:** Amy O'Leary, "Everybody Inhale: How Many People Can Manhattan Hold?" *New York Times*, March 1, 2012.

29 **In 1814:** Jon C. Teaford, *The American Suburb: The Basics* (Routledge, 2008), p. 2.

30 **By 1849:** Ibid., p. 4.

31 **Riverside's streets were specifically designed:** www.olmstedsociety .org.

32 **Automobile registrations:** Federal Highway Administration state motor-vehicle registrations.

32 **Even during the Great Depression ... bathtub:** Jackson, *Crabgrass Frontier*, p. 173.

32 **In the early 1900s, a planner named Clarence Perry:** Eric Dumbaugh and Robert Rae, "Safe Urban Form: Revisiting the Relationship Between Community Design and Traffic Safety," *Journal of the American Planning Association* 75, no. 3 (Summer 2009): 309–29.

33 **As the influential urban historian:** Lewis Mumford, *The City in History: Its Origins, Its Transformations, and Its Prospects* (Harcourt, Brace & World, 1961).

34 **From 1921 to 1936, the "golden age of highway building":** David L. Ames and Linda Flint McClelland, "Historic Residential Suburbs: Guidelines for Evaluation and Documentation for the National Register of Historic Places," National Park Service, U.S. Department of the Interior, 2002.

34 **Between 1923 and 1927, new homes were built:** U.S. Bureau of the Census, *Historical Statistics of the United States, Colonial Times to 1970*, part 2.

34 **from 1920 to 1930:** Jackson, *Crabgrass Frontier*, p. 175.

34   **For twenty years, housing starts averaged:** U.S. Bureau of the Census, *Historical Statistics of the United States, Colonial Times to 1970*, part 2.

34   **The housing shortage was so severe:** Jackson, *Crabgrass Frontier*, p. 232. Jackson's quote about sleeping in his grandparents' dining room comes from a transcript of the PBS series *The First Measured Century*, 2000.

35   **The mortgage interest tax deduction, a by-product:** Lost in the current political debate over the mortgage interest tax deduction is the fact that the Revenue Act of 1913 didn't refer to mortgage interest at all; rather, it simply provided a deduction for "all interest paid within the year by a taxable person on indebtedness." More on this can be found in Dennis J. Ventry Jr., "The Accidental Deduction: A History and Critique of the Tax Subsidy for Mortgage Interest," *Law and Contemporary Problems* 73 (Winter 2010): 233–84.

35   **Housing starts jumped from:** U.S. Bureau of the Census, *Historical Statistics of the United States, Colonial Times to 1970*, part 2.

35   **The percentage of American families who owned their own homes:** U.S. Census Bureau.

35   **The suburban surge continued:** The Jackson quote comes from *Crabgrass Frontier*, p. 190.

36   **By 1970, 38 percent:** U.S. Census Bureau, *Demographic Trends in the 20th Century*, Census 2000 Special Reports, November 2002.

36   **From 1950 to 1970 Americans' incomes nearly doubled:** U.S. Census Bureau.

37   **On a single day in March 1949:** Jackson, *Crabgrass Frontier*, p. 237.

38   **In 1950, a builder in Fullerton, California:** fullertonheritage.org.

38   **Lakewood, California, the fastest-growing community that same year:** *The Lakewood Story: History, Tradition, Values* (City of Lakewood, 2004).

38   **In 1957, first-time author:** John Keats, *The Crack in the Picture Window* (Houghton Mifflin, 1956)

39   **That year, the Urban Land Institute:** *Community Growth: Crisis and Challenge*, 1959, National Association of Home Builders and Urban Land Institute. This video is fascinating to watch.

40   **likens this setup to an "unmade omelet":** Andres Duany, Elizabeth Plater-Zyberk, and Jeff Speck, *Suburban Nation: The Rise of Sprawl and the Decline of the American Dream* (North Point Press, 2000), p. 10. The au-

thors also describe the difference between traditional neighborhood design and the sprawl-style designs that replaced it in terms of how they could be drawn: the latter can be drawn as a bubble diagram with a "fat marker pen," whereas the drafting of the dense, intricate layouts of traditional towns requires a fine-point writing instrument.

42 **Robert Putnam, a Harvard professor:** This particular quote comes from Putnam's appearance in the PBS documentary *Designing Healthy Communities*, a four-part series produced by the Media Policy Center that aired on public television stations in January 2012. But the relation between the size of one's triangle—the distance between where a person shops, sleeps, and works—and his or her happiness is a major tenet of Putnam's and one he explores in his book, *Bowling Alone: The Collapse and Revival of American Community* (Simon & Schuster, 2000), cited elsewhere in these notes. Putnam posits that when we lived in villages long ago, the distances among those three points were very small; now it might be thirty or forty miles or more. He suggests that the smaller the triangle, the happier the person, as long as there are social interactions. (He also suggests you can judge how small your triangle is by the size of your refrigerator since people with small fridges are usually able to frequent stores more often, and posits "the bigger the refrigerator, the lonelier the soul.")

43 **The nationwide home ownership rate . . . the rate for blacks was 44.1 percent:** U.S. Census Bureau. These stark differences in home ownership rates by race are almost never mentioned in the discussion of the benefits widespread home ownership has brought to our society.

44 **For one, cities all but crumbled, seeing a net out-migration of thirteen million:** Robert Fishman, *Bourgeois Utopias: The Rise and Fall of Suburbia* (Basic Books, 1987), p. 182.

44 **By 1981, half of office space:** Rodney Jennings, "Dynamics of the Suburban Activity Center: Retrofitting for Pedestrian/Transit Use," Portland State University, June 1989.

44 **By the end of the 1990s:** Terry Christensen and Tom Hogen-Esch, *Local Politics: A Practical Guide to Governing at the Grassroots*, 2nd ed. (M. E. Sharpe, 2006), p. 52.

45 **dwarfed only by the size:** Many big-box store parking lots are so large, they sublease sections of their asphalt to fast-food chains.

45   **Whether called "technoburbs":** The term "technoburbs" was coined by Robert Fishman in *Bourgeois Utopias*. "Boomburbs" was coined by the demographer Robert E. Lang in a 2001 report for the Fannie Mae Foundation that identified fifty-three boomburbs, defined as incorporated places in the top fifty metropolitan areas in the United States with more than one hundred thousand residents that are not the core cities in their metropolitan areas and that maintained double-digit population growth over consecutive censuses between 1970 and 2010. See also: Robert E. Lang and Jennifer B. LeFurgy, *Boomburgs: The Rise of America's Accidental Cities* (Brookings Institution Press, 2007).

45   **In 1991, the author and scholar:** Joel Garreau, *Edge City: Life on the New Frontier* (Anchor, 1992). Perhaps the most famous coinage of the U.S. suburbs since the phrase "bedroom community" first appeared.

45   **In places like Atlanta:** Demographia.com, U.S. Census Bureau; see also http://www.demographia.com/db-atl1960.htm.

45   **By 2000, metropolitan areas covered:** U.S. Census Bureau.

45   **That same year:** Russ Lopez, *Thirty Years of Urban Sprawl in Metropolitan America: 1970–2000: A Report to the Fannie Mae Foundation.*

46   **a massive region where two-thirds of residents:** Scott Gold and Massie Ritsch, "Swallowed by Urban Sprawl," *Los Angeles Times*, October 18, 2002.

46   **In 2002 a report:** Reid Ewing, Rolf Pendall, and Don Chen, *Measuring Sprawl and Its Impact*, Smart Growth America, 2002.

46   **"There is no 'there' there":** Gold and Ritsch, "Swallowed by Urban Sprawl."

46   **The historian Lewis Mumford:** Jackson, *Crabgrass Frontier*, pp. 237, 244; Lewis Mumford, *The Culture of Cities* (Mariner Books, 1970).

47   **Her influential 1961 book:** Jane Jacobs, *The Death and Life of Great American Cities* (Random House, 1961). The definitive critique of twentieth-century urban planning. It's hard to overstate Jacobs's role in urban planning, and her own artful explanation of the "sidewalk ballet" is worth citing in full here. She wrote that under the seeming disorder of cities, there was a "marvelous order for maintaining the safety of the streets and the freedom of the city." This order, she wrote, is "composed of movement and change, and although it is life, not art, we may fancifully call it the art form of the city and liken it to the dance—not to a

simple-minded precision dance with everyone kicking up at the same time, twirling in unison and bowing off en masse, but to an intricate ballet in which the individual dancers and ensembles all have distinctive parts which miraculously reinforce each other and compose an orderly whole. The ballet of the good city sidewalk never repeats itself from place to place, and in any one place is always replete with new improvisations."

48   **Raymond Tucker, the mayor of St. Louis:** Jackson, *Crabgrass Frontier,* p. 270.

48   **Even Victor Gruen:** M. Jeffrey Hardwick, *Mall Maker: Victor Gruen, Architect of an American Dream* (University of Pennsylvania Press, 2004). In a speech Gruen gave in London in 1978 called "The Sad Story of Shopping Centres," he further explained that Americans had corrupted his vision. Speaking of a "tragic downgrading of quality," he said the American pursuit of profits had derailed his vision and that the public should protest the further construction of shopping centers.

51   *Blue Velvet, Revolutionary Road:* These digs at suburbia weren't always movies or works of art. During the course of my reporting one suburbanite mentioned to me a greeting card she once saw that claimed to teach "the ABCs of suburbia—Adultery, Booze and Crabgrass!"

51   **"Suburbia is . . . hell":** Whether "hell" is the first word that comes up depends on your computer and what Google thinks about you. On mine, the first thing that comes up is "hell"; the second, "boring." On other people's computers, boring was first, hell second.

52   **among them the author James Howard Kunstler:** James Howard Kunstler, *The Geography of Nowhere: The Rise and Decline of America's Man-Made Landscape* (Simon & Schuster, 1993). To say that Kunstler's verbal lances are entertaining would be an understatement. In addition to his books, which also include *The Long Emergency: Surviving the End of Oil, Climate Change, and Other Converging Catastrophes of the Twenty-first Century* (Grove Press, 2006), and *Too Much Magic: Wishful Thinking, Technology, and the Fate of the Nation* (Atlantic Monthly Press, 2012), Kunstler weighs in weekly on his blog, *Clusterfuck Nation,* at Kunstler.com/blog/. A TED talk he gave in 2004 is viewable at ted.com and well worth the nineteen minutes.

CHAPTER TWO: THE MASTER-PLANNED
AMERICAN DREAM

53   **"Some rich men came and raped the land":** Words and music by Don
      Henley and Glenn Frey © 1976 Cass County Music and Red Cloud
      Music. All rights reserved. Used by permission of Alfred Music Pub-
      lishing Co., Inc.

57   **"In retrospect, I understand that it was utter insanity":** Charles
      Marohn, "Confessions of a Recovering Engineer," strongtowns.org,
      November 22, 2010.

59   **In 2010 the financial analyst Meredith Whitney:** Shawn Tully,
      "Meredith Whitney's New Target: The States," Fortune.com, Septem-
      ber 28, 2010.

60   **One study by the Denver Regional Council:** "The Fiscal Cost of Sprawl:
      How Sprawl Contributes to Local Governments' Budget Woes," Environ-
      ment Colorado Research & Policy Center, December 2003. Other states
      and municipalities have conducted similar studies with similar results.

60   **A 2008 report:** Kaid Benfield, "Sprawl Should Pay More for Infra-
      structure, but Seldom Does," *Switchboard*, the staff blog of the National
      Resources Defense Council, September 26, 2008.

61   **The mortgage interest tax deduction:** Internal Revenue Service,
      Statistics of Income Bulletin, Winter 2012.

62   **This subsidy amounts to nearly $200 billion a year:** Federal Highway
      Administration Office of Highway Policy Information, "Our Nation's
      Highways: 2011."

62   **it sparked outrage among conservatives:** Joel Kotkin, "California
      Wages War on Single-Family Homes," forbes.com, July 26, 2011; Wen-
      dell Cox, "California Declares War on Suburbia," *Wall Street Journal*,
      April 9, 2012.

63   **"The suburbs are a big government handout":** William Upski Wim-
      satt, "Five Myths About the Suburbs," washingtonpost.com, February
      11, 2011.

63   **The city of Long Beach:** Jonathan Hiskes, "Tell Me Again Why We
      Mandate Parking at Bars?" Grist.org, June 24, 2010.

63   **In the delightfully entertaining:** Andres Duany, Elizabeth Plater-

Zyberk, and Jeff Speck, *Suburban Nation: The Rise of Sprawl and the Decline of the American Dream* (North Point Press, 2000), p. 163n. This book, a seminal tome in the anti-sprawl canon, is a rollicking guide to the history, makeup, and implications of U.S. sprawl-based development. It is chock-full of similarly colorful phrasing: the automobile is "a private space as well as a potentially sociopathic device"; the NAHB convention is described as a place where "Sixty-five thousand people, mostly men, all eat lunch under large tents pitched on parking lots, where the choice of entrée ranges from beef barbecue to pork barbecue."

65   **in 1931, the author James Truslow Adams simply wrote:** James Truslow Adams, *The Epic of America* (Little, Brown, and Company, 1931), p. 415.

65   **"No man who owns his own house and lot":** Thomas Sugrue, "The New American Dream: Renting," *Wall Street Journal*, August 14, 2009.

65   **"Strengthening families, establishing communities":** William J. Clinton, "Proclamation 6807, National Homeownership Day, 1995," June 2, 1995. Online by Gerhard Peters and John T. Woolley, *The American Presidency Project*.

66   **In his remarks:** William J. Clinton, "Remarks on the National Homeownership Strategy," June 5, 1995. Online by Gerhard Peters and John T. Woolley, *The American Presidency Project*.

66   **in 2004, George W. Bush:** President's Remarks to the National Association of Home Builders, Greater Columbus Convention Center, Columbus, Ohio, October 2, 2004, available at georgewbush-whitehouse.archives.gov.

67   **Prices rose nearly 200 percent:** S&P/Case-Shiller Composite 10 home price index.

67   **A *Fortune* article:** Grainger David, "Riding the Boom," *Fortune*, May 30, 2005.

67   **The home-building industry exploded:** U.S. Census Bureau, new residential construction statistics.

68   **From 2002 to 2007:** American Farmland Trust, www.farmland.org. During that time, the site says, we were losing more than an acre of farmland per minute to development.

68   **A *New York Times Magazine* profile:** Jon Gertner, "Chasing Ground," *New York Times Magazine*, October 16, 2005.

68   **By 2009, three million Americans:** U.S. Census Bureau, 2009 American Community Survey.

69   **In the span of eleven years:** U.S. Census Bureau.

71   **By 2005, there were nearly four million homes with:** U.S. Census Bureau, American Housing Survey for the United States, 2001 and 2005.

71   **By 2006, the average home was 2,500 square feet:** U.S. Census Bureau.

71   **"Drive 10 miles and save $10,000":** Chris Serres, Jim Buchta, and Glenn Howatt, "Minnesota's New Ghost Towns," *Minneapolis Star Tribune*, April 21, 2008.

71   **All told, between 1996 and 2006:** U.S. Census Bureau, new single-family unit completions.

72   **By the end of 2009, home prices had fallen:** S&P/Case-Shiller Composite 20 home price index.

72   **All told, housing prices fell 34 percent:** Ibid.

73   **In Perris, California, owners of ranches:** "Another Skinny, Abandoned Horse Found in Inland Empire," *Los Angeles Times*, September 16, 2011.

74   **In Atlanta, the city's outer suburban ring:** "Real Estate Expert Dubs Area 'Ring of Death,'" wsbtv.com, June 2, 2011.

74   **In December 2011, one foreclosure "heat map":** Alexander Soule, "Feds Consider Changes for Seized Foreclosures," *Westchester County Business Journal*, January 23, 2012.

75   **The economist Edward Glaeser:** Edward L. Glaeser, Harvard University and the National Bureau of Economic Research, "Rethinking the Federal Bias Toward Homeownership," *Cityscape: A Journal of Policy Development and Research* 13, no. 2 (2011): 5–37. Also see "Ed Glaeser on Why Cities Matter," video produced by CEOs for Cities, December 27, 2011. Glaeser points out that by pushing people toward single-family homes at the expense of higher-density types of living (since most single-family dwellings are owner-occupied while most multifamily dwellings are rented), the mortgage interest deduction encourages people to buy bigger homes, farther away from urban centers, which has a number of negative implications: it diminishes productivity; it increases commuting distances, energy expenses, and therefore level of damage to the environment; and, by increasing the physical distance between the rich and poor, Glaeser suggests it might also increase the social

distance between them, reducing levels of empathy. Glaeser also points out that as we learned during the "housing convulsion," subsidized borrowing can lead to a " 'foreclosure' rather than an 'ownership' society."

76 **A recent study by the National Association of Home Builders:** National Association of Home Builders, "Voters Place High Value on Homeownership, Oppose Policies That Make It More Difficult to Own a Home," January 11, 2012.

76 **A recent study by the real estate Web site Trulia:** Trulia biannual American Dream survey, September 20, 2011.

CHAPTER THREE: "MY CAR KNOWS THE WAY TO GYMNASTICS"

79 **"First they built the road":** By Arcade Fire. Used here with artists' permission.

82 **In the United States, 83 percent:** Federal Highway Administration, National Household Travel Survey, 2009. Europe: Erik Olin Wright and Joel Rogers, *American Society: How It Really Works* (W. W. Norton, 2011); John Pulcher, "Public Transportation," in Susan Hanson and Genevieve Giuliano, *The Geography of Urban Transportation*, 3rd ed. (Guilford Press, 2004).

82 **We have the highest per capita:** World Bank statistics.

83 **One study found a nearly 500 percent:** Peter Swift, "Residential Street Typology and Injury Accident Frequency," June 1997; updated 2002, 2006.

83 **Jeff Speck, a renowned city planner:** Jeff Speck, *Walkable City: How Downtown Can Save America, One Step at a Time* (Farrar, Straus and Giroux, 2012), p. 172.

84 **Specifically, Dumbaugh found:** Eric Dumbaugh and Robert Rae, "Safe Urban Form: Revisiting the Relationship Between Community Design and Traffic Safety," *Journal of the American Planning Association* 75, no. 3 (Summer 2009): 309–29.

84 **A recent report authored by experts at the Centers for Disease Control and Prevention (CDC) found:** Richard J. Jackson, MD, MPH, and Chris Kochtitzky, MSP, Centers for Disease Control and Prevention, "Creating a Healthy Environment: The Impact of the Built Environment on Public Health," Sprawl Watch Clearinghouse, sprawlwatch.org, p. 11.

84   **Another study:** Ibid.

86   **Studies using pedometers:** David R. Basset Jr. et al., "Pedometer-Measured Physical Activity and Health Behaviors in United States Adults," National Institutes of Health, October 2010.

86   **In the United States, roughly half of all trips taken by car are three miles or less:** 2001 National Household Transportation Survey; also see "Complete Streets Change Travel Patterns," Smart Growth America.

86   **When it comes to trips under one mile:** Edward L. Glaeser and Matthew E. Kahn, "Sprawl and Urban Growth," National Bureau of Economic Research, May 2003.

86   **more than a third of U.S. adults:** Centers for Disease Control and Prevention, National Health and Nutrition Examination Survey, 2009–2010.

87   **As far back as 2001, a report:** Jackson and Kochtitzky, "Creating a Healthy Environment."

87   **"We have built America in a way":** From the 2012 four-part PBS series *Designing Healthy Communities*, hosted by Richard J. Jackson, MD, MPH, produced by the Media Policy Center and accompanied by a companion book copublished by the American Public Health Association (Richard J. Jackson with Stacy Sinclair, *Designing Healthy Communities* [Jossey-Bass, 2011]). The documentary series is one of the most in-depth, comprehensive looks at the social, economic, and health problems associated with sprawl-style development.

88   **The prevalence of overweight children:** Centers for Disease Control and Prevention statistics.

88   **Rates of type 2 diabetes have doubled:** Jackson and Sinclair, *Designing Healthy Communities.*

88   **In 1969, roughly half:** David Darlington, "Why Johnny Can't Ride," *Bicycling,* April 27, 2012 (citing 2009 National Household Travel Survey statistics). This in-depth article focuses on one family's fight for their son's right to be able to ride his bike to school, provides keen insight into how our development patterns became so exaggerated over the years and how hard it is to walk or bike in some communities. As Darlington reports, the Council of Education Facility Planners now recommends at least twenty acres of land and another acre for every hundred students, a policy that, according to the NTHP, amounts to "the construction of

giant educational facilities in remote, middle-of-nowhere locations that rule out the possibility of anyone walking to school." As Darlington points out, the remote location is not the only reason children don't walk: among students who lived within one mile of school, 88 percent walked or bicycled forty-three years ago; today only 38 percent do.

88   **children are four times as likely:** "Travel and Implications of School Siting," Environmental Protection Agency, October 2003.

88   **The number of trips the average child makes:** "Mean Streets," Surface Transportation Policy Partnership, 2000.

89   **a telling study came out of the University of Utah:** Ken Smith et al., University of Utah, "Walkability and Body Mass Index: Density, Design and New Diversity Measures," *American Journal of Preventative Medicine* 35, no. 3 (September 2008): 237–44.

90   **"When there is nearly nothing":** Jackson and Sinclair, *Designing Healthy Communities.*

90   **"frozen in a form of infancy":** Andres Duany, Elizabeth Plater-Zyberk, and Jeff Speck, *Suburban Nation: The Rise of Sprawl and the Decline of the American Dream* (North Point Press, 2000), p. 117.

90   **the music video of the 1982 Rush classic "Subdivisions:"** The author highly recommends this diversion, easily found on YouTube.

91   **researchers at the University of California, Davis, found:** Kristin Lovely et al., "Neighborhood Satisfaction in Suburban Versus Traditional Environments: An Evaluation of Contributing Characteristics in Eight California Neighborhoods," *Landscape and Urban Planning* 97, no. 1 (July 30, 2010): 37–48.

91   **"I started missing not just my urban friends":** Linda Erin Keenan, *Suburgatory: Twisted Tales from Darkest Suburbia* (skirt!, 2012). *Suburgatory* the book is really nothing like *Suburgatory* the TV show; it's a collection of *Onion*-style satirical news dispatches from suburbia as seen through Keenan's hilariously observant eye. Bite-size chapters are arranged by faux headlines: "Mom Plans School Auction During Dreary Sex"; "Aspergers' Dad 'Hot'"; "Dad Forcibly Removed from Mall Massage Chair"; "Mom Unaware of Two American Wars"; "Dad and Hot Nanny Really 'Just Good Friends.'" Keenan is a talent and the book is uproariously funny—it will not disappoint.

93 **Square founder Jack Dorsey:** Eric Savitz, "Jack Dorsey: Leadership Secrets from Twitter and Square," *Forbes*, November 5, 2012.

93 **Studies have shown:** Jeffrey Tumlin, *Sustainable Transportation Planning: Tools for Creating Vibrant, Healthy, and Resilient Communities* (Wiley, 2012). Tumlin focuses on the physiological and sociological benefits of walking, like how it has been found to trigger oxytocin, the powerful neurotransmitter known as the "love hormone," but also on the way we have evolved as a walking species. One way we are unique among mammals, Tumlin points out, is that we have a stark contrast between our iris and our sclera, or the whites of our eyes. In most animals, the sclera is camouflaged. That, Tumlin says, is by design, or rather by evolution; that contrast makes our eyes highly visible and our expressions highly readable, and it makes us better able to engage in nonverbal communication with one another at close to moderate distances.

94 **The average suburban resident now drives:** Jinwon Kim and David Brownstone, "The Impact of Residential Density on Vehicle Usage and Fuel Consumption," University of California Transportation Center, University of California, Irvine, March 2010.

94 **the average worker spends fifty-one minutes:** U.S. Census Bureau, 2011 American Community Survey.

94 **close to 90 percent of U.S. commuters:** U.S. Census Bureau, 2011 American Community Survey.

94 **Some 3.5 million Americans:** Transportation Research Board of the National Academies, "Commuting in America III."

94 **A few years ago local television news stations:** Brian Stelter, "TV News for Early Risers (or Late-to-Bedders)," *New York Times*, August 31, 2010.

95 **more than 40 percent of Riverside and San Bernadino county residents commute:** "An In-Depth Look at Inland Southern California Commuters," Beacon Economics for the University of California, Riverside School of Business Administration, March 10, 2011.

97 **A 2006 study on happiness:** Daniel Kahneman and Alan B. Krueger, "Developments in the Measurement of Subjective Well-Being," *Journal of Economic Perspectives* 20, no. 1 (Winter 2006): 3–24.

97 **In 2004, a pair of Swiss economists:** Alois Stutzer and Bruno S. Frey,

"Stress That Doesn't Pay: The Commuting Paradox," Institute for Empirical Research in Economics, University of Zurich, 2004.

97   **Other studies have linked long commutes:** Annie Lowrey, "Your Commute Is Killing You," Slate.com, May 26, 2011.

97   **Robert Putnam, the Harvard political scientist:** Nick Paumgarten, "There and Back Again," *New Yorker*, April 16, 2007.

98   **a study from researchers in Sweden:** Erika Sandow, "On the Road: Social Aspects of Commuting Long Distances to Work," Department of Social and Economic Geography, Umea University, Sweden, 2011.

98   **Another study of commuting couples:** Meni Koslowski, Avraham N. Kluger, Mordechai Reich, *Commuting Stress: Causes, Effects and Methods of Coping* (Springer, 1995), p. 94

98   **Nationwide, roughly 40 percent of workers:** Alan E. Pisarski, "Commuting in America III," Transportation Research Board, p. 47.

99   **the amount of time we spend stuck in traffic ... more than sixty hours a year stuck in traffic:** David Schrank, Bill Eisele, and Tim Lomax, Texas Transportation Institute 2012 Urban Mobility Report. The report found that the average urban auto commuter spent thirty-eight hours of extra time in traffic, the equivalent to almost five vacation days. The 2011 report found that rush hour (which it called "possibly the most misnamed period ever") lasted six hours in the largest cities.

99   **$120 billion a year:** Ibid.

99   **A study by the American Automobile Association:** Nancy Bartley, " 'Road Rage' Takes Deadly Detour—More Traffic Incidents Lethal as Drivers' Stress Goes Up," *Seattle Times*, April 1, 1997.

99   **In 2003, the average suburban household spent:** Bureau of Labor Statistics.

100   **Bernstein and his team found:** Barbara J. Lipman et al., "A Heavy Load: The Combined Housing and Transportation Burdens of Working Families," Center for Housing Policy, October 2006.

100   **in Kankakee County:** View and use the H+T Affordability Index at htaindex.cnt.org.

103   **From 2000 to 2008:** All gas prices from the U.S. Energy Information Association.

103 **That year, one hundred schools:** Rebekah Kebede, "Schools Eye Four-Day Week to Cut Fuel Costs," Reuters, July 24, 2008.

104 **"Exurb homeowners accepted long drives":** Christopher Steiner, *$20 Per Gallon: How the Inevitable Rise in the Price of Gasoline Will Change Our Lives for the Better* (Grand Central Publishing, 2010), p. 130.

105 **the lauded oil economist Daniel Yergin:** "How Long Will Fossil Fuels Dominate?" *Wall Street Journal*, May 25, 2012.

105 **"The various tech industries are full of":** James Howard Kunstler, "Forecast for 2009," Kunstler.com, December 29, 2008. As is per usual with Kunstler, the rest of the passage is worth including here: "The environmental movement, especially at the elite levels found in places like Aspen, is full of Harvard graduates who believe that all the drive-in espresso stations in America can be run on a combination of solar and wind power. I quarrel with these people incessantly. It seems especially tragic to me that some of the brightest people I meet are bent on mounting the tragic campaign to sustain the unsustainable in one way or another."

105 **158 million:** U.S. Census Bureau.

106 **"driving to the supermarket becomes":** Steiner, *$20 Per Gallon*, p. 120.

106 **For his part, Rubin envisions:** Jeff Rubin, *Why Your World Is About to Get a Whole Lot Smaller: Oil and the End of Globalization* (Random House, 2009).

107 **The total number of miles driven peaked in 2007:** Benjamin Davis, Tony Dutzik, and Phineas Baxandall, "Transportation and the New Generation: Why Young People Are Driving Less and What It Means for Transportation Policy," Frontier Group and U.S. PIRG Education Fund, April 2012.

107 **The total number of registered automobiles:** Federal Highway Administration state motor-vehicle registrations.

107 **In April 2012:** Davis, Dutzik, and Baxandall, "Transportation and the New Generation," p. 7.

107 **When measured per capita:** Ibid, p. 7.

107 **in addition to miles driven:** U.S. Department of Transportation, 2009 National Household Travel Survey.

108 **Rachel Meeks:** "Living as a One-Car Family in the Suburbs," small notebook.org, May 24, 2012.

110 **According to FHA data:** Federal Highway Administration, Highway Statistics, Distribution of Licensed Drivers, 1980 and 2010.

110 **the average American aged sixteen to thirty-four:** Davis, Dutzik, and Baxandall, "Transportation and the New Generation," p. 7.

110 **In a study done by MTV Scratch:** Amy Chozick, "As Young Lose Interest in Cars, G.M. Turns to MTV for Help," *New York Times*, March 22, 2012.

110 **while people between twenty-one and thirty-four purchased 38 percent:** Patrick S. Duffy, "Marketing to the Millennial Generation," *Builder & Developer* (October 2012).

110 **"Gen Y Eschewing V-8 for 4G":** Hasan Dudar and Jeff Green, "Gen Y Eschewing V-8 for 4G Threatens Auto Demand," businessweek.com, August 7, 2012.

CHAPTER FOUR: THE URBAN BURBS

113 **O'Hara quote:** From *Meditations in an Emergency* (Grove Press, 1957).

120 **All told, there are an estimated five to six hundred:** Estimate provided by Rob Steuteville, ed., *Better! Cities and Towns*. Steuteville estimates that there are another thousand-plus neighborhoods or more that have been revitalized in the last ten to twenty years in which New Urbanism thinking has played a part in the vision, building design, codes, street design, public design, or all of the above.

126 **one blogger described New Urbanism:** Chris DeWolf, "Why New Urbanism Fails," Planetizen.com, February 18, 2002.

127 **celebrity author and urban theorist Richard Florida:** Florida continues this theme in the foreword to Ellen Dunham-Jones and June Williamson's *Retrofitting Suburbia: Urban Design Solutions for Redesigning Suburbs* (Wiley, 2011): "It's happening everywhere. Suburbia isn't as suburban as it used to be."

127 **there are by some estimates as many as four hundred "city replicas":** Jonathan O'Connell, "Can City Life Be Exported to the Suburbs?" Washingtonpost.com, September 7, 2012.

128 **Morristown, New Jersey:** Jamie Duffy, "A Suburban Town Sees Housing Where Retail Rules," *New York Times*, August 16, 2011.

129 **last year, two of its penthouse apartments:** "Two New Penthouse

Sales Just Days Apart at 40 Park Reflect Limited Collection's Sensational Appeal," blognj.com, March 1, 2012.

129   **Salon.com cities columnist Will Doig:** Will Doig, "Invasion of the Faux Cities," Salon.com, September 22, 2012.

129   **what the *New York Times* has referred to as "hipsturbia":** Alex Williams, "Creating Hipsturbia," *New York Times*, February 15, 2013.

130   **calls these new urban-suburban markets:** Christopher B. Leinberger, "DC: The WalkUP Wake-Up Call: The Nation's Capital as a National Model for Walkable Urban Places," Center for Real Estate and Urban Analysis, George Washington University School of Business, 2012.

130   **A 2001 study that analyzed:** Charles C. Tu and Mark Eppli, "An Empirical Examination of Traditional Neighborhood Development," Marquette University, October 1, 2001.

131   **Kevin Gillen, a housing economist:** Kevin C. Gillen, PhD, "The Correlates of House Price Changes with Geography, Density, Design and Use: Evidence from Philadelphia," Congress for the New Urbanism, October 2012.

131   **A separate study of metropolitan Washington, DC:** Christopher B. Leinberger and Mariela Alfonzo, "Walk This Way: The Economic Promise of Walkable Places in Metropolitan Washington, D.C.," Brookings Institution, May 2012.

132   **Using data from Walk Score:** Joe Cortright, Impresa Inc. for CEOs for Cities, "Walking the Walk: How Walkability Raises Home Values in U.S. Cities," August 2009.

133   **Media, Pennsylvania, fits this description:** As close as it is to Media's downtown, the Walk Score of my childhood house is 48, making it "car-dependent."

134   **Marianne Cusato, designer and author:** Marianne Cusato with Daniel DiClerico, *The Just Right Home: Buying, Renting, Moving—Or Just Dreaming—Find Your Perfect Match!* (Workman Publishing, 2012). According to Cusato, homes can sacrifice more square footage when they are located in close proximity to a walkable "public realm." The closer you are to cafés and movie theaters, the smaller your house can be because it doesn't need to "do everything for you": when a commuter comes home fresh off the freeway from a long drive, the last thing he or

she wants to do is get back in the car; dinner is much more likely to be had at home, which requires more space. But if there is more to do nearby, Cusato maintains, the house has to carry less of the "entertainment burden." (An extreme version of this theory is routinely channeled by New York City real estate brokers when they try to sell you a two-hundred-square-foot studio: "Manhattan is your living room!")

136   **In 2007, the average square footage of U.S. homes built:** U.S. Census Bureau.

136   **983 square feet:** U.S. Department of Labor, "New Housing and Its Materials 1940–56," Bureau of Labor Statistics Bulletin no. 1231.

136   **NAHB found they expected home size to drop:** Rose Quint, NAHB, "The New Home in 2015," Housingeconomics.com, March 2, 2011; "NAHB Predicts Average Home Size Will Shrink over the Next Few Years," Trilogybuilds.com, April 13, 2011.

136   **The median "ideal home size":** Kaid Benfield, "What's Going On with New Home Sizes—Is the Madness Finally Over?" *Switchboard*, February 9, 2012.

136   **Only 9 percent of respondents:** "The McMansion Era Is Over: Trulia's Latest Data About American Attitudes Toward Home Sizes," Trulia.com, August 20, 2010.

136   **Two-thirds of new homes built in 2011 had one:** Haya El Nasser and Paul Overberg, "Front Porches Making a Big Comeback," *USA Today*, September 19, 2012.

137   **The percentage of homes built without a garage:** Ibid.

138   **the so-called Tiny House movement:** Alec Wilkinson, "Let's Get Small," *New Yorker*, July 25, 2011.

139   **In a TED talk:** See Graham Hill's talk at ted.com. For a hilarious take on the same topic, watch George Carlin's classic bit on "stuff."

CHAPTER FIVE: THE END OF THE NUCLEAR FAMILY

143   *Friends* **quote:** Used with permission from Warner Bros.

144   **The U.S. birth rate:** All birth rate data from the U.S. Centers for Disease Control and Prevention's National Center for Health Statistics, National Vital Statistics System.

144 **The percent of people 65 and over hit a record 13 percent:** U.S. Census Bureau.

144 **From 2000 to 2010, the ranks of:** William H. Frey, "The Uneven Aging and 'Younging' of America: State and Metropolitan Trends in the 2010 Census," Brookings Institution Metropolitan Policy Program, June 2011, p. 1.

144 **the median age in the United States:** Frey, "Uneven Aging," p. 4.

145 **The change is more pronounced in the suburbs:** Ibid., pp. 1, 11.

145 **one-third of all suburbs saw an absolute decline:** Ibid., p. 11.

145 **by 2025, an estimated 72 percent of American homes:** Arthur C. Nelson, "Leadership in a New Era," *Journal of the American Planning Association* 72, no. 4 (Autumn 2006): 393–409.

145 **the Janssens (four kids):** Names in this sentence have been changed.

145 **from 2007 to 2009, the height of the recession:** Paul D. Sutton, PhD, Brady E. Hamilton, PhD, and T. J. Mathews, MS, "Recent Decline in Births in the United States, 2007–2009," National Center for Health Statistics Data Brief, March 2011, p. 1.

145 **Married households now make up:** "The Decline of Marriage and Rise of New Families," Pew Research Center, November 18, 2010.

146 **in the 1950s, half of men and women who married:** U.S. Census Bureau.

146 **now, the average age is twenty-eight for men:** Centers for Disease Control and Prevention, National Center for Health Statistics.

146 **Between 2007 and 2009, while the birth rate in the United States fell:** Sutton et al., "Recent Decline in Births," p. 2.

146 **a record 27 percent of all households:** U.S. Census Bureau, America's Families and Living Arrangements, 2012.

148 **According to an AARP survey:** Nicholas Farber, Douglas Shinkle, et al., "Aging in Place: A State Survey of Livability Policies and Practices," AARP and the National Conference of State Legislatures, December 2011.

148 **"In some ways, current senior growth":** Frey, "Uneven Aging," p. 10.

148 **Fairfax County, Virginia:** Carol Morello, "If Baby Boomers Stay in Suburbia, Analysts Predict Cultural Shift," *Washington Post,* June 28, 2011.

150 **In Levittown, Pennsylvania:** Haya El Nasser and Paul Overberg, "Census Reveals Plummeting U.S. Birthrates," *USA Today,* June 24, 2011.

151   **The average Manhattan apartment:** The Corcoran Report, 3rd
Quarter 2012.

151   **There are now twenty-six hundred more married families:** U.S.
Census Bureau.

151   **the financial district, where fifty-seven thousand people:** Downtown Alliance, Lower Manhattan Fact Sheet, Q3 2012.

152   **In 2011, 22 percent of twenty-five- to thirty-four-year-olds:** Kim
Parker, "The Boomerang Generation: Feeling OK About Living with
Mom and Dad," Pew Research Social & Demographic Trends, March
15, 2012, p. 2.

152   **Overall, 53 percent of all adults:** Ibid., p. 6.

152   **best captured by a *New Yorker* magazine cover:** *New Yorker,* May 24,
2010.

153   **the Pew Research Center found:** "Millennials: A Portrait of Generation Next," Pew Research Center, 2010. For much of human history, it
was actually quite normal and even expected for people to live with
their parents until their twenties or thirties—typically, until they got
married. In the seventeenth and eighteenth centuries, it was even ille-
gal for unmarrieds to live alone in the United States. Until the 1940s it
remained common that young adults lived with their parents or other
family until they were married.

154   **William May:** Name has been changed at subject's request.

155   **From 2009 to 2011, just 9 percent:** Ben S. Bernanke, "The U.S. Hous-
ing Market: Current Conditions and Policy Considerations," Federal
Reserve white paper sent to the U.S. Senate Committee on Banking,
Housing and Urban Affairs.

155   **the record 30 percent of households:** U.S. Census Bureau.

157   **"21 percent of millennial moms":** "21 Percent of Millennial Moms
Use Their Phone in the Bathroom and 12 Percent Use It During Sex,"
PR Newswire, May 9, 2012.

157   **77 percent of millennials:** Shyam Kannan, "Suburbia, Soccer Moms,
SUVs and Smart Growth," Robert Charles Lesser & Co., Public Strategies Group, February 2, 2012, p. 11.

157   **A National Association of Realtors study found:** "The 2001 National
Community Preference Survey: What Americans are looking for when

deciding where to live," National Association of Realtors, March 18, 2011.

157 **say they'd rather live in a neighborhood with:** G. M. Filisko, "How Millennials Move: The car-less trends," *On Common Ground*, National Association of Realtors, Summer 2012.

157 **many are willing to pay for the ability to walk:** S. Mitra Kalita and Robbie Whelan, "No McMansions for Millennials," *Wall Street Journal*, January 13, 2011.

158 **the 2011 figures showed birth rates:** "Births: Preliminary Data for 2011," CDC National Vital Statistics Reports.

159 **Similar efforts are under way:** Vanessa Wong, "Micro-Apartments in the Big City: A Trend Builds," *Bloomberg Businessweek*, March 14, 2013.

159 **Arthur C. Nelson:** Heather LaVarnway, "The Changing American Dream: Shifting Trends in Who We Are and How We Live," February 2012; coverage of Nelson's December 2011 address at Pace University Land Use Law Center's conference on sustainable development.

160 **William Lucy, professor of urban and environmental planning:** William H. Lucy, Lawrence Lewis Jr. Professor of Urban and Environmental Planning, "A Different Path to a Housing Rebound," University of Virginia, September 20, 2010.

CHAPTER SIX: WHERE THE WEALTH IS MOVING

163 *Mad Men* **quote:** Courtesy of AMC Network Entertainment LLC.

164 **"unerringly contextual:"** Robbie Whelan, "A Departure from Mc-Mansions," *Wall Street Journal*, August 22, 2011.

165 **"Fortress of Glassitude":** One sample: Pete Davis, "Fortress of Glassitude Ready to Rise at 400 Park Avenue South," curbed.com, July 16, 2012.

166 **Toll's City Living division:** As Toll Brothers' Bob Toll wrote in a regulatory filing in 2003: "We see great demand from affluent buyers for dramatic residences in exciting urban locations. The resurgence of American cities, fueled by population growth, increasing affluence and the appeal of bright city lights, is a catalyst."

166 **Toll Brothers City Living "is our best market...":** Vivian Marino, "Square Feet: Douglas C. Yearley Jr.," *New York Times*, March 24, 2011.

166 **Highbrow publications:** See www.theatlanticcities.com and Salon .com's Dream City column, authored by Will Doig, at salon.com/topic/ dream_city/.

167 **Reversing a ninety-year trend:** William H. Frey, "Demographic Reversal: Cities Thrive, Suburbs Sputter," Brookings Institution, State of Metropolitan America series, June 29, 2012.

167 **In many of the biggest cities:** U.S. Census Bureau.

167 **cities like New York, which saw the population within:** Steven G. Wilson et al., U.S. Census Bureau, "Patterns of Metropolitan and Micropolitan Population Change: 2000 to 2010," September 2012, p. 28. The exact number was a gain of 37,422 people or 9.3 percent.

167 **and where new census numbers show:** David Seifman, "The Bigger Apple: Population Spike Reverses Exodus," *New York Post*, March 15, 2013.

167 **In Philadelphia, the 2010 census revealed:** U.S. Census Bureau; also, "Leading the Way: Population Growth Downtown," Central Philadelphia Development Corporation and the Center City District, September 2011.

167 **Of all cities, Chicago showed the biggest gain:** Wilson et al., U.S. Census Bureau, "Patterns of Metropolitan and Micropolitan Population Change: 2000 to 2010."

167 **The population of the Loop area alone:** David Roeder and Art Golab, "Loop Transforms into More Residential Area over Last Decade," *Chicago Sun-Times*, February 25, 2011.

167 **Manhattan is expected to add:** "New York City Population Projections by Age/Sex & Borough, 2000–2030," the City of New York, Department of City Planning, December 2006; also, Amy O'Leary, "Everybody Inhale: How Many People Can Manhattan Hold?" *New York Times*, March 1, 2012. The current population of Manhattan as of the 2010 census is 1,585,873.

168 **When it was mulling locations:** "Room and Board Buys into 14th Street," dcmud.com, June 10, 2009.

168 **In St. Louis, an old abandoned:** These look pretty great. See www .warehouse7lofts.com.

168 **In Boston, a West Coast development firm:** Casey Ross, "West Coast Firm Takes on Fort Point," *Boston Globe*, October 20, 2011.

168   **In 1975, the *New York Daily News*:** *New York Daily News* front-page headline, "Ford to City: Drop Dead," October 30, 1975.

169   **In Philadelphia, much of the population increase:** U.S. Census Bureau; also, "Philadelphia: The State of the City, a 2012 Update," Pew Charitable Trusts and the Philadelphia Research Initiative, 2012.

170   **She listed ten more benefits:** Daily's full list of things she likes most about living in Boston is here, verbatim:

-Access to museums for quick visits (kid-length)

-Fun, quick access to free events—fireworks, free music, cliff diving (Red Bull sponsored a contest last weekend where people dove off the top of the Institute of Contemporary Art into Boston Harbor)

-People visiting town—easier to see extended network of people

-I'm still living my life—e.g., restaurants, music

-Access to sports—friends with tickets they can't use for professional sports are frequently offered to us b/c we can use them on a last-minute basis

-More time by not having to take care of a house

-Not more expensive, just a trade-off of space (vs. a house in the suburbs)

-kids get a lot of activity—lot of walking, parks, even in winter

-Internet shopping makes things much easier (can't imagine not having that!)

-Can get groceries delivered (I don't do this all the time)

172   **Walmart has said it is planning "hundreds":** Laura Heller, "Hundreds of Small Walmarts Are Coming Soon," *Daily Finance*, March 11, 2011, and Tom Ryan, "Walmart's View from 15,000 Square Feet," Retailwire.com, March 14, 2011; store info at corporate.walmart.com.

172   **By 2016 Best Buy plans:** Zach Honig, "Best Buy to Close 50 Big Box U.S. Retail Stores, Open 100 Mobile Stand-Alone Outlets in 2013," engadget.com, March 29, 2012.

172   **Even Target:** Matt Townsend, "Target's City Ambitions," *Bloomberg Businessweek*, May 31, 2012.

172   **"You have a massive rush throughout retail":** Miguel Bustillo, "As Big Boxes Shrink, They Also Rethink," *Wall Street Journal*, March 3, 2011.

172   **As of this writing, JCPenney:** Lois Weiss, "Penney Shines Images with Lafayette Lease," *New York Post*, May 2, 2012.

173   **in 2007, United Airlines left:** "United Airlines Moving Its Headquarters to the Willis Tower," *Chicago Tribune*, August 13, 2012.

173   **This year, Hillshire Brands:** Hillshire Brands 10K report.

173   **Motorola Mobility is shuttering:** Sandra Guy, "Motorola Mobility Leaving Libertyville for Merchandise Mart," suntimes.com, July 26, 2012.

173   **"The whole corporate campus seems":** Eddie Baeb, "Crain's Special Report: Corporate Campuses in Twilight," *Crain's Chicago Business*, May 30, 2011.

173   **In New York City, UBS:** Charles V. Bagli, "Regretting Move, Bank May Return to Manhattan," *New York Times*, June 8, 2011.

173   **Twitter, Zynga, Airbnb, Dropbox:** A notable exception to the tech moguls' fascination with cities is Steve Jobs, who lived and worked his whole life in the suburbs (he lived in a Tudor house in Palo Alto, and Apple's headquarters were in nearby Cupertino). But when Apple-owned Pixar moved to a new headquarters in Emeryville, California, Jobs pushed the designers to emphasize central locations where employees could mingle with one another with the hope of fostering creativity. Another exception is Mark Zuckerberg, who has built Facebook's headquarters into a massive campus in Menlo Park, but one that attempts to approximate urbanism, with a walkable commercial strip that includes a dry cleaner, gym, doctor's office, and various eateries.

174   **Zappos, the online shoe giant:** Leigh Gallagher, "Tony Hsieh's New $350 Million Startup," Fortune.com, January 23, 2012.

175   **In keeping with the findings of:** Glaeser found that, for example, that innovation happens faster in cities because proximity to others breeds creativity. Ideas, Glaeser said in his book *Triumph of the City*, "cross corridors and streets more easily than continents and seas." He writes of a contagion or osmosis effect that occurs when people work in close physical proximity to others in their field. He writes that studies of patents bear this out, showing that patents have a tendency to cite other patents that are geographically close. Productivity is higher in cities, too: doubling density rates, Glaeser found, raises overall productivity anywhere from 6 to 28 percent.

176   **For most of the 1970s, the trend in stadium construction:** David Dobkin, "Fair or Foul?: Ballparks and Their Impact on Urban Revital-

ization," *Panorama*, 2011. All of the information in this paragraph comes from Dobkin, including the informal list he put together for me of ball-parks built since 1990.

176 **It was a seminal moment in sports:** Mark Byrnes, "The Islanders' Move: A Harbinger of Suburban Decline?" theatlanticcities.com, November 9, 2012.

177 **as early as 2005, the suburban poor:** Alan Berube and Elizabeth Kneebone, "Two Steps Back: City and Suburban Poverty Trends, 1999–2005," Brookings Institution, 2006.

177 **"We think of poverty as a really urban phenomenon":** Tami Luhby, "Poverty Pervades the Suburbs," CNNMoney.com, September 23, 2011. Elizabeth Kneebone and Alan Berube, *Confronting Suburban Poverty in America* (Brookings Institution Press, 2013).

178 **nearly three-quarters of suburban nonprofits:** Scott W. Allard and Benjamin Roth, "Strained Suburbs: The Social Service Challenges of Rising Suburban Poverty," Brookings Institution, October 7, 2010.

178 **In Grand Rapids, Michigan:** Theresa Everline, "Surviving Suburbia," *Next American City*, no. 27, 2010.

178 **In Long Island's Suffolk County:** "Struggling in the Suburbs," *New York Times*, July 7, 2012.

178 **"Soaring poverty rates threaten":** Lisa McGirr, "The New Suburban Poverty," nytimes.com, March 19, 2012.

179 **In 2012 federal prosecutors in northern Virginia:** Pierre Thomas and Marisa Taylor, "Gang Members Arrested on Charges of Sex Trafficking Suburban Teens," abcnews.go.com, March 31, 2012.

179 **After a tragic gang rape:** Aliyah Shahid, "Girl, 11, Lured into Park Bathroom in Moreno Valley, Calif. and Gang Raped by 7 Teens: Cops," *New York Daily News*, March 29, 2011.

179 **While overall homicides:** Cameron McWhirter and Gary Fields, "Crime Migrates to Suburbs," *Wall Street Journal*, December 30, 2012. Many of the nation's highest-profile shootings have occurred in the suburbs as well, from Columbine to Aurora, Colorado, to, of course, the horrific shooting in Newtown, Connecticut, on December 14, 2012. The urban scholar Richard Florida studied data from mass shootings in recent years and found that, while the data does not cover every single episode and the

geographic information is limited, the "wide majority" of such shootings, and especially mass school killings, have occurred not in urban centers of large cities but in the "small towns, burgs and villages of our suburban and rural areas." (See "Gun Violence Is an Everywhere Issue," theatlanticci-ties.com, December 15, 2012.) The data shows that like other kinds of crime, gun violence is as much a suburban problem as an urban one.

180　**Only one enclosed indoor shopping mall has opened in the United States since 2006:** Kris Hudson and Vanessa O'Connell, "Recession Turns Malls into Ghost Towns," *Wall Street Journal*, May 22, 2009.

180　**Cleveland's Galleria at Erieview:** Stephanie Clifford, "How about Gardening or Golfing at the Mall?" *New York Times*, February 5, 2012.

180　**Ellen Dunham-Jones:** See Ellen Dunham-Jones and June Williamson, *Retrofitting Suburbia: Urban Design Solutions for Redesigning Suburbs* (Wiley, 2011). Also see Dunham-Jones's TED talk on the subject at ted.com.

182　**The number of restaurants:** William Neuman, "Slicing Costs, and Still Serving," *New York Times*, December 27, 2011.

183　**crop prices had soared . . . Don England Jr.:** Robbie Whelan, "U.S. Farmers Reclaim Land from Developers," *Wall Street Journal*, November 14, 2011.

184　**In a seminal article published in 1987, the Poppers argued:** Deborah Epstein Popper and Frank J. Popper, "The Great Plains: From Dust to Dust," *Planning* magazine, December 1987.

184　**The controversy around their idea inspired:** Richard S. Wheeler, *The Buffalo Commons* (Tor Books, 2000); Anne Matthews, *Where the Buffalo Roam: Restoring America's Great Plains* (University of Chicago Press, 2002); *The Fate of the Plains* (Nebraska Educational Television, 1995); *Facing the Storm: Story of the American Bison* (PBS, 2010).

184　**started endorsing their idea:** "New National Park Could Save High Plains in Kansas," *Kansas City Star*, November 15, 2009.

185　**Now the Poppers also study shrinkage:** Deborah E. Popper and Frank J. Popper, "New England and the Subtracted City," Communities & Banking, Spring 2011; Deborah E. Popper and Frank J. Popper, "Planning on Shrinking," *Shelterforce*, Spring 2011.

185　**Buffalo, they point out:** Deborah Popper and Frank Popper, "Smart Decline in Post-Carbon Cities: The Buffalo Commons Meets Buffalo, New York," in *The Post Carbon Reader Series: Cities, Towns, and Suburbs*, edited by Richard Heinberg and Daniel Lerch (Watershed Media Press, September 2010), p. 3.

185 **Justin Hollander:** Justin B. Hollander et al., "The New American Ghost Towns," *Land Lines*, Lincoln Institute of Land Policy, April 2011.

186 **In California's San Bernardino County:** "9 Worst Recession Ghost Towns in America," Thefiscaltimes.com, August 3, 2011.

187 **Wall Street giants like Blackstone Group:** Janet Morrissey, "Big Money Bets on a Housing Rebound," *New York Times*, December 8, 2012.

187 **As of this writing, we have a 4.4-month supply:** National Association of Realtors.

188 **In the late 1990s, when measured per square foot:** Christopher B. Leinberger, "Now Coveted: A Walkable, Convenient Place," *New York Times*, May 25, 2012.

CHAPTER SEVEN: THE FUTURE

191 **"With your head full of brains . . .":** Used with permission from Random House.

193 **Joel Kotkin:** Joel Kotkin, *The Next Hundred Million: America in 2050* (Penguin Books, 2011). Also see Kotkin's writings on the topic of demographics and migration patterns at joelkotkin.com and newgeography.com.

195 **A recent public radio story:** "The Changing Face of Suburbia," *The Takeaway*, July 14, 2010. To read the many entertaining comments, see thetakeaway.org (or: http://www.thetakeaway.org/2010/jul/14/start-conversation-whats-good-about-suburbs/).

195 **"I can get to the city when I need to":** David Dobkin, a recent urban planning graduate whom I enlisted to read my manuscript, noted in the margins that this benefit is particularly one-sided: "Who ever said, 'I can get to the suburbs when I need to'?"

196 **In Prince George's County:** Lori Aratani, "Effort to Bring Whole Foods to Prince George's Highlights Complexity of Process," Washingtonpost.com, April 28, 2012.

196 **In Lower Merion, Pennsylvania, meanwhile, during a debate:** Inga

Saffron, "Changing Skyline: Suburbia's Outer Ring Losing Shine, Some Economists Say," philly.com, January 6, 2012.

197   **single-family housing starts had climbed:** U.S. Census Bureau, new residential construction statistics.

197   **new home sales were on track:** National Association of Realtors data.

198   **One of the hottest areas is in multifamily:** U.S. Census Bureau, new residential construction statistics.

198   **The number of renters surged by more than five million:** "The State of the Nation's Housing, 2012," Joint Center for Housing Studies of Harvard University, p. 1.

198   **Toll Brothers' recent plans:** This came from my conversations with Toll, but also see coverage including Jeff Clabaugh, "Toll Brothers Plans Bethesda Condos," *Washington Business Journal,* January 16, 2013.

201   **In 2010,** *Travel and Leisure*: Daniel Derouchie, "Coolest Suburbs Worth a Visit," *Travel and Leisure*, August 2010.

201   **In a recent travel section write-up:** Jeff Heilman, "Road Trip: Delaware County," *New York Daily News*, September 30, 2012.

202   **these neighborhoods' smaller-scale houses:** To get an idea of what these suburbs look like, picture the neighborhood where Bradley Cooper romanced Jennifer Lawrence in *Silver Linings Playbook*, filmed mostly in Ridley Park, an inner-ring Philadelphia suburb not far from where my father grew up in inner-ring, grid-planned Drexel Hill. The Llanerch Diner, where Cooper and Lawrence go on a date, is down the street from my father's childhood house. After the movie came out, flocks of tourists went to the area on the weekends, visiting sites from the film.

202   **In Pittsburgh, the former rust belt inner-ring suburbs:** Mike Madison, "Rust Belt Chic Goes Mainstream, or Hip and Hipsters in Lawrenceville," Pittsblog.com, August 13, 2011.

202   *Pittsburgh* **magazine proclaimed it as:** Christine H. O'Toole, "City Guide: Best of the 'Burbs," *Pittsburgh* magazine, August 2011.

204   **in their book** *Megapolitan America*: Arthur C. Nelson and Robert E. Lang, *Megapolitan America: A New Vision for Understanding America's Metropolitan Geography* (American Planning Association/Planners Press, 2011).

204   **America 2050, a think tank arm:** See america2050.org under "Megaregions" (don't skip the maps).

205 **Some foreclosed McMansions in exurbs are finding:** Barbara Kiviat, "Reinventing the McMansion," *Time*, September 28, 2009; Patricia Leigh Brown, "Animal McMansion: Students Trade Dorm for Suburban Luxury," *New York Times*, November 12, 2011; Norimitu Onishi, "Foreclosed Houses Become Homes for Indoor Marijuana Farms," *New York Times*, May 6, 2012.

205 **Some creative underwater owners:** Alyssa Abkowitz, "Room for Rent—in a Mansion," *SmartMoney*, February 14, 2011.

INDEX